INSIGHT GUIDES

Tasmania

APA PUBLICATIONS

Part of the Langenscheidt Publishing Group

L

INSIGHT GUIDE
Tasmania

Project Editor
Jerry Dennis
Managing Editor
Tom Le Bas
Art Director
Klaus Geisler
Picture Editor
Hilary Genin
Production
Kenneth Chan
Cartography Editor
Zoë Goodwin
Editorial Director
Brian Bell

Distribution

UK & Ireland
GeoCenter International Ltd
Meridian House, Churchill Way West
Basingstoke, Hampshire RG21 6YR
Fax: (44) 1256-817988

United States
Langenscheidt Publishers, Inc.
36–36 33rd Street 4th Floor
Long Island City, New York 11106
Fax: (1) 718 784-0640

Australia
Universal Publishers
1 Waterloo Road
Macquarie Park, NSW 2113
Fax: (61) 2 9888 9074

New Zealand
Hema Maps New Zealand Ltd (HNZ)
Unit D, 24 Ra ORA Drive
East Tamaki, Auckland
Fax: (64) 9 273 6479

Worldwide
**Apa Publications GmbH & Co.
Verlag KG (Singapore branch)**
38 Joo Koon Road, Singapore 628990
Tel: (65) 6865-1600. Fax: (65) 6861-6438

Printing

Insight Print Services (Pte) Ltd
38 Joo Koon Road, Singapore 628990
Tel: (65) 6865-1600. Fax: (65) 6861-6438

©2006 Apa Publications GmbH & Co.
Verlag KG (Singapore branch)
All Rights Reserved

First Edition 2006

ABOUT THIS BOOK

The first Insight Guide pioneered the use of creative full-colour photography in guidebooks in 1970. Since then, we have expanded our range to cater for our readers' need not only for reliable information about their chosen destination but also for a real understanding of that destination. Now, when the internet can supply inexhaustible (but not always reliable) facts, our books marry text and pictures to provide that much more elusive quality: knowledge. To achieve this, they rely heavily on the authority of locally based writers and photographers.

How to use this book

The book is structured to convey an understanding of Tasmania:

◆ To understand a place, you need to know something of its past. The first section covers Tasmania's people, history and culture in lively essays.

◆ The Places section provides a full run-down of all the attractions worth seeing. The main places of interest are coordinated by number with full-colour maps.

◆ Photographic features illuminate aspects of the state's wildlife, its two best-known national parks, and the Port Arthur convict labour camp.

◆ Photographs are chosen not only to illustrate landscapes and buildings but also to convey the moods of Tasmania and the life of its people.

◆ The Travel Tips listings section provides information on travel, hotels, shops and outdoor pursuits. Information may be located quickly by using the index printed on the back cover flap – and the flaps are designed to serve as bookmarks.

a regular conributor to *The Monthly* magazine. The writer of the People chapter will be no stranger to Tasmanians. **Tim Cox** is presenter of ABC Tasmania's *Statewide Mornings* programme every weekday from 8.30–11.30 on 936 AM and various FM frequencies. Cox's regularly out on the road and, through his show's talkback slots, has his finger firmly on the pulse. He writes a column in *The Mercury* newspaper.

Also out and about a lot is **Gabi Mocatta**, but in her case, it's in a pair of hiking boots and waterproofs. She is a freelance travel writer who undertakes commissions for *Australian Geographic* amongst others. She contributed the features on the environment and outdoor activities.

The food and drink essay as well as most of the restaurant and café listings have been prepared by **Roger McShane and Sue Dyson**, who specialise in all aspects of cuisine for *Gourmet Traveller* magazine and ABC Tasmania. They also run the website www.foodtourist.com.

The Travel Tips represent a phenomenal feat of research by **Christine Long**, a journalist of several years' experience, currently working for the *Sydney Morning Herald*. Another *Herald* writer, **Dugald Jellie**, walked the Overland Track for us.

The project was managed by **Tom Le Bas**, with the assistance of **Jeffery Pike**, **Richard Carmichael** and **John Mapps**. **Sylvia Suddes** proofread the text, and **Helen Peters** compiled the index.

The contributors

This book was written and photographed by **Jerry Dennis** – an Englishman living in Melbourne who is now also the possessor of an Australian passport. It means he'll drink the local beer but warm it up first. Dennis has worked on countless Insight Guides, primarily as a photographer, and his work has been appearing in travel publications and other media for many years. He's been a regular visitor to Tasmania and jumped at the chance to make several more trips across the Bass Strait.

To create this guidebook, he enlisted the skills of several writers and researchers who had special knowledge of the island.

Zora Simic, author of the history feature, teaches Australian History at the University of Melbourne and is

CONTACTING THE EDITORS

We would appreciate it if readers would alert us to errors or outdated information by writing to:

Insight Guides, P.O. Box 7910, London SE1 1WE, England. Fax: (44) 20 7403-0290. insight@apaguide.co.uk

www.insightguides.com
In North America:
www.insighttravelguides.com

Contents

Travel Tips

THE BEST OF TASMANIA

The great outdoors, activities for children, fabulous beaches, historic sights and gourmet delights... Here, at a glance, are our top recommendations for a visit

BEST WALKS

ABOVE: some of the finest views are to be found in Freycinet National Park. **BELOW:** even on short walks it's advisable to go well-equipped conditions can change without warning.

- **Overland Track**
  The rite of passage for many is the 5-day (or more) journey from Dove Lake in Cradle Valley to the southern end of Lake St Clair. *See page 206.*
- **Mount Strzelecki**
  Climb from an elevation of 20 metres (65ft) to 756 metres (2,480 ft) in this 4–5-hour walk on Flinders Island to the peaks of Mount Strzelecki. *See page 227.*
- **Bay of Fires**
  Join the organised Bay of Fires Walk. Starting in Mount William National Park, the route heads south along this spectacular coast for 4 days and 3 nights. *See page 154.*
- **Maria Island**
  There are a number of walks to be enjoyed on this car-free island so it's worth booking to stay for a few days. *See page 140.*
- **South Cape Bay**
  Starting from a point about as far south as you can get by road, follow the path from Cockle Creek even further south to South Cape Bay. The intrepid can continue along the South Coast Track for the 7-day walk to Port Davey. *See page 112.*

- **Wineglass Bay**
  No visit to Freycinet National Park is complete without a walk to see Wineglass Bay, either from the lookout (1 hour + return) or on down to the bay itself (2 hours + return). *See page 143.*
- **Walls of Jerusalem**
  The climb to the top of Mount Jerusalem rewards the 12 hours (return) that it takes with fabulous views. *See page 205.*
- **Cataract Gorge**
  Launceston's back yard provides a lovely scenic stroll, right next to the downtown area. *See page 171.*

NATIONAL PARKS

● **Mount Field**
Pleasant cool walks to Russell Falls or Lady Barron Falls in the summer and one of Tasmania's two ski fields in the winter. *See page 120.*

● **Rocky Cape**
A craggy headland on the northwest coast with a few caves and the popular Sisters Beach. *See page 194.*

● **Mount William**
Access to the top of the Bay of Fires as well as a rare chance to see some Forester kangaroos. *See page 157.*

● **Tasman**
There is some spectacular cliff erosion down on the Tasman Peninsula, creating caves and blowholes. *See page 94.*

● **Strzelecki**
Mountains and dramatic coastlines are the main features with Trousers Point a highlight. *See page 227.*

● **Narawntapu**
Unspoiled coastal heathland and teeming wildlife are the attractions. *See page 187.*

● **Cradle Mountain-Lake St Clair**
One of the must-see destinations in the state is well set up for visitors. *See page 208.*

ADVENTURE ACTIVITIES

● **Diving**
Plenty of opportunities around the north and east coasts as well as off the islands. Check out Low Head for unique underwater diversity.

● **Rock climbing**
While there are no iconic mountains to climb, enthusiasts can test themselves in Cataract Gorge, on Mt Wellington, and perhaps the Hazards. *See pages 171, 81 and 142.*

● **Skiing**
Ben Lomond, east of Launceston, and Mount Field National Park are the options. *See pages 145 and 120.*

● **Rafting**
The best known and most testing destination for white-water rafting is the Franklin River in the west. Several tour operators will take groups for anything from a few hours to many days. *See page 213.*

ACTIVITIES FOR KIDS

● **Tasmazia**
Lose the kids in one of the seven mazes or take in the wacky pleasures of the model village of Lower Crackpot. *See page 207.*

● **The Ship that Never Was**
Amusing and informative play performed nightly at the Visitor Centre in Strahan. *See page 218.*

● **Penny Royal World**
Segments of the 19th century are re-created in this small-scale Launceston theme park. *See page 170.*

● **Cadbury Factory Tour**
Every child's fantasy fulfilled in this fascinating tour. Lots of tasting too. *See page 85.*

● **Queen Victoria Museum**
The Discovery Plus gallery as well as the Planetarium are especially good for children in this Launceston favourite. *See page 170.*

● **Alpenrail**
See a detailed model Swiss village and railway in suburban Hobart. *See page 85.*

ABOVE: walk this way. Spoiled for choice in Strzelecki National Park. **ABOVE LEFT:** paddling in Dove lake in Cradle Mountain NP. **BELOW:** a maze at Tasmazia, Lower Crackpot just beyond.

8

LOCAL PRODUCE

- **Chudleigh Honey Farm**
  There's every flavour of honey imaginable and it's not far from Deloraine. *See page 203.*
- **King Island Dairy**
  Don't miss the

fromagerie where some of Australia's best, and best-known, cheese is made. *See page 229.*
- **Christmas Hills Raspberry Farm**
  Blow in to this finely targeted shop and café near Elizabeth Town. *See page 187.*
- **Hursey Seafoods**
  This Stanley favourite is one of several places around the coast providing huge freshly caught crayfish and giant crabs. *See page 196.*

SHOPPING

- **Salamanca Market**
  Every Saturday morning this market gets into full swing selling everything from political tracts to a bag of apples. *See page 73.*
- **Reliquaire**
  Part shop, part tourist attraction, this treasure trove of toys and oddities is in Latrobe's Gilbert Street. *See page 185.*
- **Southern Forest Working Craft and Furniture Centre**
  Geeveston's home to a variety of artisans who sell their wares at competitive prices. *See page 110.*
- **Penguin Old School Market**
  Pick up a bargain every second and fourth Sunday of the month. *See page 191.*

HISTORIC SIGHTS

- **Port Arthur**
  Landmark early colonial penal settlement. *See page 95.*
- **Battery Point**
  Some of Hobart's earliest housing still feels like a Georgian village. *See page 73.*
- **Sarah Island**
  Fearsome convict station isolated in Macquarie Harbour. *See page 218.*
- **Clarendon**
  Neoclassical mansion in the Midlands. *See page 131.*
- **Launceston**
  Prosperous Victorian-

era streetscapes are well preserved. *See page 164.*
- **Richmond**
  Thought by many to be the perfect colonial township. Famous bridge. *See page 91.*
- **Ross**
  Another beautifully preserved old town, with another picturesque bridge. *See page 129.*
- **Maria Island**
  The old buildings of this former penal settlement are now within a National Park. *See page 140.*

TOP LEFT: honey is available from small producers all over the state. **ABOVE LEFT:** product of the "Apple Isle". **BELOW:** the Port Arthur Historic Site.

BEACHES

- **Binalong Bay**
  Wonderful beach at the southern end of the Bay of Fires with a lagoon just behind it. *See page 153.*
- **Bicheno**
  A choice of beautiful shaded bays at this family resort town. *See page 144.*
- **Trousers Point**
  Idyll on Flinders Island. *See page 228.*
- **Spiky Beach**
  Easily missed, this is a perfect little beach

south of Swansea on the East Coast, over the road from Spiky Bridge. *See page 141.*
- **Yellow Rock Beach**
  Deserted swathe of sand on King Island even comes with its own shipwreck. *See page 230.*
- **Boat Harbour Beach**
  On a quiet stretch of the northwest coast, this pristine stretch of sand is perfect for families avoiding the crowds. *See page 194.*

SPECIALIST MUSEUMS

- **Australasian Golf Museum**
Bothwell has this and the oldest golf course in the country. *See page 136.*
- **Tasmanian Angling Hall of Fame**
One of the esoteric attractions in the grounds of the Salmon Ponds outside New Norfolk. *See page 118.*
- **Copping Colonial and Convict Collection**
In reality a paean to one man's dedication to never throwing anything away, no matter how useless it may be. *See page 93.*

- **Huon Valley Apple and Heritage Museum**
Is there really anyone crying out for a whole museum dedicated to the apple? Yes, apparently. *See page 109.*
- **Australian Axeman's Hall of Fame**
A large centre in Latrobe dedicated to woodchopping and run by champion axeman David Foster. *See page 185.*
- **Tasmanian Cricket Museum**
Combine a tour of Bellerive Oval – the test cricket ground in Hobart – with a visit to this modern homage to the great game. *See page 83.*
- **Pearn's Steam World**
Huge hangars on the edge of Westbury contain a vast collection of steam engines, tractors, motorbikes and anything else that can be fitted in. *See page 178.*

GARDENS

- **National Rose Garden**
Colourful walled garden in the grounds of the Woolmers Estate near Evandale. *See page 133.*
- **Royal Botanical Gardens**
Established in Hobart in 1818, recent additions include an Antarctic Plant House. *See page 83.*
- **Table Cape Tulip Farm**
During September and October, the fields are awash with colour. *See page 194.*

LEFT: detail from Pearn's Steam World. **ABOVE:** display at the Royal Botanical Gardens. **BELOW:** an artist's impression of the Tasmanian tiger, extinct since the 1930s

MONEY-SAVING TIPS

National Parks: There are admission fees to National Parks throughout Tasmania, so if you want to see any of the signature sights, such as Cradle Mountain or Wineglass Bay, you'll need to pay. Daily fees can add up, whether for individuals or vehicles (allowing up to 8 occupants), so look at buying an 8-week permit, which pays for itself within 3 days. Since the majority of parks don't have staffed offices and only allow for on-the-spot purchases of day passes, make sure you get your long-term permit in advance from Visitor Centres at the bigger parks or some state Visitor Information Centres. More details at www.parks.tas.gov.au/natparks/current_fees.

BYO: There are restaurants and cafés across Tasmania which do not have licenses to sell alcohol but are happy for you to bring your own (advertised as BYO) for which they add a small corkage charge to the bill. This not only allows wine buffs to drink exactly what they want with their meal, but also seriously reduces the cost of dining out. Even some establishments that *do* have licenses will allow BYO wine but the corkage tends to be set a bit higher.

Roadside stalls: Keep a look out for people selling cheap produce by the roadside. Often there will just be a hand-painted sign and a basket of whatever's in season, with an honesty box alongside. Occasionally, you'll even see a big box of apples with the invitation: "help yourself".

LOCATING THE GOOD LIFE

Tasmania packs an enormous amount into its compact frame – with the important exception of people. Giving visitors a chance to get away from it all is a key part of its attraction

It may look like stray punctuation trailing off the edge of Australia – indeed, careless cartographers have on occasion neglected to include it in their maps of the continent – but Tasmania makes a compelling case to be a priority for travellers, whether they come from overseas or across the Bass Strait. Mainland Australia has scale, but most of it is endless stretches of empty, infertile outback. Tasmania, on the other hand – comprising less than 1 percent of the Australian landmass, crams a great deal into a small space.

In this island half the size of England (but with a tiny fraction of the population) there are lakes, mountains, an abundance of ancient rainforest, beaches, surf and elegant towns and villages. Many of the latter are throwbacks to the time, nearly 200 years ago, when as Van Diemen's Land, Tasmania was one of the first areas to be colonised by the British. Wander around Hobart, Launceston or, especially, some of the settlements on the Midlands Highway connecting those cities, and the sense of Georgian-Victorian England transported across the world is irresistible. It is to the visitor's advantage that the post-colonial economic boom largely bypassed the state, leaving so much of that history intact.

Today the island is prospering again, helped in no small part by tourism. The colonial history and its attractive sandstone residue is a significant factor, particularly the deeply atmospheric Port Arthur penal settlement. A belated recognition of prior Aboriginal occupancy is adding another dimension. However, more important still is Tasmania's reputation as a place of phenomenal natural beauty. The attractions of Cradle Mountain, Freycinet National Park or the southwestern wilderness are just the beginning. Follow any road and be open to serendipitous discovery: a tumbling waterfall, an alpine tarn, perhaps a million-year-old rainforest.

Allied to the glorious environment, there's something about the way of life that draws people back once they've made that first visit. As the British poet laureate Andrew Motion has noted, Tasmania is "jam-packed with people who have deliberately chosen it as the site of the good life: somewhere to be kinder, more composed, more appreciative of important things". True enough, although "jam-packed" is rather extreme… ❏

PRECEDING PAGES: hiking across the southwestern wilderness; cricket at Hobart on a fine summer day. **LEFT:** tree ferns are common in the rainforests of western Tasmania.

TANLEBOUEYER
A Native of the District of Oyster
Bay & the wife to Manalargerna
was attached to the Mission in 1830

THE MAKING OF TASMANIA

From a sparsely populated Island glimpsed by explorers, to a convict colony for hardened criminals, to a "little England" farmed by vigorous settlers, to a hotbed of environmental politics… Tasmania has a unique and distinctive history

It is both Tasmania's fortune and curse to be cut off from the rest of Australia. Now separated from the mainland by the Bass Strait, Tasmania has not always been an island, but its present-day identity has been very much formed by its geography. The divide from the rest of the country is both physical and metaphorical. Many characteristics of historical and contemporary Tasmania are unique, from its early indigenous occupants and their fate, and the particular brutality of its penal period, to the supposed insular nature of its present population. Yet for every negative critique of Tasmania, there's an equally compelling positive argument derived from its extraordinary natural beauty, energetic political activism and inspiring cultural scene.

Tasmania's colonial history reflects the history of all Australia, but with distinctive twists. Like New South Wales, it shares the dubious honour of being settled primarily as a penal colony. But although transportation of convicts to New South Wales ceased in 1840, it continued to Tasmania, or Van Diemen's Land as it was first known, until 1853. As with the other six Australian states, Tasmania has British colonial foundations, but these origins are more obviously reflected in its British-dominated population, architecture, patterns of land use and social and political development. And while few Aborigines anywhere in Australia were immune from the ravaging effects of

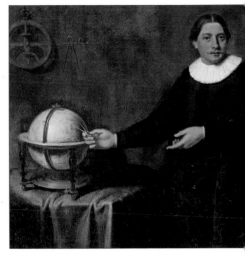

LEFT: painting of Tanlebouyer in the Tasmanian Museum and Art Gallery.
RIGHT: portrait of Abel Tasman.

disease and dispossession, the common perception is that the state's indigenous population was wiped out altogether. Not surprisingly, Tasmanians have sometimes struggled with their history, yet for the smallest Australian state, and one of the least populated, Tasmania has disproportionately inspired Australia's historical and literary imagination.

Van Diemen's Land

Aborigines settled in the region about 40,000 years ago, originally on the wider Bassian Plains and eventually on the island that was formed about 12,000 years ago when the seas rose and cut off the peninsula from Australia proper. As a consequence of their island experience, the indigenous occupants developed a culture that was distinctive from mainland Aborigines and later a source of international scientific and anthropological fascination.

Approximately 5,000 Aboriginal people were said to be living on the island at the time of the Europeans' arrival. By 1833 the native population had dwindled to 300. Truganini, the last "full-blooded" Tasmanian Aborigine, died in Hobart in 1876. Her skeleton remained on display in the Tasmanian Museum until 1947. Truganini has become as synonymous with Tasmania's colonial history as Port Arthur, the island's infamous convict prison.

orders, Lieutenant John Bowden set up the first settlement on the banks of the Derwent River in 1803. Meanwhile, Captain David Collins and his fellow colonists went south, establishing Hobart, the administrative hub of a colony characterised in its early years by colonial neglect. Collins was promoted to first governor, but it was hardly a role he relished. He died in 1810.

Those early years of European settlement were marked by the classic colonial combination of isolation, near starvation and improvisation. Isolation was a particular problem. Van Diemen's Land settlers survived on eating native game such as emus and kangaroos and

Dutch explorer Abel Tasman saw and named Van Diemen's Land on 24 November 1642. Captain James Cook caught a glimpse in 1777, but it was the French Naval Officer Nicolas Baudin who, throughout the 1790s, first properly mapped and explored the island. England's Matthew Flinders followed in his wake. The French Government hoped to claim Van Diemen's Land, but a strategically obsessed Britain, eager to ensure their dominance in the Pacific, acted quickly. British exploitation began with Bass Strait sealing in the 1790s, followed by formal colonisation in 1803–4 in both the south and north. With contingents of mostly convicts, and under British

by the timely arrival of supplies by sea. Shelter was typically found in huts under a leaky roof of bark or thatch. When more substantial buildings were erected, architectural options were limited by the difficulty of transporting heavy materials.

The landscape itself was often threatening. The island's wild forests were the home of snarling Tasmanian devils and the thylacine, the marsupial equivalent of a wild dog, later known locally as the Tasmanian tiger. The last known Tasmanian tiger died in captivity in 1936, though island legend insists on repeated sightings, all unconfirmed. Soon enough, the same forests would also conceal escaped convicts as Van Diemen's Land was transformed into perhaps the harshest penal colony of them all.

The convict stain

If the British didn't quite know what to do with Van Diemen's Land in its first few years, the re-direction of convicts from the notorious Norfolk Island (1,000 miles off the coast of New South Wales) soon established the southern colony as the natural home of the most cunning and recalcitrant convicts. Before too long, many of them were escaping to the hinterlands to take up bushranging and related forms of banditry. A bandit economy thrived,

As the pastoral stretches between Hobart and Launceston began to open up, colonial settlers, convicts and Aborigines became locked in an inevitable battle over land. And so began the years of the Black War, highlighted by an effort to capture the Aborigines by forming the "Black Line" of civilians and soldiers across the island to push Aborigines towards the fringe: Forestier's Peninsula in the southeast. Yet this much-publicised effort succeeded in netting only two captives. Inevitably, the inexhaustible reserves and increasing firepower of the Europeans wore down the indigenous population, but it was hardly an easy struggle for either side.

as hamlets of beleaguered settlers fell under bushranger control. Governor Thomas Davey declared martial law, but without much support from Sydney and with convicts-turned-bushrangers such as Michael Howe elevated to local infamy, it had little effect. Farmers were left to battle the outlaws themselves and the free use of firearms resulted in accidental deaths. Settler William Abel shot his own son, and William Roadknight did the same to his neighbour's convict servant.

FAR LEFT: the early colonisation of Tasmania is commemorated. **LEFT:** Truganini, the last Aborigine. **ABOVE:** convicts arrive on the island.

Rampaging bushrangers, prepared to kill for their stake in available land, added a further ferocious element to the volatile mix in an expanding Van Diemen's Land.

Anarchy continued to prevail until the appointment of the officious George Arthur as governor in 1824. Wool became a significant export, especially after local pastoralists sponsored the settlement of the Port Phillip district on the mainland during the 1830s. Maritime industry was flourishing and the colony was becoming a viable commercial centre. Under the supervision of George Augustus Robinson, a Wesleyan builder with a knack for establishing trust with the Aboriginal people, the Aborigines were eventually rounded up and exiled on Flinders Island in 1833, in what was intended as an attempt to save the few remaining indigenous inhabitats from marauding white settlers. However, with Robinson's departure, conditions deteriorated and few of the Aborigines survived. This left the green pastures of the mainland to be populated with enterprising and increasingly respectable settlers. The island economy was soon booming on the back of sheep farming and whaling combined with a surplus of convict labour.

Yet commercial success was secondary amongst Arthur's concerns. An ex-army officer, he was also a serious student of crime and punishment, eager to ensure that Van Diemen's Land evolved into what the British wanted it to be, an efficient gaol. And indeed on Arthur's watch, Van Diemen's Land became a most impressively run outdoor penitentiary. Prisoners, most of them men, were landed at an average rate of 2,000 a year and immediately set to work, building bridges, making roads and toiling on the farms of the growing gentry. Arthur offered the incentive of tickets of leave and conditional pardons for the industrious convicts, and the threat of the chain gang and the penitentiary to the troublesome. He famously expounded: "The most unceasing labour is to be extracted from the convicts... and the most

THE GULAG PENINSULA

In 1830 a new penal settlement was formed at Port Arthur, deliberately chosen for its splendid isolation. The prison was built 100 km (60 miles) from Hobart on a peninsula that could be reached only by a narrow isthmus. Port Arthur was originally a timber station, though as its importance as a penal institution grew, so too did its industries; in 1842 a huge flour mill and granary was erected. By 1848 Port Arthur was well on its way to becoming one of the largest institutions of punishment in the colonies. The flour mill was converted into a penitentiary, which meant convicts would continue to pour into Port Arthur in the decades after the end of transportation.

The isolation of the settlement was crucial. Escape from the southeastern peninsula was next to impossible, and if a convict did manage to make it as far as Eaglehawk Neck, baying dogs were there to greet him. Many of the 12,000 convicts shipped to Port Arthur between 1830 and 1877 would die on the settlement, where they were buried in mass graves on the Isle of the Dead. Port Arthur was but one of many convict stations established during this period, but its size and later history as an asylum, fire-ravaged relic and massacre site have meant ongoing historical fascination. Today it is Tasmania's most visited tourist site (see pages 95–98 and 100–101).

harassing vigilance over them is to be observed."

Objections to the transportation of convicts were first raised in Britain, among liberals and especially the clergy, who questioned its ability to deter or reform. When transportation ceased to New South Wales in 1840, the abolitionist protests focused on Van Diemen's Land. In addition to their forceful moral arguments, abolitionists spoke also of the importance of self-government and of the economic benefits that would surely flow from the cessation of the convict system. However, in reality this was an economy and society heavily dependent on convict labour; when transportation finally ceased in 1852, the economy suffered. The abolitionists had been so successful in denouncing the evils of the penal colony that it would be some time before Van Diemen's Land could remove the stigma of convictism. A name change seemed a good way to start the island's rehabilitation.

The last convict vessel docked at Hobart on 26 May 1853. This was followed by the island's governmental independence from New South Wales in 1856, a cause for much celebration in the freshly minted "Tasmania".

A green and pleasant land

Contemporary Tasmania is a much-loved place. Locals and visitors alike effuse affectionately about the lush, green landscape and the strong sense of community that pervades both cities and towns. These endearing qualities and appreciation of them are not new. As early as the 1820s, visitors such as Edward Curr of the Van Diemen's Land Company were struck by the locals "degree of nationality" and their passionate references to the "good old days". James Ross, writing in the *Hobart Town Courier* in 1829, identified a love of country in the "native Van Diemener", who he believed would pine away in exile, longing for the magnificent mountains and verdant plains of his own island. Such passionate identifications were apparent within a generation, a striking characteristic in a colony essentially of exile. Yet despite Tasmania's

distance from London, its cool maritime climate and appealing landscape of mountains, forests, rivers and lakes were familiar to the settlers. Such vistas were reminiscent of the Scottish Highlands much celebrated in the cult of the picturesque at the time. Elsewhere, in the open grasslands of the midlands for instance, Tasmania exuded a romantic, pastoralist air. More than the other southern colonies, for settlers and convicts alike, Tasmania felt and looked like "home".

Not surprisingly, the contrast between the pure natural environment and the corrupt degeneracy of a penal society featured prominently in anti-transportation literature.

One crusader's lament was typical: "I always thought that of all the British colonies, the beautiful island of Van Diemen's Land is the last which ought to be subjected to this cruel degradation". And while the end of transportation meant a decline in Tasmania's fortunes, the demographic and economic effects of the slump proved vital to fostering an emerging sense of place. As Tasmanians grew accustomed to their peripheral status to the rest of the Australian colonies and its lack of allure for migrants, local ties were strengthened through intermarriage and a uniquely Tasmanian version of the Australian nationalism that was sweeping the mainland

ABOVE LEFT AND RIGHT: the penitentiary at Port Arthur penal settlement, from a contemporary etching, and as it appears now.

by the 1880s. "Australia for the morphed "Tasmania for the Tasmanians".

Self-government

Tasmanians were always understandably inclined to put Tasmania first. This sense of distinctiveness and autonomy was, ironically, profoundly informed by the island's image of itself as a little England. One of its first gestures as a self-governed colony was to enthusiastically display their patriotism as Britain entered the Crimean War. Huge sums of money were donated to the cause Tasmanian newspapers were engulfed with emotional responses to the events in Europe.

Conscious of its place on the fringes of the Empire, aware of the need to overcome its violent and unrespectable past and proud of its physical affinities with the mother country, Tasmania pronounced itself Tasmanian and proudly British. The Church of England established an early and ever-increasing presence. Empire builders who fought and lived in India were invited to Tasmania to relax. As elsewhere in the Empire, the emerging school system slavishly modelled the British in both protocol and syllabus.

When Britain passed the Constitution Act of 1855, ushering in formal self-government in Tasmania, it was celebrated as a reinforce-

PUTTING DOWN ROOTS

The present-day landscape of Tasmania owes much to the early British settlers, who planted hedgerows across the island and eradicated native flora in favour of roses and oak trees.

ment of responsible government rather than an opportunity for radical change. The system of government – an ostensibly democratic lower house that was still dependent on land ownership for voting, and a powerful legislative assembly stacked with wealthy gentlemen – symbolised Tasmania's British allegiance.

Yet the apparent homogeneity of Tasmania's population has always been deceptive. A landscape abundant in trees, seals, sheep, apples and, eventually, gold encouraged a plethora of regional identities, not all of them finely tuned to the prevailing Britishness. On the margins of the "genteel" society that dominated politics were the Bass Strait Islanders – descendents of the sealers and Aboriginal women. Timber gatherers, especially "piners" in the south west, argued for their share of the spoils. Small farmers in the southeast (apples) and northwest (potatoes) and trappers and shepherds from the central plateau would also come to express increasing dissatisfaction with Hobart-dominated politics.

Launceston emerged as a base for serious challengers to vested interests. And the disenfranchised found an advocate in the outstanding liberal reformer Andrew Inglis Clark (1848–1907), a staunch proponent of proportional representation and the Federation of Australia. However, while Clark's reformist dreams would mostly be realised, regionalism and jealousies continued as staples of Tasmanian political life.

The Tasmania that emerged from the spectre of transportation was a struggling colony, committed to survival. In a demographic trend that would come to be repeated in the 20th century, a significant number of Tasmanians headed north to Victoria in search of their share of the gold-rush bounty. Many who stayed on the island were rewarded in the 1860s and 1870s with growing markets for Tasmania primary products and the discovery of gold and tin. As the rest of the colonies were consumed by economic depression in the 1880s, a silver and copper mining boom on the west coast in the 1890s helped ease Tasmania's hardship.

Tasmania's population was growing and it was finally attracting migrants, while the opening of the University of Tasmania in 1890 was testimony to faith in the future. But in 1891 things took a turn for the worse when the Bank of Van Diemen's Land collapsed. Such was the impact of the crash that for many years afterwards Tasmanians dated events from "the year the VDL Bank went broke". It was hardly a promising sign for the island's prospects on the eve of Federation.

nia for the Tasmanians" continued to conclude the speeches of both the gentleman-dominated Tasmanian Native's Association and local unions. When Tasmanians voted overwhelmingly in favour of the federation of the colonies in the 1898 referendum it was in the spirit of enabling, rather than impairing, island autonomy. It would do Tasmania more harm than good to stay outside a united Australia.

So Tasmania entered the 20th century committed to the new Australia as a practical move, while staying resolutely loyal to Crown and Empire. The island's national reputation as the state that lagged behind the rest, in a nostalgic imperial glow, was further encour-

Federation and war

Occasional proposals that Tasmania should amalgamate with Victoria provoked partisan Tasmanian responses. Geography, wrote one Tasmanian to *The Bulletin* in 1898, meant Tasmania was the "only naturally separate province of Australia". Tasmania's distinct terrain and climate had produced "a people of more virile temper and stronger physique than the people on the other side of the Strait".

Meanwhile, the refrain "let us have Tasma-

LEFT: 19th century Hobart. **ABOVE:** the Discovery Museum in Stanley on the north coast.
RIGHT: wartime recruitment poster.

aged by the slow growth of the Labor Party and the fervent response to the Boer War.

It was perhaps the most passionate of all states in its commitment to World War I, voting "yes" for conscription in the first referendum and unleashing a new wave of loyalist organisations. From a population of roughly 200,000, more than 14,000 men enlisted and nearly 2,500 were killed. Island political sympathies shifted back to conservative after a flirtation with Labor, following their debut on the Tasmanian political scene in 1909.

By the 1920s, with primary industry in decline, Tasmanians came to suspect federation had doomed the island to redundancy as it struggled to compete alongside larger and more influential states. Still, when Tasmanian J. A. "Honest Joe" Lyons ascended to the Prime Ministership of Australia in 1932, he was able to make sure Tasmania was not forgotten in the Great Depression relief effort. Joe and his wife Enid caught the popular imagination and to the end the pair were convinced their Depression schemes "saved the nation from ruin".

After Joe's death in 1939, Enid entered the federal House of Representatives as its first woman member, having won a Tasmanian seat. Joe and Enid's "Home Hill" in Devonport is open to the public and celebrates both

Australia laments a brain and talent drain of their youngest and brightest, Tasmania has to suffer two-fold, losing locals to the mainland first.

The island's population size varied as its fortunes rose and fell over the course of the 20th century. The state was hit hard by losses during World War II, but recorded its first population growth above the national average in the immediate post-war period. Yet this was a blip, facilitated by the growth of industrialisation, as the Hydro-Electric Commission became its directing force. Before too long such industrial largesse was to become a source of island conflict, as "progress" was

their domesticity and Enid's impressive collection of Empire memorabilia. The significant place of the Lyons of Tasmania in Australian political history is one example of how Australia's electoral system – which allocates seats per state, rather than per capita – has granted this smallest state political influence out of proportion to its diminutive size.

Joe Lyons wasn't the only Tasmanian to make an off-island splash in the 1930s. Errol Flynn (1909–1959; *see panel on page 80*) remains the most famous local hero, and his move from Hobart to Hollywood was the kind of journey that has become a classic Tasmanian rite of passage. If contemporary

increasingly pitted against Tasmania's oft-declared heartland, the wilderness.

Saving the wild places

In Tasmania, there are monuments to Abel Tasman, doomed governor-explorer John Franklin, all the wars fought for Empire, the father of Australian landscape painting John Glover (in Evandale, near the family farm, Patterdale, where he painted his most memorable landscapes) and David Boon, the test cricketer (at Hobart's Bellerive Oval). The convict past has been rehabilitated at Port Arthur, where convicts are reborn as skilled workers. Yet even affection for Errol Flynn cannot match

Tasmania's first and most prominent love – the beauty of its natural environment.

Tourism became a booming industry over the course of the 20th century and while visitors may delight in the restored colonial charm of Battery Point or the historical homesteads of Launceston, what really brings people to Tasmania are the natural wonders of Cradle Mountain, Cataract Gorge, Lake St Clair National Park, the Gordon River and Huon Valley, to name just a few. Tasmanians have been celebrating these landscapes since the beginning, rooting their Tasmanian identity in the earth, sea and skies.

Before the Hydro-Election Commission threatened to flood the glorious Lake Pedder in southwestern Tasmania in 1972, environmental activism was a fringe activity. After, Tasmania's identification with the wilderness became political. The Lake Pedder case suggested the stakes were high. On 8 September, environmental activist Brenda Hean and pilot Max Price set off in a Tiger Moth biplane, flying to Canberra to lobby politicians against the flooding. They never arrived and the wreckage of their plane was never found. The leader of today's Green Party, Senator Bob Brown – who competes with Denmark's Princess Mary as the best-known Tasmanian alive today – is still calling for an investigation.

It was the flooding of Lake Pedder that saw the birth of the United Tasmania Group, the first Green political party in the world. Despite the protests, more than 240 hectares (600 acres) of Tasmania's wilderness were drowned. Several years later, however, when the Tasmanian Government passed the Hydro-Electric Commission's development plan to flood the Franklin River, Tasmanian's last wild river, the conservation movement rallied harder than ever before, arousing the emotions of urban dwellers on the mainland and abroad. This time they won – in 1983 the High Court overturned the case and prevented the flooding. There was even the suggestion that the Franklin River helped the Hawke Labor government win the federal election in 1983.

Since this landmark case, Tasmania's wilderness has continued to define not only Tasmania's sense of place, but also its role in federal politics and the national imagination. With each election Australians have grown accustomed to the sight of prospective candidates inspecting endangered forests and staking a claim either for the preservation of national wonders or the continued employment of hardworking Tasmanians in the logging industry. Political pundits most recently blamed the Federal Labor Party's loss in the 2004 election on their clumsy, ad hoc policy responses to Tasmanian environmental, union and logging interests. Politically and culturally, Tasmanians can both confound and

entrance mainlanders. Federal senators such as the now-retired Brian Harradine yield considerable power and have proved predictable only in their unpredictability.

Tasmania has been known to drop off maps of Australia, cartographers apparently forgetting about its existence. Yet its history and beauty are indelibly part of the Australian psyche. And for every princess that heads across the seas to find her future elsewhere, there is an author such as Richard Flanagan or a committed activist such as Bob Brown, who decide to stay, celebrating the natural wonders and defending them as the enduring heart of Tasmania. ❑

LEFT: soldiers parade through Hobart prior to departing for Europe, October 1914.
RIGHT: Senator Bob Brown, leader of the Green Party.

Decisive Dates

c. **40,000 BC** The first human inhabitants reach Tasmania. They arrive over a sand dune desert known as the Bassian Plains.

c. **12,000 BC** Tasmania is separated from the mainland of Australia.

1642 Abel Janszoon Tasman, the Dutch explorer, sails past the west coast island. He names it Van Diemen's Land after the governor of Batavia.

1772 Captain James Cook sails past the east coast of Tasmania. The first Europeans (from the expedition of the French explorer Marion du Fresne) come ashore at Marion Bay.

1788 The First Fleet arrives in Sydney Cove, bringing the first convicts to Australia.

1798 Matthew Flinders becomes the first man to circumnavigate Tasmania.

1803 Lieutenant John Bowen, a British soldier, chooses Risdon Cove on the eastern shore of the River Derwent in the southeast for the first settlement of Europeans.

1804 Lieutenant-governor David Collins moves the settlement across the river and Hobart is founded.

1805 Europeans settle near the mouth of the River Tamar on the north coast.

1806 This settlement moves upriver and Launceston is founded, at first independent of Hobart.

1815 Governor Davey proclaims martial law against bushrangers.

1820–40 European population of Van Diemen's Land grows from 4,300 to 57,000.

1822 The Sarah Island penal settlement is established in Macquarie Harbour on the west coast.

1824 George Arthur appointed Governor of Van Diemen's Land. He holds this position until 1836 and transforms the lawless colony into a proper settlement.

1825 Van Diemen's Land, which had been part of the colony of New South Wales, becomes a colony in its own right. Convict station established on Maria Island, off the east coast.

1828 Martial law declared and soldiers used to clear the land of Aborigines.

1829 Europeans settle what later becomes Burnie, on the north coast.

1830 The Black Line, a military plan to round up Aborigines, is started. George Augustus Robinson begins his mission to protect Aborigines in a settlement on Flinders Island. Port Arthur timber station founded. Henry Savery's *Quintus Servinton*, Australia's first novel, published in Hobart.

1832 "Escape-proof" prison established at Port Arthur.

1833 Sarah Island penal settlement is closed.

1834 John Batman sails from Launceston to Port Phillip in Victoria: he and his associates found the city of Melbourne. Theatre Royal built in Hobart – Australia's oldest theatre.

1842 Hobart Town becomes a city. Convict transportation reaches its peak – 5,329 in one year.

1843 Royal Society of Tasmania founded to promote science.

1847 Marcus Clarke's *For the Term of his Natural Life* published, the great epic of the penal system.

1852 Gold is discovered near Fingal, near the east coast. Elections held for the first municipal councils in Hobart and Launceston. Transportation officially ended.

1853 The last shipment of convicts arrives.

1854 The two houses of Parliament (upper and lower) established.

1856 Van Diemen's Land's name is changed to Tasmania. The title "Governor" is conferred on the representative of the English Crown.

1861 Population of Tasmania reaches 90,000.

1871 Tin is discovered at Mount Bischoff near the west coast.

1876 Truganini, the last of the "full-blooded"

Tasmanian Aborigines, dies in Hobart. The Elwick racecourse opens north of Hobart.

1877 The penal settlement at Port Arthur is closed.

1879 Tin discovered at Mount Heemskirk.

1880 The first telephone installed, with a line from Hobart to the Mount Nelson Signal Station, just south of the city.

1884 Fears of a Russian invasion lead to the island's defences being strengthened.

1890 The University of Tasmania is founded.

1897 Queenstown founded after gold, silver and copper are discovered at nearby Mount Lyell.

1900 Tasmanian forces leave to fight in the Boer War in South Africa.

1901 The Commonwealth of Australia is proclaimed: Tasmania becomes a state of Australia.

1909 Errol Flynn is born in Hobart. The first Labor government is elected in Tasmania.

1914 The first aeroplane flight in Tasmania. Tasmanian forces leave to fight in World War I.

1920 Chocolate factory north of Hobart built for English company Cadbury's.

1932–9 Joseph Aloysius Lyons the first (and only) Tasmanian to be Prime Minister of Australia.

1936 Last known thylacine, otherwise known as the Tasmanian tiger, dies in captivity.

1940 Tasmanian forces leave to fight in World War II.

1972 Protests over proposed flooding of Lake Pedder. United Tasmania Group, the world's first Green party, is born.

1973 The first legal casino in Australia opens at Wrest Point, Hobart.

1974 Tasmania's State Wages Board awards women equal pay.

1975 The *Lake Illawarra*, a bulk ore carrier, crashes into the Tasman Bridge in Hobart, causing part of it to collapse. Twelve people, from the bridge and the ship, die.

1977 Rebuilt Tasman Bridge opens.

1978 Passenger train services cease operating in Tasmania.

1979 Tasmania's first ombudsman appointed.

1983 The High Court of Australia rules against the building of the Gordon-below-Franklin dam, planned for the Gordon River in the southwest. Bob Brown elected to Tasmanian parliament as its first Green member.

1984 Theatre Royal, Hobart, gutted by fire.

1986 Archaeologists working in the southwest discover Aboriginal rock paintings thought to be 20,000 years old.

1987 Archaeologists find Aboriginal stencils of handprints dating back to the last Ice Age.

1989 Green independents gain the balance of power in Tasmania's parliament and enter into an accord with Groom's Labor government.

1993 The $53-million Henty Gold Mine opens near the west coast. Speed cameras introduced on Tasmania's roads.

1995 The Aboriginal Land Act is passed and 12 significant historic and cultural sites are returned to Aboriginal Tasmanians.

1996 Martin Bryant kills 35 people at and around the Port Arthur Historic Site. Prominent environmentalist Bob Brown elected to the Federal Senate. David Boon's 12-year career in first-class cricket ends. He has played in 107 matches and scored 7,422 runs.

2002 The original *Spirit of Tasmania* Victoria to Tasmania ferry is replaced by two superfast ferries, *Spirit of Tasmania I* and *Spirit of Tasmania II*. Richard Flanagan wins the Commonwealth Writer's Prize for *Gould's Book of Fish*.

2004 Hobart-born Mary Donaldson and Crown Prince Frederik are married in Copenhagen Cathedral. She becomes Her Royal Highness The Crown Princess of Denmark. ❑

LEFT: Governor Arthur, appointed in 1824.
RIGHT: logging is still on the political agenda.

TASMANIAN IDENTITY AND SOCIETY

No longer the isolated country bumpkins,
today's Tasmanians are proud, opinionated,
often quirky – but still undecided
about their true place in Australian life

Not so very long ago, many mainland Australians – or "mainlanders" as Tasmanians insist on referring to them – saw Tasmania as a backwater, a joke. Indeed jokes about Tasmanians, not to mention their two heads, were as commonplace here as jokes about the Irish or the Polish in other parts of the world. Not many of these mainlanders, let alone international visitors, saw any reason to visit, and Tasmania was treated as the dim cousin in the Commonwealth family. Its residents – "Apple Islanders" at best, or "pointyheads" at worst – were as low on the totem pole as could be. All of this was determined from a distance and without much, if any, experience of the place or its people.

Tasmanians didn't pay much heed to it, though, and continued about their business: farming, mining, working out whether or not the "convict stain" on one's family was something to claim or deny, and producing some of the country's best Australian Rules footballers (records fail to show just how many elite athletes have honed their skills on the infamous gravel grounds around Queenstown in the state's rugged southwest).

Along the way came a movie star in the dashing Errol Flynn. A mental image of Short Beach in Battery Point, a century ago, exemplifies the way Tasmania has changed: there's young Flynn, wetting his feet in the cold, clean waters of the River Derwent, learning to

swim without fanfare or fuss. Tasmania was an uncomplicated and provincial place, a backwater content to promote itself as "Australia's food basket", exporting the bulk of its best produce interstate and overseas.

The Tasmanians you will meet today are, by and large, enormously different from those of Errol Flynn's day. The "convict stain" no longer exists, Queenstown's gravel footie ground is still there but the jokes are long gone, and Tasmania is now firmly entrenched as both a desirable brand name and destination, and is becoming increasingly cosmopolitan, particularly in its "twin capitals" Hobart and Launceston.

PREVIOUS PAGES: British Admiral Beach, King Island.
LEFT: watermelon man.
RIGHT: park ranger with wombat.

Hobart, in the south, is the seat of government, the university and the state's leviathan public service. It has sent apples, chocolate and latterly beer, ultra-fast passenger and vehicle ferries, and at least one princess to the outside world. To the north is Launceston, an old-money town, where a conservatism borne of the city's former life as an agriculture hub remains today. Launceston, though, is a more stylish city than Hobart. Some locals claim that's due to its (relative) proximity to Melbourne, others reckon Melbourne's mantle as Australia's most stylish metropolis is purely due to its being so close to Launceston.

Tasmanians, like most Australians, are fiercely proud of where they live. It should be noted that Hobart is truly (as well as officially) the state capital. And while they're only 200 km (125 miles) apart, Launcestonians and Hobartians are as different as are Londoners and Mancunians or New Yorkers and Los Angelinos. Tasmanians from other parts of the state are, individually and collectively, different again; all in a state that's about the same size as Scotland and has a population that has yet to reach half a million.

You will still find pockets of the countryside – and not always particularly remote ones – where life has changed very little over the past few decades. And the locals, while not

ABORIGINAL ISSUES

Tasmania's Aboriginal community is perpetually divided over its origins and how, or indeed whether, it fits into today's society. That Europeans treated the island's indigenous peoples deplorably is not at issue; what remains to be settled is what it means to be Aboriginal today. Following the recent return of Aboriginal land on Cape Barron Island (in Bass Strait), Tasmania looks likely to be the first Australian state to grant financial reparation to the "stolen generations" of Aborigines, taken from their families and placed into state-run care. How that might unite or further divide the Aboriginal community is not easy to foresee.

inherently resistant to change, kind of like it that way. Whole communities are brought together by their town fairs or, in larger communities by their royal shows. These are once-a-year gatherings that still feature displays of the latest farming machinery and sales of homemade preserves, bric-a-brac and livestock – often as children's pets. Save for the type of games on offer at the sideshow alley and the presence of the satellite TV sales stand, it's difficult to imagine today's fairs and shows being much different from those of 50 years ago. Mothers still talk about whether or not their children will stay with them or move "into town"; fathers still fret over how wet or dry it has been (Tasmanians are obsessed with the weather); courtships are commenced, knees are scraped, stomachs upset.

Local colour

In recent years Tasmania has enjoyed a boom in its visitor numbers, and tourists are made to feel welcome. Locals love to hear about other places and other cultures. You'll hear plenty about Tasmania's too, sometimes to the point of what's known as "copping an earbashing", often embellished with a dubious claim or two. You may need to discount half of what you hear – but it's up to you to determine which half.

Two centuries of European history have

The state has an abundance of Australia's "oldests": the oldest bridge (in Richmond), the oldest golf course (at Bothwell), the oldest theatre (Hobart's Theatre Royal), the oldest brewery (also in Hobart) and, as Tasmania was settled as a British outpost and convict repository, the country's oldest military establishment, Anglesea Barracks.

Mistrust of the new

You'll also find some challenging, fascinating and often award-winning modern architecture. What's particularly interesting, though, is how little most Tasmanians seem to care for it. Indeed, it's surprising how scornful they are

thrown up genuine oddities of which Tasmanians (who are renowned for their quirky sense of humour) are proud, and for which visitors can keep an eye out. For example, Hobart is home to Australia's oldest synagogue, though the Jewish congregation has shrunk to the point where the synagogue has a website but not a rabbi. No one considers it a setback, just another opportunity for a tiny Tasmanian community to call on the sort of remarkable resourcefulness that has seen it survive for more than 160 years.

of most modern buildings, and how quickly they'll claim, "they're ruining the look of our cityscapes".

Hobart's architecture was altered – and not for the better – by a spate of post-World War II investment that led to the creation of a number of spectacular eyesores. They are, though, in their way, noteworthy and of interest to the visitor, though more of an ordeal for the civic pride of the recalcitrant Hobartian. Launceston missed out on that rush of investment and is a better city for it today: there remain sizeable pockets in the inner city where rows of Georgian houses and other spectacular architecture remain intact and in use.

LEFT: taking advantage of the pleasant climate.
ABOVE: greengrocer in Salamanca Market.

You'll hear – and rightly – plenty about the magnificent Government House at Pavillion Point in Hobart. Commanding a still-stunning view across the Derwent, the "early Victorian country house in neo-Gothic style", 73-room vice-regal residence is a hugely popular attraction when open to the public (once a year on Australia Day) and a source of much pride and boasting when it isn't. While the historic Hobart waterfront around Sullivan's Cove is the source of considerable debate, not to mention regret at some less-than-wise development, you won't hear so much about some of the breathtaking work that has also been done. Take a peek inside the Henry Jones Art Hotel in Hunter Street (actually on Hunter Island): this is the spot where Governor Collins first stepped ashore and where the Henry Jones trading empire was based. It was a jam factory, which lay idle for decades before being refashioned into magnificent, modern accommodation. If you take time to see it, you'll wonder why locals aren't more vocal about it.

Modern life

Tasmanians are living with – and thriving through – an uncharacteristically rapid period of change. From shedding a largely unwarranted "country bumpkin" tag to creating what many consider to be Australia's most socially

IMMIGRATION IN TASMANIA

After a century and a half of largely British and Irish immigration, the makeup of Tasmania was altered by a wave of migrants and "displaced persons" in the years immediately following World War II. People arrived in their thousands from the Netherlands, Germany, Poland and Italy, with a large number from what statisticians call "other continental European countries". They came to Tasmania not just to flee their war-ravaged homelands, but on contracts to continue the expansion of Tasmania's massive network of hydroelectric dams. Many of them stayed only for the duration of their contracts; many more of them, and their offspring (and their offspring's offspring) remain today.

The early part of the 21st century is seeing a similar influx of settlers from Sudan, Ethiopia, Sierra Leone and, to a lesser extent, Eritrea, Liberia, Rwanda, Somalia and Tanzania. And, although the state has received little more than a ripple from the waves of immigration into Australia from Asia, there are small numbers of Tasmanians from Vietnam and the Philippines, and even smaller numbers from other parts of Asia.

Students from a variety of Asian countries are found in a similar mix to that in every large city throughout Australia. There are also small numbers of migrants from the Middle East, particularly Lebanon and Syria.

progressive state, Tasmania has become a buzzword for "fresh" and "natural", while still embodying a way of life that is unhurried but unmistakeably contemporary. The Tasmanian you will meet today is sure to have strong views on any issue that directly affects his or her way of life, and a better-informed world view than ever before. Despite having Australia's most repressive and archaic anti-homosexuality laws only a decade ago, the state now embraces same-sex couples at all levels, and indeed leads the rest of Australia in legal recognition of gay and lesbian rights. Many predict Tasmania will be the first state to recognise gay marriage: a far cry from the

expressed as debate rages about the environment, how much of it should be preserved, and how much should be exploited. You're unlikely to meet a single Tasmanian who doesn't want to have a say in this debate.

Tasmania, rightly, considers itself the birthplace of the environmental movement in Australia, but not everyone you'll meet is happy about it. From the debate over the flooding of Lake Pedder *(see page 44)* in 1972, through the much larger, far more passionate protests, street marches and, ultimately, arrests less than 10 years later, as the iconic Franklin River was saved from a similar fate, environmentalists have been centre-stage. However, preservation

days not so long ago when gay rights protestors were carted away in police "divvy-vans".

Because of the state's electoral system and multi-member electorates, Tasmanians are as astute and politically aware a populace as you'll ever encounter. There are many issues of importance that unite and divide them, but none like management of the environment. Even in the suburbs, about as far as you can get (in Tasmanian terms) from the state's stunning wilderness areas, passionate views are

LEFT: looking down to Wineglass Bay from a viewpoint in Freycinet National Park. **ABOVE LEFT:** King Island Dairy. **ABOVE RIGHT:** law enforcement.

of wilderness comes at a cost (jobs lost, particularly in remote areas) and while the squabble itself was decided long ago – by politicians in Canberra, as it happens – some of the acrimony remains and occasionally surfaces.

The divisions are still there today, though it's not rivers but old-growth forests that are now at issue. Large tracts of the "old" Tasmania, its beliefs and its practices remain, while a newer Tasmania, full of "sea-changers" and bright young things who'd have once headed interstate, never to return, is emerging fast, jostling for space. As you'll see, today's Tasmanian tends to be one or the other, rather than a little of each. ❑

GEOGRAPHY

A mosaic of landscapes, Tasmania is famed for its natural
beauty. Pristine temperate rainforest, dramatic
coastlines and unique flora and fauna form a large
part of the appeal of this isolated southern land

Tasmania, the "Apple Isle", lies some 240 km (150 miles) adrift of Australia's southeastern coast across the Bass Strait. Hobart, its capital (latitude 42°50' south, population 180,000) is one of the world's most southerly cities: polewards of 40° south, only Christchurch and Dunedin in New Zealand are comparable – the outposts of Patagonian Chile, Argentina and the Falklands are further south but far smaller. Beyond Tasmania there are only the stormy waters of the Southern Ocean – the Roaring Forties – and then the Antarctic ice sheet. To the east lies the Tasman Sea, extending 1,600 km (1,000 miles) to the south island of New Zealand.

This southern annexe to Australia is famous for its natural beauty, with extensive tracts of pristine forest and mountains complemented by magnificent coastal scenery. Together with areas of farmland and pasture, it's all packed into the state's 68,332 sq. km (26,350 sq. miles) – an area around half the size of England, which equates to less than 1 percent of the total area of Australia. In more meaningful terms, Tasmania measures approximately 300 km (200 miles) north to south, and 320 km (215 miles) from east to west. Some 6 percent of the state's land area is comprised of smaller islands, the most significant of which are King and Flinders islands off the northwest and northeast coasts. The population is around 480,000, around 2.5 percent of the Australian total.

The lay of the land

Flat land is in short supply in Australia's most mountainous state, the most extensive areas being in the north around Devonport, the Tamar and Derwent rivers and Launceston, and further south around Hobart.

The wildest part of Tasmania is the west and southwest, much of which is encompassed within national parks. Rugged mountain ranges clothed in temperate rainforest alternate with treeless plains (mainly buttongrass moorland), while the coast is marked with sheer cliffs and isolated windswept beaches. The grandeur and scale of the scenery bears a certain resemblance to the Scottish Highlands. The splendour continues into the northwestern corner, with further stands of forest and beautiful beaches.

The highest land, however, runs across the west-centre of the island. A large plateau is studded with various ranges and peaks, the loftiest of which is Mt Ossa – at 1,617 metres (5,305 ft) Tasmania's highest point. Numerous sizeable lakes dot the landscape, bearing witness to the glaciation of the region.

To the east of these ridges are the Midlands, an area of natural grasslands lying between Hobart and Launceston which have been gradually replaced by farmland. Another chain of uplands runs along the beautiful east coast, with Legges Tor (1,573 metres/5,160 ft) the island's second-highest peak in the northeast of the island.

eroded and worn down (in contrast to a range of more recently formed mountains such as New Zealand's Southern Alps). In fact, the ancient geology of the island can be traced back to the time of the Gondwana supercontinent: together with Antarctica, Tasmania was one of the blocks of land to separate from Gondwana, and although part of the general Australian landmass, it was originally connected to New Zealand, South America and Antarctica. Tasmania's geology has much in common with Antarctica, in particular the presence of dolerite rock which does not occur elsewhere in Australia. The ancient link is further supported by the

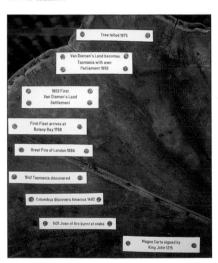

Geology

Tasmania only separated from the rest of Australia around 11,000 years ago, when rising sea levels flooded low-lying areas. Evidence of this can be seen in the broad estuaries (rias) of many of the state's rivers. Reminders of the island's glacial past abound in the U-shaped valleys of the uplands.

Much of the bedrock of Tasmania is extremely old and, in common with the rest of Australia, its mountains are considerably

discovery of fossilised plant life in the Antarctic ice sheet which bears strong resemblance to the unique species found in Tasmania today. Similar species exist in southern Chile and New Zealand.

Mining is an important part of the economy, with rich deposits of copper, iron, tin and zinc.

Vegetation

Despite the considerable pressure from logging concerns *(see pages 45–47)*, much of Tasmania remains forested. A great swathe of pristine temperate rainforest – one of the largest such environments on earth – extends across the southwest, rich in various types of

LEFT: where the mountains meet the sea.
ABOVE: some trees date back hundreds of years.
RIGHT: a Huon pine.

eucalyptus and other species, many of which are found nowhere else on earth.

Among the many indigenous species of tree found in the state are several conifers, the most notable of which is the Huon pine *(Lagarostrobos Franklinii)*. Highly valued by the boat-building trade for its remarkably water-resistant wood, these majestic trees can grow to over 40 metres (130 ft) and live for 2,000 years. Huon pines thrive best in riverine environments in southwestern Tasmania – some fine examples can be seen on a cruise along the Gordon River.

Another noteworthy species is the Southern beech *(Nothofagus gunnii)*, which, perhaps

tree, famous for the honey produced from the pollen of its summer flowers.

Approximately one seventh of the area of Tasmania is covered in Buttongrass moorland; buttongrass itself is a type of sedge, and co-exists with other sedges and grasses in this ecosystem. It is the main vegetation type in poorly drained areas, most common in the southwest and west. Another common species is *Anodopetalum biglandulosum*, commonly known as horizontal scrub. The sub-alpine plant grows in dense thickets and is familiar to any hiker who has attempted to stray off piste in the wilderness areas of the southwest.

Tasmania's upland moors are found in

surprisingly, is the only native tree that loses its leaves in winter. There is a splendid autumnal display of foliage colour from these trees in the Cradle Mountain National Park (the species favours cool, wet environments). It is closely related to the beeches of New Zealand and southern South America, an indication of their shared ancient ancestry on the supercontinent of Gondwanaland.

The swamp gum *(Eucalyptus regnans)*, mainly found in the forests of the south, can reach heights of over 100 metres (330 ft), making it the largest flowering plant on earth. Other notable species include the tree fern *(Dicksonia antarctica)* and the leatherwood

exposed areas with poor soil, most of which are on the central plateau. Often these treeless areas are quite limited in extent, as the topography and soil conditions, which dictate vegetation cover, vary greatly over relatively small areas. This variety is a characteristic of Tasmania. The frequency of bushfires (more especially in the east) also plays a part in the patchwork nature of parts of the landscape.

For details on the wildlife of Tasmania see pages 40–41.

Climate

The southerly location and the influence of the ocean means that Tasmania is considerably cooler, and rainier, than the rest of Australia, particularly in the south and west of the island. Summers are still warm and mostly sunny, however, with heatwaves bringing temperatures over 30°C (86°F) for short periods, particularly in the north. Late summer usually brings the most prolonged spells of good weather. Winter can be cold, and snow is common on higher ground. *See climate chart on page 259.*

National Parks, Reserves and World Heritage Areas

For most visitors, a major part of the appeal of Tasmania lies in its landscapes and nature, the ern Tasmania, which lies within the boundaries of several National Parks. The Reserves, of which there are several different categories including State Reserves, Conservation Areas, Nature Reserves and Regional Reserves, are areas which are accorded varying statutory protection. Land in any of the Reserves does not overlap with that in the National Parks, and unlike the Parks no pass or fee is required to enter. There are also a handful of Marine Reserves dotted around the Tasmanian coasts.

Some of the most rewarding National Parks are Cradle Mountain–Lake St Clair *(see pages 207–11)* in the highlands – the starting point for the famous Overland Track, Freycinet on

highlights of which can be found in the numerous National Parks – in total there are 19 of them, while the Tasmanian Parks and Wildlife Service manages over 400 reserves. Together these amount to more than a third of the land area of the state. Around 20 percent of the state is also designated a World Heritage Area. There is some overlap between the three categories: the Tasmanian Wilderness World Heritage Area (as recognised by UNESCO to protect an area of outstanding universal significance) covers a large swathe of southwest-

the east coast *(see pages 142–4)*, the Franklin–Gordon Wild Rivers *(see pages 213–14)* and the Walls of Jerusalem *(see pages 205–7)*. The largest and most pristine of all is the magnificent Southwest National Park. Other notable National Parks include Ben Lomond, Hartz Mountains, Mt Field, Mt William, South Bruny, Strzelecki and Tasman, which between them offer visitors almost every aspect of the Tasmanian outdoors. ❑

● *For more information on visiting National Parks and Reserves see page 257, or visit the Tasmanian Parks and Wildlife Service website at www.parks.tas.gov.au, and the Wilderness Society site at www.wilderness.org.au*

LEFT: open Hartz. The Hartz Mountains National Park.
ABOVE: alpine flowers on Ben Lomond.

WILDLIFE

Not only is Tasmania rich in wildlife, but for a number of species it's the last safe haven

Australian wildlife is distinctive enough with its marsupials and monotremes, but Tasmania, by dint of its physical isolation from the mainland, adds its own ingredients to the mix with the unique Tasmanian devil and the last remaining habitats for such creatures as the Eastern quoll and the Eastern barred bandicoot. Its bird population, too, contains some of the rarest species in the country: the forty-spotted pardalote is only found on Bruny Island or within Mt William National Park, and the orange-bellied parrot is so rare that huge infrastructure projects on the mainland have been abandoned or redesigned to accommodate it.

Marsupials, where the mother gives birth to a glorified embryo, which then grows in a pouch, are well represented; most common are Bennetts wallabies, which grow up to a metre (3 ft) tall. Pademelons are much smaller wallabies and harder to spot in their forest home, while the quolls and bandicoots are rarely seen.The only kangaroos are Foresters, now found only in National Parks in the northeast. However, a range of possums are relatively easy to spot.

The platypus and echidna are both examples of monotremes: mammals that lay eggs and then suckle the young. Both are most likely to be seen at dusk.

BELOW: the skink is distinctive for its stubby tail which looks as if it's had a couple of centimetres lopped off and, in some varieties, its blue tongue.

ABOVE: the echidna, or spiny anteater, an egg-laying mammal unique to Australia, is a fairly common sight in most parts of Tasmania.

LEFT: there are plenty of wallabies to be seen from the walking trails and, at dusk, along the roadside. Some are tame enough to search for food in campsites or even to pester tourists on beaches.

THE THYLACINE

The Tasmanian tiger – or thylacine – was a dog-like meat-eating marsupial. A fast runner, possessed of a fantastic set of jaws, the tiger was thought by early colonial settlers to be responsible for killing and maiming sheep. The government offered a generous bounty for dead thylacines, and in consequence, by the early 20th century the creature was becoming rare. The last captive individual died in a Hobart zoo in 1936 – and the species was officially declared extinct. In subsequent years, thylacines were still spotted in the wild, but reported sightings have become few and Tasmania's tiger is now confined to the realm of myth. The ultimate test – a A$1 million cash reward – was offered by The Bulletin magazine in 2005 for a confirmed sighting of a thylacine. There were no takers.

Today all that remains is a few seconds of black and white film of a tiger pacing its cage in the zoo, and its image reproduced everywhere, most notably on Cascade beer bottles.

ABOVE: Tasmanian devils are carnivorous marsupials which are unique to the state. In recent years a cancerous facial tumour disease has seriously reduced the size of the population.

ABOVE RIGHT: despite the warnings, motorists account for significant quantities of wildlife, and some roads can seem to be awash with roadkill. The most dangerous times are dawn and dusk.

BELOW: although there are numerous places supposedly good for seeing platypus in the wild, in reality the chances are quite slim. Ideal times are early morning or evening but the best bet may be Platypus House at Beauty Point *(see page 176)*.

ABOVE: Tasmania's last thylacine, photographed at Hobart Zoo in 1936.

RIGHT: little penguins (and guides are rigorous in avoiding the old term "fairy penguin") can be found at various locations around the coast. Guided viewing can be arranged at Stanley, Low Head, Bicheno, Bruny Island, King Island, Grassy (Flinders Island) and, of course, at Penguin on the north coast. The hide at Burnie is good too. Dusk is one of the best times to see them.

THE ENVIRONMENT

Conservation or exploitation? Fierce
arguments rage over how Tasmania's
wild places should be managed

No subject divides the people of Tasmania so thoroughly as the environment. It is an issue that has launched political movements and brought down governments; even national elections have swung on the struggle to preserve Tasmania's wild places.

With so much of nature's bounty still intact here, and money to be made from exploiting it, it's no wonder that the environment looms so large. Ask any Tasmanian for an opinion on the matter and, one way or the other, it's likely to be a passionate view. The history and current status of the environmental debate is complex and dramatic; and it's essential background knowledge for a deeper understanding of Tasmania.

Early exploitation

In pre-colonial Tasmania, nature must have been close to pristine. The island's Aboriginal population numbered only about 5,000 – and their nomadic way of life meant that no area was utilised for long. The real exploitation of Tasmania's resources began with the arrival of the Europeans in 1803. The island's tall hardwood forests were a perfect source of timber for the ships of the British colonies. In particular, Huon pine *(Dacrydium franklinii)*– miraculously rot resistant – was highly sought after, and convicts were quickly put to work felling in western Tasmania, the central plateau and the Huon Valley. Land was cleared for agriculture and livestock, and native

LEFT: beautiful and dammed.
RIGHT: Dove Lake in Cradle Mountain National Park.

animals were ruthlessly hunted for their meat. The thylacine – Australia's largest marsupial carnivore and a supposed threat to sheep – was hunted to extinction *(see page 41)*.

Whaling and sealing were big business in the early days of the colony. It is said that in old Hobart Town, residents could sometimes not sleep at night for the noise of whales in the harbour. In fact whales were so plentiful that they could be hunted from shore. By 1841, there were 53 whaling stations in Tasmania, and sealing was also a major industry. Within 50 years of European arrival, much of this was gone thanks to over-hunting. One hundred thousand seals and sealions had been killed for their skins, and by the 1850s, the southern right and sperm whales here had been hunted to the brink of extinction.

In the first 100 years of European settlement, the landscape of Tasmania was altered irrevocably – but this was only a taste of what was yet to come.

The anti-dam movement

As Tasmania moved into the 20th century, its wild rivers began to prove a hydro-industrialist's dream. In 1929, the Hydro Electric Commission (HEC) was formed with a view to supplying power for the island's intended industrialisation, and between the

mega-dams. There was a sustained, highly vocal anti-dam protest and Pedder soon became a major political controversy. In March 1972, with the dam waters already rising, the Tasmanian parliament collapsed as a result of the dispute. When elections were called the following month, a new political movement, the United Tasmania Group, put forward candidates on a conservation and anti-dam mandate – and the world's first Green party was born.

Despite the political upheaval and community opposition, the Strathgordon scheme went ahead, drowning Lake Pedder and making the environmental movement even more determined to save what was left of wild Tasmania.

1930s and the 1950s it built many ambitious hydro power schemes.

As remaining undammed river catchments in Tasmania's watery Central Highlands became few, the HEC's surveyors started to look to the rivers of the wild southwest – even though many of these waterways were by then already officially protected within national parks. In the early 1960s, the first road was bulldozed into the Southwest Wilderness, and in 1968, work on the immense Lake Pedder/Strathgordon power scheme began. Lake Pedder – a geological and aesthetic wonder – and much of the surrounding wilderness, would be drowned under the impact of these

When, in the early 1980s, there were rumblings of a new HEC dam, protest was swift and passionate.

The Gordon-below-Franklin scheme called for a 100-metre (330-ft) dam in the rainforests of the west coast's Gordon River, below its confluence with the Franklin. The scheme would have flooded 35 percent of the remaining Southwest Wilderness – by 1982, listed as a UNESCO World Heritage Area.

Intense Australia-wide protests climaxed in the Franklin Blockade: thousands of volunteers placed themselves in front of bulldozers and, in a flotilla of hundreds of small boats, blocked river access to barges carrying machinery to the dam site. There were 1,300 arrests. All over Tasmania tensions were high.

The Franklin debate became a tussle between the Tasmanian and Commonwealth (Federal) governments. National elections in early 1983 saw the Labor party campaigning on anti-dam promises, and when they won the election, new Prime Minister Bob Hawke's first announcement was an immediate cessation of works. Still dam-determined, the Tasmanian government took its argument to the High Court, which, after months of debate, ruled in favour of the Hawke government. The dam was finally abandoned, and the Franklin left to run free.

est are cleared in Tasmania every year, and the state has one of the highest rates of native forest destruction anywhere in the world.

In the early days of the colony, the clearing of forest for timber and farming was excruciatingly difficult – a battle of axe, handsaw and fire against giant trees up to 90 metres (300 ft) tall and 20 metres (65 ft) in girth. This was dangerous, backbreaking work, and a painstakingly slow process compared to the mechanised clear-felling that would follow.

Industrial forestry did not begin in Tasmania until the 1960s, with the advent of power machinery such as chainsaws, bulldozers and cable logging rigs. Since the 1970s, clear-

The Franklin victory had huge political and social costs. It divided Tasmania ideologically along pro- and anti-conservation lines, and set the stage for the vehement forest debate that currently cleaves the state.

The forest debate

At the time of European settlement, most of Tasmania was covered by forest. Two hundred years on, less than 20 percent of Tasmania's original old-growth forests remain. Some 30,000 hectares (74,000 acres) of native for-

felling has been the order of the day. By this method, selected areas are razed of all vegetation, straight saw-logs removed, and the remaining timber burnt before replanting, usually with single-species plantations of non-native trees.

POISONED FORESTS

One of the most controversial practices of the logging industry is to scatter poisoned carrots in new plantations to kill native wildlife – particularly wallabies and brushtail possums – that might eat the seedlings. This was banned on public land in 2005 but continues in privately owned plantations.

LEFT: pipes from the hydro scheme.
ABOVE: environmental protesters take to the streets.

Woodchipping for export began in Tasmania in 1972, first to process waste from sawmills, then as an industry in its own right. By 2000, some 5.1 million tonnes of matchbox-sized woodchips were being sent annually to Japan to be used in paper mills. Over 90 percent of timber taken from Tasmania's native forests now becomes woodchips (worth on average about A$10–12 per tonne) and only 3–4 percent becomes high-quality saw log and veneer. The success of the export woodchip industry has contributed some A$300 million to the state's economy each year, and employed over 8,000 people – but that could be about to change.

Green activists, who have objected to what they see as Gunns' ruthless exploitation of Tasmania's old-growth forests, claim it as a victory for conservationism. But the explanation could be simple economics: the Asian demand for woodchips is falling, and at the same time South American countries are increasing their output, at lower prices. Gunns now have plans to build a controversial A$2.4-billion pulp mill on the Tamar River. The company has already received millions of dollars of state support for the development, which would enable Gunns to process woodchips on home territory instead of exporting them, then sell the resulting pulp to the world.

Forests on public land in Tasmania are managed by the government corporation Forestry Tasmania, and harvested mostly by the private company Gunns Limited – Australia's largest forestry company, exporting more woodchips to Asia than all the other Australian states put together, for an annual profit in 2004 of A$105 million. But early in 2006 most of the state's 170 forest contracting businesses had their log purchase contracts with Gunns cut by at least 40 percent, with other long-term contracts between timber firms and Gunns and Forestry Tasmania not renewed. It resulted in several harvesting contractors closing their businesses and many more workers losing their jobs.

Objectors claim that the change of emphasis would do nothing to halt the destruction of Tasmania's ancient forests. Their opponents insist that changes in forestry practices are vital to preserve jobs and the economy of rural communities.

Just like the Franklin battle before it, the forest debate has created a fundamental division that goes to the very heart of Tasmania, an ideological clash between "rednecks" and "greenies" that shows little sign of abating.

Those who suggest that forestry in Tasmania should continue as today point out that much of the state is already protected: close to 40 percent of the landmass currently lies within a World Heritage Area, national parks or reserves. To this camp, any reduction in forestry that would cost jobs is unacceptable. Those who call for a reduction in the harvesting of old-growth forests point out that, though much of Tasmania's land area is reserved, little of this encompasses tall, biodiverse, old-growth habitat. Just 10 percent of original old-growth forest cover, they say, falls inside reserves: the rest is still vulnerable. Even the greenest of the green acknowledge that the state must have a forestry industry of some kind – but, they believe, Tasmania should stop selling its best asset cheap as woodchips or pulp.

In a world where wilderness is becoming harder to find, natural places may be the island's most valuable asset. Tourism has boomed in Tasmania since the 1990s. It adds A$1.74 billion to the state's economy each year, and employs 38,500 people. Most visitors now come here, at least in part, because of the island's natural environment.

Strahan on the west coast is perhaps the best case study of environmental preservation's benefits. Once the base for works on the Gordon-below-Franklin dam, Strahan would have been busy for a few years of dam building then probably returned to its west coast sleepiness – with few jobs or hope for its inhabitants. However,

Meanwhile the logging of old-growth forests continues and Tasmania's forest debate is still far from resolved. There have been promises that logging will be phased out in high conservation value old-growth forests on public land by 2010. But many fear that by 2010, there may be little old growth left to argue over.

Another way?

Since Europeans first went into Tasmania's tall forests and wildernesses, many have stood in awe at the natural beauty that resides there.

Strahan today is a thriving tourist town. The nearby rivers and rainforests that would have gone under the dam are now one of the state's greatest tourist drawcards. In hindsight, preserving the Franklin undoubtedly made both environmental and economic sense – as perhaps the fight to preserve the last old-growth forests will do in years to come.

The future for Tasmania's environment will no doubt lie somewhere between preservation and exploitation. Ecotourism will probably increase in the protected parts of the island, while industrial forestry continues in others. Tasmania's vociferous conservation campaigns will undoubtedly continue too. ❏

FAR LEFT AND LEFT: from this… to this: wood chips.
ABOVE: peering into the Devil's Gullet.

OUTDOOR PURSUITS

From white-water rafting to mountain
biking, golf to big-game fishing,
Tasmania offers plenty of ways to make
the most of the great outdoors

alk to most Tasmanians and you'll discover a great love of the outdoors. Whether it's boating, fishing, hiking or careering down a hillside on a mountain bike, many spend time being active in Tasmania's wonderful natural surroundings. More than 40 percent of the island is protected in World Heritage areas, parks and reserves. There's temperate rainforest, alpine meadows, glacial valleys and jagged – sometimes snowcapped – peaks, hundreds of pristine beaches, clean oceans, lakes, wild rivers, and plenty of quiet roads, walking paths and forest tracks.

To enjoy Tasmanian nature, you don't have to be fabulously fit or "oudoorsy". Much of it is accessible even in short trips, and the tourist infrastructure here is certainly geared up to offer outdoor experiences. If you can put up with mud and the occasional leech, and make a stab at reading a map, getting out there yourself is hugely rewarding.

Being outdoors in Tasmania famously means being prepared for any weather. The prevailing westerly winds, the Roaring Forties, rip across these southern latitudes, changing conditions in the blink of an eye. Expect sunburn or snow flurries on any day of the year, carry warm layers, wet-weather gear and sunscreen; and if you're going seriously remote, on land or sea, take an EPIRB – an Electronic Position Indicating Radio Beacon – for transmitting your position in the event of an emergency.

LEFT: a pause on the Frenchmans Cap trail.
RIGHT: start of the trek.

Bushwalking

For people who love to hike, Tasmania is heaven. Almost 3,000 km (1,864 miles) of walking tracks (more than the state's road network) criss-cross the island, and there's everything from tough, two-week expedition walks to strolls of a few hours on carefully manicured tracks. Tasmanians are avid bushwalkers – and kitted out in the de rigeur outfit of stripy thermal long johns under shorts – they're to be seen relishing wilderness walks all over the state, come sun, rain or snow. Some 350,000 visitors also partake of a Tasmanian bushwalk each year – but with so many kilometers of track, there's plenty of space for all.

Tasmania's best-known multi-day bush-walk is the **Overland Track**, a 65-km (40-mile) trek through the alpine scenery of the Cradle Mountain–Lake St Clair National Park *(see page 206)*. Walkers can stay in huts or camp; walk independently, or join a guided, catered trip with one Tasmania's several bush-walking operators *(see page 256)*. Another classic bushwalk is the **South Coast Track** – a 10-day adventure through the remote World Heritage wilderness of Tasmania's southwest.

For walkers who seek a real challenge, there's the **Western Arthurs Traverse**, known as Australia's most difficult walk. Covering just 20 km (12 miles), it takes in 25 major peaks in

Cycling

Cyclists love Tasmania. For tourers, the short distances, uncrowded roads and splendid scenery are hard to beat. Intrepid bikers can try the 480-km (300-mile) **Tasmanian Trail**, which traverses the island from Devonport to Dover. The track is shared with walkers and horse riders. A heart-thumping, lung-bursting journey is the spectacular, winding **Lyell Highway** that makes up most of the 290 km (180 miles) between Hobart and Strahan. In the northwest, the 100-km (62-mile) **Western Explorer** is an easier – but extremely remote – ride through the buttongrass plains of the Tarkine Wilderness *(see page 220)*.

12–14 days through fabulously rugged country. The most bragged-about prize in Tasmanian bushwalking is surely **Federation Peak**. Although only a modest 1,300 metres (4,265 ft), the peak is surrounded by precipitous cliffs and razorback ridges.

But walking in Tasmania is certainly not all hardcore – there are plenty of rewarding day walks of all grades. Hobart's forested Mount Wellington alone offers more than 50 different routes. And the classic short Tasmanian bushwalk – the well-made track to the east coast's legendary **Wineglass Bay**, a breath-takingly lovely curve of sand and ice-blue water – takes only three hours there and back.

MULTISPORT EVENTS

Tasmania leads the way in combination sports. The Freycinet Challenge, Australia's Multisport Championships, is held every September at Coles Bay. This gruelling two-day combination of running, mountain biking, road biking and sea kayaking is designed for teams as well as individuals. There's also the daredevil mountain-biking/canoeing/running race, the Ben Lomond Descent, in August, and numerous triathlons and long-distance endurance races right through the year. One of the most gruelling is April's Three Peaks Race, a sailing/running battle that demands its competitors risk seasickness on the high seas in between running up three mountains.

East coast touring is gentler: towns are closely spaced, gradients are moderate – and the clear, blue seas and beaches lend a relaxed, holiday feel. For mountain bikers the trails on forest-shrouded Mount Wellington, just behind Hobart, offer challenging rides, and just south of Hobart, Snug Tiers and the hills of the Huon Valley have as much mud, rocks and waist-deep puddles as any dedicated mountain biker could hope for. In the north are the rocky slopes of Ben Lomond. The highlight of the mountain biking year is Wildside in February, a gruelling four-day, 200-km (124-mile) race from Cradle Mountain to Strahan. An easier ride is the 15-km (9-mile) **Intercity Cycleway** between

fairways. The greens are fenced to keep these mobile mowers at bay.

Fifteen minutes from downtown Hobart is the Tasmania Golf Club. The course is bounded on three sides by the waters of beautiful Barilla Bay. It has narrow, tree-lined fairways and large, open greens. The third hole, a tricky cliff-top par five, is said to be Tasmania's most infamous.

And then there's Barnbougle Dunes Links near Bridport, described in *Australian Golf Digest* as "a course so jaw-droppingly spectacular that it will be love at first sight for even the most travelled golfer". Set amid the natural dune landscape, it incorporates a nature reserve. *(See page 255 for a list of golf courses.)*

Sullivans Cove in Hobart and Berriedale. Built on a disused railway track, it is pleasantly flat. *(For details of tour companies and bicycle hire, see page 236.)*

Golf

Tasmania has Australia's oldest golf course – possibly the first in the southern hemisphere – at Bothwell in the Midlands. This is true country golfing: the club, which dates from the 1830s, leases the course from property owners who continue to graze sheep on the

Fishing

Tasmania is known internationally in angling circles for its clean inland waters and its feisty brown trout. Between October and April, the small, clear streams of the Central Highlands teem with fish, and stocked lakes and dams provide fine sport for the keen fly fisherman. Many operators offer a guide service. *(See page 257.)*

On the sea a Tasmanian favourite is flathead, a tasty estuary fish, and the most prized catch to be found close to shore. There's great reef fishing for stripy trumpeter, coral perch and squid – and for divers, wonderful abalone. Further out, deep sea game fish like marlin, tuna, mako and blue shark put up an athletic fight.

LEFT: penny farthing racing in Evandale.
ABOVE: one of the most gruelling multisport events.

River rafting and kayaking

With so many lakes and wild rivers, Tasmania is prime white-water rafting and kayaking country. The **Franklin River** provides the state's peak white-water experience – 10 days of wilderness immersion in an environment as untouched and primeval as it was in the days before European settlement. The river navigates the World Heritage area's Franklin-Gordon Wild Rivers National Park, winding through dramatic gorges, tranquil pools, and ancient myrtle rainforest. Several operators offer guided trips through the summer months. With several grade-6 rapids, and stretches like The Cauldron, The Coruscades and The

Sea kayaking

In the early 1990s, sea kayaking Tasmania – and since then its popularity has skyrocketed. Locals hoist kayaks on to roof racks at the weekend, and head for a leisurely paddle on one of the state's more protected waterways.

Near Hobart, the **D'Entrecasteaux Channel** is the perfect place to paddle – a sheltered stretch of water between beautiful Bruny Island and the southern mainland. The east coast's **Freycinet Peninsula** is also prime sea kayakers' habitat. A multi-day trip down the peninsula, and around uninhabited Schouten Island provides a wonderful taste of coastal wilderness. There are pristine white beaches, soaring

Churn, kayaking the Franklin River is most definitely not for the inexperienced.

Cataract Gorge in Launceston is another high-skill paddle. When the power company Hydro Tasmania lets water out of Trevallyn Dam upstream, all hell breaks loose – with white-water and slalom sections considered more difficult than those used in Olympic competition. Somewhat tamer river kayaking (grade 1–2) can be enjoyed on the **River Derwent**, upstream of Hobart, and there's also relatively gentle rafting (grade 2–3) on the **Mersey River** in the north of the island. *(Find details of rafting companies in Travel Tips, pages 255–6.)*

cliffs, and wildlife including seals and dolphins.

Ask any sea kayaker to name Tasmania's most unforgettable paddle, however, and you're likely to hear the words **Bathurst Harbour** and **Port Davey**. These isolated inlets surrounded by the southwest's World Heritage wilderness lure most sea kayakers eventually. The majority fly into Port Davey by light plane as part of an organised group, for three- and seven-day paddles with all equipment and food provided.

Sailing

Mention Hobart to a yachtie and you'll get an instant reaction. The name conjures images of yachting triumph as the end point of the tough annual bluewater classic, the Sydney–Hobart Yacht Race. The world's top racing teams and their high-tech boats start to arrive just before New Year, and there's an almighty celebration in Hobart's dockside precinct. The Shipwrights' Arms on Trumpeter Street, Battery Point, is where the yachtsmen traditionally celebrate, and the walls are lined with boating pictures and memorabilia.

Sailing is big in Hobart in summer. There's the annual King of the Derwent Race on 2 January, Sailing South Race Week, a four-day regatta, also in January, and Regatta Day – a public holiday – in mid-February. On Saturdays during summer and every Wednesday and Thursday evening, 100 white sails grace the harbour. There are races organised for everything from dinghies to cruising yachts. The Royal Yacht Club of Tasmania plans much of it and can sometimes find crew places for visiting sailors.

For sailors more taken with cruising, there's no shortage of tranquil waterways. Macquarie Harbour and the Gordon River, Port Davey, the Tamar and Huon rivers, the D'Entrecasteaux Channel and the Freycinet Peninsula all provide perfect cruising and handsome scenery.

Head for Hobart's excellent Maritime Museum *(see page 77)* to absorb Tasmania's colourful seafaring history. One can also take a cruise aboard the Lady Nelson, a replica of the tall ship that brought Tasmania's first permanent European settlers from Sydney in 1803.

Surfing and windsurfing

Take an island in the open ocean, big swells and plenty of wind power and you have the perfect ingredients for sports of the waves and water. Tasmania has some coveted surf breaks – Clifton Beach, Roaring Beach, Pirates Bay and the huge waves of famous Shipstern Bluff of the Tasman Peninsula. Bring your wet suit.

Marrawah on the northwest coast is known as the home of Tasmanian windsurfing. Here perfect winds and swells that frequently reach 8 metres (26 ft) or more combine to make this possibly the best wave-sailing spot in the whole of Australia.

LONG-DISTANCE SAILING

The Sydney–Hobart Yacht Race has become an icon of Australian summer sport, as keenly followed as the Melbourne Cup or a cricket Test match against England. Yachts leave Sydney Harbour on Boxing Day at the start of a 628 nautical mile course, one of the toughest in the world. The winning boat usually reaches Hobart's Constitution Dock around two days later.

Scuba Diving

The temperate waters off Tasmania provide good conditions for divers, with visibility ranging from 12 metres (40 ft) in summer to

more than 40 metres (130 ft) in winter. Attractions for divers include the 30-metre (100-ft) giant kelp forests off the Tasman Peninsula and rare marine species such as the weedy sea dragon and big-bellied seahorse on a dive in Tasmania. *(See page 255.)*

Other adventure sports

Rock climbing is popular along Cataract Gorge, Mt Wellington and the Hazards, while abseiling off the Gordon Dam – one of the highest in the world – should more than satisfy any dangerholic. Caving around the Western Tiers at Mole Creek is also popular. For a list of tour operators, *see page 256.* ❑

LEFT: grin and snare it.
RIGHT: gently down the stream.

FOOD AND DRINK

These days, the Island's delectable fruit, vegetables, meat and seafood are available in a host of top-quality restaurants and food stores. The wine's not bad, either

With its cool climate and four distinct seasons, Tasmania has been a larder to the rest of the country for almost 200 years. Look closely at just about any menu in Sydney or Melbourne's top restaurants and you'll find Tasmanian ingredients play a starring role. Products such as abalone, scallops, oysters, saffron, sea-run trout, venison and black truffles are all shipped north, while premium fruits, such as cherries and apricots are exported to Europe and Asia.

But the state is not just a source of luxury products. Tasmanian farmers also grow most of the processed vegetables eaten in Australia. The country's supermarkets are full of beans, peas, broccoli, cauliflower and potatoes that grew in northwest Tasmania. Under threat from imported foods, Tasmania's farmers have recently fought a high-profile national campaign to force better labelling of origin for fresh and packaged food.

While Tasmania has many other attractions, it would be possible to devote an entire visit to the state just to the thrill of the hunt for great food and wine. While it's not laid out on a plate, it's not all that hard to find either.

Where to eat

Though the best choices for restaurants are in Launceston and Hobart, in recent years there has been a significant improvement in the dining options in country towns. It's possible, with careful planning, to eat out well in most

parts of the state. Towns as widely spread as Strahan, Woodbridge, St Helens, Penguin, Devonport and Deloraine can all provide good, and sometimes excellent, meals.

Launceston and Hobart vie competitively for the title of culinary capital, with the pendulum moving from one to the other every five years or so. At present, Launceston probably wins. For its size, it is one of Australia's best eating cities, with good dining options across many styles of food and prices. Stillwater River Café's degustation menu is one of Australia's most exciting culinary experiences, Mud serves up beautifully cooked Italian-inspired grills, and the ribs at Smokey Joe's

LEFT: eating out in Hobart.
RIGHT: Tasmania is well known for its apples.

little down-home café are always excellent.

In Hobart, the two dining hubs are the waterfront and North Hobart, but relying only on those areas would be to miss memorable experiences such as Lebrina, where Scott Minervini serves some of Australia's best bread with his near-perfect dishes, and Stuart Prosser's delicious local seafood at Prosser's on the Beach.

What to eat

Your best bet is to seek out local food that's in season *(see box below)*. You can be confident that it will be fresh. If you do end up in a restaurant that looks as if it could be disap-

pointing, the best things to choose are usually oysters – unless it's high summer – and either beef or lamb. The beef and lamb served in Tasmanian restaurants is nearly always locally produced and will usually be excellent. You can't go wrong with fresh berries in summer and in autumn and early winter desserts featuring apples or pears should be good.

There's usually a good choice of fish throughout the year but if you're ordering fish or shellfish in a restaurant be sure to check that it's fresh, not "freshly frozen". Look for Spring Bay mussels and scallops, farmed baby abalone from Bicheno, Bruny Island or Barilla Bay oysters, stripey trumpeter, trevalla (blue-eye cod) and sea-run trout, and remember that if you see prawns on a menu, they won't be local.

And, given the largely Anglo nature of the Tasmanian population, it's not surprising that fish and chips are popular, and generally a safe bet. There are a few renowned fish and chipperies around the state where you can be sure of a good, inexpensive meal.

Shopping for food

When you leave Hobart or Launceston, it pays to be prepared. While there are good restaurants in other parts of the state, you can't rely on finding somewhere you want to eat in every country town, particularly if it's early in the week. Buying good bread and other supplies can also be fraught. A good solution is to book yourself into self-catering accommodation, stock up on supplies in one of Hobart's or Launceston's superb food shops, then be

SEASONAL SPECIALITIES

Once you know your restaurants, you need to be familiar with what's in season. In summer the highlights are berries, including raspberries, strawberries and blueberries, and less familiar fruits such as tayberries and loganberries. Apricots, cherries and peaches are also abundant.

In autumn, Tasmania is famous for apples and pears (hence its long-standing moniker "the Apple Isle"), but new season's walnuts and hazelnuts are also worth seeking out. Restaurant menus also often feature quince and blackberries. Just occasionally, you might also find wild mushrooms, although to eat these you generally need to

know someone who lives in the right area. The locations for cèpes and slippery jacks are closely guarded secrets.

In late winter a few restaurants feature fresh truffles, one of Tasmania's newest luxury crops. For the most part, though, you'll do well eating long-cooked stews, served with purées of local potato. It's also a good time of year to eat game, such as hare and wallaby, and oysters are at their flinty best.

Spring signals scallops, new pinkeye potatoes, broad beans, peas, asparagus, lobster, lamb and the return of Tongola fresh goat cheeses after the goats' winter rest from milking.

prepared to forage along the way. When you're in a town with a good restaurant, make the most of it. Otherwise, cook yourself a feast, using the produce you've found along the way.

It's a good idea to buy a decent-sized polystyrene box from somewhere like the Wursthaus Kitchen in Hobart, and a couple of ice packs that you can replenish in the freezer each night. Then you'll be ready for what is one of the great pleasures of driving around Tasmania; hunting for blackboards advertising the wares at roadside stalls and shops.

If you see a roadside blackboard, always try to stop. This is one the best ways to buy

GRUB GUIDES

To help you find fresh food and good wine around the state, Tourism Tasmania publishes a free *Cellar Door and Farm Gate Guide*, and Graeme Phillips' *Eat Drink Tasmania* is also a good resource.

Anvers chocolates near Latrobe, Kate's Berry Farm at Swansea, and Sorell Fruit Farm, where you can pick your own. Some roadside shops, such as Oyster Cove Fruit and Vegetables and The Big Spud at Sassafras, also carry lots of local produce.

On weekends there are also usually markets where you can supplement your roadside pur-

ripe, seasonal produce and you'll rarely be disappointed. They range from a backyard shed in Hamilton selling ripe raspberries to extremely sophisticated operations such as Barilla Bay just outside Hobart, which sells its own oysters and usually also scallops from Spring Bay.

Some producers worth seeking out are Yorktown Organics, just north of Beaconsfield, for fresh fruit and vegetables, Freycinet Marine Farm for its oysters and mussels,

---

LEFT: ewe's cheese straight out of the mould in the Huon Valley. **ABOVE:** chargrilled octopus in the bistro at Grassy on King Island.

chases. Hobart's Salamanca Market is well known but if you're travelling in the north, ask about local markets and farmers' markets. Wynyard, Burnie, Penguin, Devonport, Latrobe, Deloraine and Launceston have markets where you might be able to find produce that has literally just been picked.

Food shopping in Launceston and Hobart is one of the great pleasures of any visit to Tasmania. These human-scale cities mean that it's easy to visit several shops without spending hours driving from one suburb to the next, and the quality and variety is excellent.

In Hobart, the stand-out is the Wursthaus Kitchen, just off Salamanca Place. Whether you're picnicking or planning to cook a full-scale meal, you can satisfy most of your needs there. It's also worth visiting The Hill Street Grocer, especially for fruit and vegetables, Raw for cheese, Jackman and McRoss for bread, and French patissier Jean-Pascal for pastries and tarts.

Mures fishmonger and the fish punts at Constitution Dock are also excellent. Take a few minutes to wander past the punts to see what's being advertised. You'll soon work out what has just arrived and that's what you should buy.

In Launceston if you're looking for a one-stop shop for supplies, the best option is Australia's most unlikely food store; a 24-hour service station called Davies Grand Central. No matter where you live, even New York or London, you're likely to feel just a little envy towards people who live in Launceston and have access to such groaning shelves at any time of the day or night. Delicacy and the Mill Provedore are also well worth a visit. And a stop at the Swiss Chocolatier, one of Australia's best chocolate makers, is a must.

Shopping for food at source can lead to some great experiences as well, especially if you plan ahead. Barilla Bay and Freycinet Marine Farm offer farm tours and tastings; you can watch cheese being made at Pyen-

gana, Ashgrove and Grandvewe; visit breweries in Launceston and Hobart; or charter a fishing boat on the east coast. Most of these require booking in advance.

PERSONAL SERVICE

When travelling around Tasmania, particularly away from the cities, bear in mind that many restaurants and pubs stop serving food early in the evening– around 8 or 8.30pm. Mondays can be bad nights for eating out, too. In several small towns and villages, eateries will take that evening off, leaving innocent travellers to fend for themselves. Check in advance.

Service is generally friendly, and you will often find yourself on first-name terms with the waiting staff. Indeed they will sometimes share their life-stories with you before providing an insight into all the goings-on in the village, especially that couple in the end cottage.

Tasmanian wines

Although Tasmania's wine industry roots are in the 19th century, winemaking has taken off dramatically over the past 30 years. After years of experimental plantings, where many grape varieties were grown, the industry has reached a certain maturity. Tasmania is now renowned for its sparkling wines, riesling, pinot noir and chardonnay and, more recently, sauvignon blanc and pinot gris. There are, though, exceptions where microclimates lend themselves to grape varieties that don't do well across the state as a whole.

The best wine regions for touring are the Tamar Valley, the Coal Valley, the southern vineyards in the Huon and Channel region and the east coast, south of Bicheno. If you don't have time for the full wine tourist experience, there are even excellent vineyards in the northern suburbs of Hobart, including Moorilla which also has a spectacular restaurant and antiquities museum.

Virtually every restaurant worth its salt has some Tasmanian wines on its wine list and the best will also have a good selection

available widely beyond Tasmania, a visit to the state also provides the chance to hunt out some of the smaller producers that are hard to find elsewhere. Look for pinot gris and merlot from Tamar Valley producer Grey Sands; pinot gris and pinot noir and from d'Meure in the southern channel; Frogmore Creek's organic rieslings, pinot noir and iced riesling; Domaine A's Lady A fumé blanc, cabernet sauvignon and pinot noir; and, on the east coast, Apsley Gorge pinot noir and Craigie Knowe cabernet.

Good places to shop for wine in addition to cellar doors are Benchmark or Davies Grand Central in Launceston, and Gasworks 9/11 or

by the glass, often matched to specific dishes. If you're not familiar with Tasmanian labels, especially some of the smaller ones, following the menu's advice is an excellent way to order. Restaurants such as Glo Glo's in Latrobe, Peppermint Bay at Woodbridge, and some cellar-door restaurants, such as Daniel Alps at Strathlynn, match wines to each dish.

While iconic wines, such as Pipers Brook, Moorilla, and Freycinet are well known and

the Tasmanian Wine Centre in Hobart. And, each March, just before harvesting gets underway, there are northern and southern vineyard open weekends.

Edible souvenirs

Finally, Tasmania's food and wine make great souvenirs and presents. You can have wine shipped from most cellar doors; if you're leaving from Hobart Airport call into Barilla Bay to pick up some oysters, especially packed for taking on the plane; saffron, olive oil and honey travel well; and a whole wheel of Pyengana cheddar will remind you of Tasmania for weeks after you've returned home. ❏

FAR LEFT: brownies at the Petty Sessions in Franklin. **LEFT:** sampling at the Cascade Brewery. **ABOVE:** wine for people who don't like wine.

CULTURE

Tasmania cannot offer large-scale international
events, but the local arts scene is flourishing,
if you know where to look for it

H obart and, to a lesser extent, Launceston
are the places to go for most performing
arts. The Tasmanian Symphony Orchestra under its dynamic young German conduc-
tor Sebastian Lang-Lessing is building a
reputation as a world-class operation and
consistently attracts internationally renowned
soloists. Most concerts are in the striking
Federation Concert Hall near the Hobart waterfront, but there are also regular appearances in
Launceston and one-offs around the state.

Music and drama

By dint of its larger population, Hobart is also
the most likely destination for visiting rock,
roots and folk artists. The big names play at
the Derwent Centre in Glenorchy or the Wrest
Point complex in Sandy Bay. For a more
informal night out with good local or touring
indie bands, modern jazz bands, perhaps some
reggae, head for one of the many music pubs
in either North Hobart or the bars around Salamanca Place. There are usually buskers tar-
geting tourists in the daytime, and the free
concert each Friday evening in the courtyard
of the Salamanca Arts Centre attracts an
enthusiastic crowd.

Many of the best venues for live music are
listed in the Travel Tips section *(see page
250)*, along with recommendations for dance
and club nights. Pick up a copy of the free
paper *Sauce* from cafes, bars and music stores
for listings. There is a small but vibrant
popular music and club scene in Launceston,
and weekends are the time for action in
Burnie and Devonport.

Larger theatrical productions are more or less
confined to the delightful Theatre Royal in
Hobart and the Princess Theatre in Launceston,
and are usually visiting shows from the likes of
the Bell Shakespeare Company. Smaller venues
such as the Salamanca Arts Centre are worth
checking out. Keep an eye open for performances of *The Tank*, an entertaining tale of life
in Tasmania over a couple of generations, which
has been touring on and off for a few years now.

Visual arts

There doesn't seem to be a town or village on
the island that doesn't have its own gallery
displaying work by local painters, sculptors or

photographers. If, unaccountably, there is no gallery then a sympathetic café will be found with its walls festooned with keenly priced decorative work. Quality varies but it seems that a disproportionate number of talented artists have grown up here or been attracted over by the easy (and inexpensive) lifestyle.

Aboriginal work has been enjoying a higher profile in the wider community in recent years and a funding programme under the aegis of Arts Tasmania specifically aimed at fostering projects with Aboriginal cultural content means that this trend is likely to continue. The most high-profile outlet is probably Art Mob on Hunter Street in Hobart.

numerous works in both urban and natural settings by Stephen Walker (*see panel, page 128*) and, of course, the transformation of Sheffield into a town of murals.

Festivals

Every so often, a festival comes along, gathering events according to a theme or genre. The biggest is the biennial *Ten Days on the Island* festival held every odd-numbered year at the end of March and beginning of April. A host of visiting and local theatre practitioners, dance companies, musicians and artists present events all round Tasmania under the loose banner of "island life". Visiting artists all have

Particularly fine examples of Aboriginal art can be found in the Queen Victoria Museum at Inveresk, Launceston. The Tasmanian Museum and Art Gallery in Hobart is another prime destination for historic and contemporary Aboriginal work, as well as paintings and sculptures produced by the European migrant population since the earliest colonial times.

Public art has been strongly supported since those days, particularly sculpture. More recently a receptive populace has embraced sculpture trails in Deloraine and Geeveston,

LEFT: part of the sculpture trail in Deloraine. **ABOVE:** hands up if you've seen *The Ship That Never Was*.

to come from islands themselves so there is usually a strong presence from the Pacific.

Launceston hosts its Festivale every February and, as at so many events in Tasmania, the emphasis is as much on the food and drink as the entertainment. Hobart's two-week Summer Festival every January certainly follows this pattern: the Taste of Tasmania is the focal point, surrounded by other, more cultural, activity.

Recent additions to the calendar have included the Falls Festival at Marion Bay on the southeast coast, featuring international and Australian rock bands. There is also a fledgling comedy festival attempting to find its feet in Hobart in November. ❑

PLACES

A detailed guide to the state, with the
principal sites clearly cross-referenced
by number to the maps

Make sure to allow plenty of time when travelling in Tasmania. It's not so much the laid-back lifestyle or the unpredictable weather – although neither should be disregarded – but the geography. It's never very far from one place to another, it's just that there are rather more mountains and lakes and other obstacles than elsewhere in Australia. You only need to run up behind a timber lorry as you're negotiating the narrow dirt road down to Cockle Creek, and your journey time will have to be revised significantly upwards. Whole areas across the mountains in the west can become inaccessible to normal cars for days on end in the winter. But this is the essence of Tasmania and its entire character would change were there to be a wholesale introduction of dual-lane highways.

So surrender to the pace of the island. Plan each journey and then add a chunk of time for contingencies. These may include spontaneous detours to historic sites when one of the brown heritage signs pops up, a pause to photograph a wombat or echidna loitering at the edge of the road, or a cream tea at Kate's Berry Farm on the Tasman Highway south of Swansea.

But what else to plan? If a family beach holiday is the priority, then look at the coast in the east and the north. If you want wilderness, it's the rivers and forests of the south and west. For colonial history, consider taking in Hobart and Port Arthur before running up through the Midlands to Launceston and beyond. If it's peace and quiet, well, almost anywhere will do; the ultimate tranquil antithesis to urban pressure is probably on Flinders or King Islands, where there are so few people about that every driver acknowledges every other. Everywhere you'll find good local produce, interesting cafés and restaurants, idiosyncratic craft shops and galleries.

Think about selecting two or three bases and look at the route map at the back of the book for ideas on how to make the most of everything on offer in surrounding areas. Above all, be flexible; it's the capricious response to a new setting that can make travelling so memorable – and if you miss one of the island's attractions, it'll be there next time. And, very likely, there will be a next time. ❏

PRECEDING PAGES: rural idyll – Dennes Point, Bruny Island; view of Lake Pedder from the hills above Strathgordon. **LEFT:** Christ Church at Low Head, Tamar Valley.

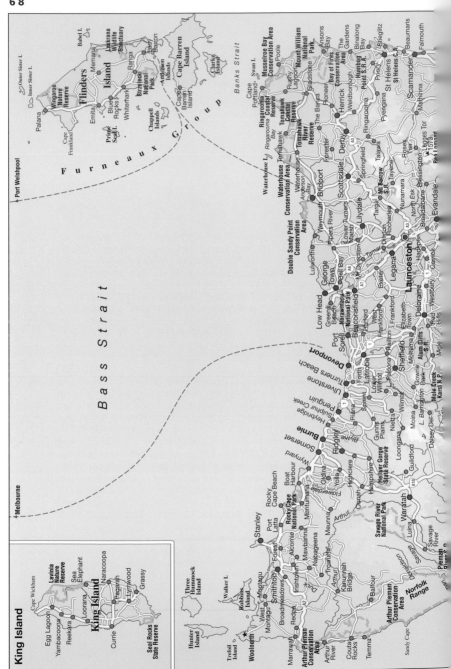

Bass Strait

Furneaux Group

Melbourne

Port Welshpool

Banks Strait

King Island

Cape Wickham
Egg Lagoon
Yambacoopa
Reekara
Loorana
Currie
Lavinia Nature Reserve
Naracoopa
Pegarah
Lymwood
Grassy
Sea Elephant
King Island
Seal Rocks State Reserve

Three Hummock Island
Walker I.
Robbins Island
Hunter Island
Trefoil Island

Flinders Island
Outer Sister I.
Inner Sister I.
Babel I.
Memana
Palana
Wingaroo Nature Reserve
Emita
Cape Frankland
Blue Rocks
Whitemark
Prime Seal I.
Ranga
Lackrana Wildlife Sanctuary
Strzelecki National Park
Chappell Islands
Badger Corner
Anderson Islands
Clarke's Island
Cape Barren Island

Cape Barren Island
Banks I.
Cape Portland
Swan I.
Poole
Musselroe Bay Conservation Area
Mount William National Park
Ansons Bay
The Gardens
Binalong Bay
Stieglitz
Beaumaris
Falmouth
Scamander
St Helens
St Helens C.K.
Priory
Pyengana
Goshen
Goulds Country
Lottah
Ringarooma Bay
Gladstone
Herrick
Derby
Branxholm
Legerwood
Springfield
Ringarooma
Talawa
Roses Tier
Legges Tor
1572
Ben Lomond
Pioneer
Tomahawk Coastal Reserve
Ringarooma Coastal Reserve
Tomahawk River Reserve
Tomahawk
Forester
Waterhouse
Waterhouse Conservation Area
Anderson Bay
Double Sandy Point Conservation Area
Bridport
Scottsdale
Nabowla
Lilydale
Tonganah
Tayene
Nunamara
Targa
Mathinna
Evandale
Brassington
Blessington
North Esk
Mt Barrow S.R.
Lisle
Myrtle Bank
Golconda
Karoola
Lalla
Turners Marsh
Lebrina
Retreat
Pipers River
Weymouth
Lulworth
Bellingham
Bridgenorth
Exeter
Legana
Hadspen
Carrick
Westbury
Launceston
Hagley
Whitemore
Deloraine
Birralee
Frankford
Elizabeth Town
Kimberley
Sheffield
Mole Creek
Mole Creek Karst N.P.
L. Barrington
Moina
Gowrie Park
Lorinna
Daisy Dell
Cradle Valley

George Town
Low Head
Bell Bay
Narawntapu National Park
Greens Beach
Kelso
Beaconsfield
Beauty Point
York Town
West Frankford
Gravelly Beach
Tamar
Mt Direction
Dilston
Rocherlea
Rosevears

Devonport
Turners Beach
Ulverstone
Leith
Forth
Don
Spreyton
Latrobe
Sassafras
Wesley Vale
Port Sorel
Squeaking Point
Harford
Moriarty
Northdown
Railton
Barrington
Nook
Acacia Hills
Paloona
Wilmot

Penguin
Sulphur Creek
Heybridge
Burnie
Somerset
Wynyard
Boat Harbour
Rocky Cape Beach
Doctors Rocks
Blythe
Ridgley
Highclere
Yolla
Oldina
Calder
Flowerdale
Preolenna
Meunna
Takone
Hampshire
Guildford
Loongana
Luina
Waratah
Savage River National Park
Savage River
Arthur Pleman Conservation Area
Norfolk Range
Sandy Cape
Temma
Balfour
Couta Rocks
Arthur River
Marrawah
Redpa
Arthur Pleman Conservation Area
Kanunnah Bridge
Trowutta
Roger River
Nabageena
Mawbanna
Montumana
Alcomie
Edith Creek
Forest
Stanley
Port Latta
Rocky Cape National Park
Smithton
West Montagu
Montagu
Broadmeadows
Irishtown
Woolnorth

Hellyer Gorge State Reserve
Sisters Creek
Gunns Plains
Nietta
Sprent
Lower Wilmot
Riana
Gawler
Arthur Pleman Conservation Area
Corinna
Donaldson River
Pieman River S.R.

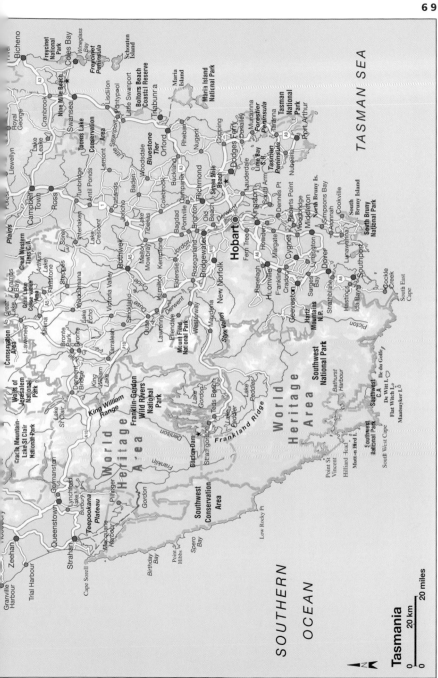

Tasmania

HOBART

Australia's oldest city after Sydney nestles attractively under Mount Wellington. As the state's administrative and commercial capital, Hobart embraces tradition in its numerous well-preserved colonial buildings and balances this with a buzzing modern outlook

For a state capital, Hobart is remarkably low key and compact. But with a population some way short of the 200,000 mark, it could hardly be anything else. Its size is largely dictated by its position, with growth restricted by water and mountains. When the city was founded in 1803, it was the shelter of the Derwent estuary that proved the prime attraction for pioneer settlers seeking a place to establish the next penal settlement after Sydney. As to the mountains, they are never far away anywhere in Tasmania. But it's to Hobart's advantage, especially these days when tourism is one of the state's prime industries, that it has Mount Wellington to act as a backdrop to the multitude of dramatic vistas which loom up all over the city. Take your camera and you're guaranteed at least one good picture.

The most commonly reproduced view of all is shot down on the waterfront across one of the docks, fishing boats in the foreground, Mount Wellington up at the back. This is where sandstone meets sea, where the commercial hub of the docks meets the legislative fulcrum of parliament, and where it makes sense to begin a tour of the city. The advantage of a confined city centre is the ease of reaching most of the major sights on foot, albeit occasionally encountering some steep climbs on the way.

The waterfront

The main **visitor centre** is only a block away from the water on the corner of Davey and Elizabeth streets (Mon–Fri 8.30am–5.30pm, Sat–Sun 9am–5pm; tel: 03-6230 8233). Once you've tied up any accommodation issues and collected a small tree's worth of brochures, you can drop down Elizabeth Street

Maps: pages 72, 82

LEFT the General Post Office is one of the grandest of Macquarie Street's imposing buildings.
BELOW: Hobart: between water and mountain.

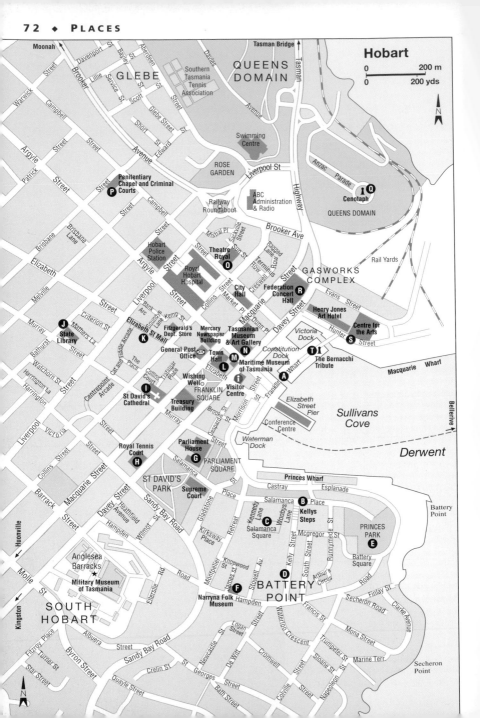

Hobart

0 — 200 m
0 — 200 yds

N

Moonah

GLEBE

QUEENS DOMAIN

Tasman Bridge

Southern Tasmania Tennis Association

Swimming Centre

ROSE GARDEN

Liverpool St

Railway Roundabout

ABC Administration & Radio

Anzac Parade

Cenotaph

QUEENS DOMAIN

Q

Penitentiary Chapel and Criminal Courts
P

Brooker Ave

Rail Yards

Hobart Police Station

Theatre Royal
O

GASWORKS COMPLEX

Royal Hobart Hospital

City Hall

Federation Concert Hall
R

Henry Jones Art Hotel

Centre for the Arts

State Library
J

Fitzgerald's Dept. Store

Mercury Newspaper Building

Tasmanian Museum & Art Gallery

Victoria Dock

S

Elizabeth St Mall
K

General Post Office

Town Hall

Maritime Museum of Tasmania

Constitution Dock

The Bernacchi Tribute
T

Macquarie Wharf

St David's Cathedral
I

Wishing Well

FRANKLIN SQUARE

Visitor Centre

A

Bellerive

Treasury Building

Elizabeth Street Pier

Sullivans Cove

Royal Tennis Court
H

Parliament House
G

PARLIAMENT SQUARE

Conference Centre

Waterman Dock

Derwent

ST DAVID'S PARK

Supreme Court

Princes Wharf

Castray Esplanade

Battery Point

Salamanca Place
B

Kellys Steps

PRINCES PARK
E

Anglesea Barracks

Military Museum of Tasmania

Kennedy Lane

Salamanca Square

Mooneys Lane

Battery Square

SOUTH HOBART

Narryna Folk Museum
F

BATTERY POINT
D

Arthur's Circus

Secheron Point

N

to **Franklin Wharf** . To either side the various docks and wharfs will be playing host to a colourful selection of fishing boats, pleasure craft, tourist ferries, floating fish shops, occasionally a vast ocean liner and regularly a ship or two preparing for the next sortie to one of the Antarctic research stations for which Hobart is a major jumping-off point.

Head south towards the imposing stone facade of **Salamanca Place** **B**. This is the well-preserved heart of old maritime Hobart. A terrace of warehouses built in the 1830s, it is now home to bars, cafés, galleries, shops and a vibrant arts centre. For much of the week it's a relaxed haunt, although overrun by cars in search of that elusive parking spot. On Saturday mornings a vast **market** takes over, running all the way up to Davey Street.

The market has become the city's primary tourist attraction and the evidence is there in the hordes that process slowly from stall to stall. It's an appealing mix of crafts, gourmet foodstuffs, self-published novels, open-air massage, fortune telling, home-made musical instruments, fruit and vegetables, and bric a brac stalls. Grab a snack at one of many food outlets and just follow the flow, perhaps ending up one of the side alleys to **Salamanca Square** **C**.

This modern development over an old quarry is always car-free and a favourite destination for weekend brunch. Then, even more than usual, the buskers are out in force. They dispense unrelenting bonhomie to passing lovers, paddlers in the fountains, admirers of the requisite public sculptures, and to parents trying to drag children away from the strange man with the musical hose.

Battery Point

Respite can be found in the quaint old streets of **Battery Point** **D**. Access is via the steep **Kelly's Steps**, back out in Salamanca Place and right. The streets up here are narrow and contain a hefty proportion of the numerous National Trust-listed houses of which the city is so proud. Most of them are small fishermen's cottages, and the apogee is the delightful **Arthur's Circus** where a dozen or so dwellings surround a little village green. This is still a residential area, although the residents probably tire of tourists peering through the lace curtains. A good number have solved this problem by turning their properties into bed and breakfast establishments. Evenings are scarcely quieter since a whole string of fine restaurants is to be found along **Hampden Road**.

Down at the eastern end of Battery Point is **Princes Park** **E**. It houses a few of the cannons that gave the area its name, as well as one of a number of signal stations which made up the chain of semaphore relays that once connected Hobart with Port Arthur. It's a quiet place to relax and there's a pirate ship play area for children.

Back along Hampden Road on

Battery Point, an enclave of early colonial homes.

BELOW: slightly foxed in Salamanca Market.

Raising standards at Anglesea Barracks. If it's Tuesday there's a chance to look around and visit the museum.

the way out of Battery Point lies the **Narryna Folk Museum** (Tues–Fri 10.30am–5pm, Sat–Sun 2–5pm; admission charge; tel: 6234 2791). This used to be the house of a merchant and has been preserved as it might have looked in Victorian times. It's evocative of the life of the privileged few and there are rarely crowds of fellow visitors to get in the way.

Military past and present

Continuing northwest, Hampden Road ends at the junction with Davey Street. To the left and a block up the hill is **Anglesea Barracks**, the oldest military base in Australia. It was founded in 1811 and many of the buildings date from the early days of the foundation of Van Diemen's Land. Inside is the **Military Museum of Tasmania**, open one day a week when there are also tours of the barracks (Tues 10am–noon; tour 11am; admission charge; tel: 6237 7160).

Return down the hill and dip into **St David's Park**, pausing to look at some classical statuary and a scat-tering of old gravestones. Turn down Salamanca Place and consider the clean lines of the **Supreme Court**. There is an interesting sculpture by Stephen Walker fixed to the wall by the entrance. Opposite on Salamanca Place is the 1835 **Parliament House**, originally built as the customs office. This imposing sandstone edifice is home to the State Legislative Council and the House of Assembly. Tours are available when the house isn't in session (Mon–Fri 2–5pm; free; tel: 6233 2200; www.parliament.tas.gov.au), but at least as interesting is a visit to the public gallery in either the lower house with its green décor, reflecting the Westminster colour-coding system, or the red-themed upper house. As with legislative sessions the world over, be prepared for grindingly dull discussions of procedure, broken up just occasionally by outbursts of inventive invective.

Backtracking slightly, there's a small sign dangling in Davey Street over the unremarkable frontage of the building housing the **Royal Tennis Court**. Visitors are

One of the simplest pleasures to be had in Hobart is strolling along the waterfront and dipping into a parcel of fish and chips bought fresh from one of the floating stalls.

permitted inside and may be lucky enough to see players engaging in the sport of real tennis (also called court tennis or royal tennis), which evolved in medieval Europe and was the precursor to modern (lawn) tennis. The game is played on an enclosed court and players use smaller racquets and slightly different balls to regular tennis. Spectators sit along the side, watch through netted slits in the wall, as if in a bunker, and try to work out the scoring.

From the cathedral to the Maritime Museum

St David's Cathedral ❶, begun in 1868 to replace a wooden building, was not completed until 1936 but its style is resolutely Georgian and its dignified sandstone fits perfectly with the grandeur of Macquarie Street. It's all a far cry from the days when public executions were conducted in the gaol, now demolished, on the opposite corner with Murray Street. The interior of the cathedral is quite plain, with an interesting pulpit and choir stalls and a small museum in the cloisters. When the

first church was built it was actually administered under the diocese of Calcutta. That ceased in 1836, when Sydney took over, and the first bishop of Hobart was finally appointed in 1842.

Further down Murray Street, the **State Library ❿** houses the **Allport Library and Museum of Fine Arts** (Mon–Fri 9.30am–5pm, last Sat of month 9.30am–2.30pm; free; www.statelibrary.tas.gov.au), with its antique books, artworks and furniture from the late 17th century to the early 19th century in reconstructed period rooms. The collection was bequeathed in 1965 by Henry Allport, a Hobart solicitor whose family arrived in Tasmania in 1831. It's all sympathetically displayed in modern, dark-panelled and carpeted rooms where there's nobody to disturb the hum of the air conditioning. The family collection of fine art is on display for short periods two or three times a year.

Head round the corner of the library into Bathurst Street to the intersection with Elizabeth Street. The route back down towards the

Map on page 72

Keeping it real. The Royal Tennis Court is still used for royal (or real) tennis. The roof is handy in this climate.

BELOW: Hobart's pleasant waterfront.

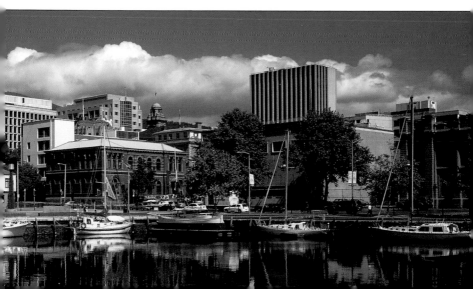

TIPS

The long-established TASAIR operate a 30-minute flight over Hobart City and Derwent Estuary, with views of Hobart landmarks. Other scenic flights offered include a 1-hour flight to the Tasman Peninsula, 2-hour flights over the Southwest National Park or the east coast, and half-day wildlife trips. For more details tel: 6248 5088, or see www.tasair.com.au.

BELOW: Sir John Franklin's statue oversees Franklin Square.

waterfront takes in the **Elizabeth Street Mall** , the heart of Hobart's downtown shopping precinct, where all the major stores are represented. It is worth looking beyond the plate glass and above the awnings, to see fine original stonework and ornamentation on yet more of the National Trust-listed structures which give Hobart its character. Of particular note is the old **Fitzgerald's Department Store** down Collins Street, with its ornate facade, although there is little to be gleaned inside what is now a Harris Scarfe outlet other than a sense of scale.

Running west off Elizabeth Street is the **Cat and Fiddle Arcade** where children may be amused by the automata on the wall in the food court. These re-enact the nursery rhyme and feature the eponymous characters along with a cow, moon, spoon, etc. Adults may find the cramped, low-ceilinged passageways, where the only light is from fluorescent strips, less appealing. The arcade runs through to Murray Street where, across the road, there's

the **Centrepoint Arcade**. It is marginally airier and houses more up-market shops until, with a clunk, you hit the Chickenfeed Bargain Store.

Back on Elizabeth Street, the route continues to the junction with Macquarie Street. On the right is the stately, tree encrusted, **Franklin Square**. On sunny lunchtimes workers spill out from neighbouring offices and occupy the seats around the fountain and the statue of Rear Admiral Sir John Franklin. Franklin was appointed Lieutenant Governor of Van Diemen's Land in 1837 and served until 1843. However, his fame derives primarily from his voyages of exploration in the Arctic, where he was the first to prove the existence of the North West Passage linking the Atlantic and Pacific oceans, although it must be said, he was unable to find it.

The grand regency pile at the end of the square is the **Treasury Building**, originally built in 1841 as a police station and used as such until 1858. It is not open to the public.

On the opposite side of Elizabeth

Street but with its main entrance on Macquarie Street is the **Town Hall** . It is yet another sandstone monument to 19th-century civic pride. There are guided tours twice a week (Tues 2.45pm, Thur 10.45am; free), but access to the entrance hall and, up at the top of the grand staircase, the ballroom, with its ornate painted ceiling and fine plasterwork, is often possible at other times. Ask at the front desk.

Opposite the Town Hall on Macquarie Street is the imposing **General Post Office** and next door the immaculate Art Deco lines of the brilliant white **Mercury Newspaper Building**. Carry on past and turn right on Argyle Street where the **Maritime Museum of Tasmania**  is at the bottom on the right (daily 10am–5pm; admission charge; tel: 6234 1427; www.maritimetas.com.au). The museum covers all the angles of Tasmania's seafaring past from the early convict ships through the trading vessels, whalers, fishing fleets, wartime activity and Antarctic expeditions. There are model boats, historic artefacts, videos and interpretive displays sufficient for an hour or two of browsing. Upstairs in the **Carnegie Gallery** there are changing exhibitions of contemporary art (daily 10am–5pm; free).

Tasmanian Museum

After a quick peek in the **Lark Distillery**, which is really a room of equipment attached to a bar, albeit one where free tastings of various home-produced spirits are readily available, it's time for the splendours of the **Tasmanian Museum and Art Gallery** . The entrance is in Macquarie Street (daily 10am–5pm; free; tel: 6211 4177; www.tmag.tas.gov.au).

The museum occupies a jumble of buildings, including old convict-built warehouses, one being the oldest building in Tasmania, dating all the way back to 1808. Alongside is a discreetly modernist 1960s block, which houses much of the art collection. The exhibits cover all aspects of the state from the wildlife, with a diorama cramming in as many of the extant fauna as it can, to a special display tracking the origins and destruction of the thylacine or Tasmanian tiger *(see page 41)*.

There is a section devoted to the indigenous peoples and their horrific demise at the hands of the settlers. The **Colonial Art Gallery** includes busts and paintings of Aboriginal people along with the usual depictions of colonial life.

Also featured is the impressive **Wongs' Collection of Chinese Art and Antiquities**, donated to the museum in 2003. The main art gallery has a changing selection of works from the museum's collection. There's a fine café in the courtyard open to all. Work is in progress to expand into adjoining buildings, used, up to now, for storage. Plans include a new Antarctic exhibit, featuring a unique viewing system to allow full appreciation of

Map on page 72

The Colonial Gallery in the Tasmanian Museum and Art Gallery.

BELOW: the Maritime Museum of Tasmania's collection.

Figures from Wongs' Collection of Chinese Art and Antiquities in the Tasmanian Museum and Art Gallery.

BELOW: inside Hobart's grandiose Theatre Royal.

stereoscopic photographs from one of Shackleton's expeditions.

Campbell & Collins streets

Further down Macquarie Street take a left up Campbell Street to the **Theatre Royal** ⓞ. Unless there's a production in rehearsal, it's usually possible to have a look at the sumptuous interior of what appears to be a perfectly preserved Victorian auditorium. In fact, the interior was gutted in a fire in 1984 and what you are looking at has been completely reconstructed from plans and photographs. It now hosts a mixture of touring theatre, opera, music and comedy with the odd in-house production thrown in. The main season is in winter. (Tel: 6233 2299.)

Carrying on up Campbell Street, a sandstone wall on the left indicates the original extent of the old Hobart gaol, but all that remains now is the **Penitentiary Chapel and Criminal Courts** ⓟ. This is one of the city's hidden gems and there is usually only a handful of people on the regular tours conducted by National Trust volunteers. It is a fascinating introduction to the remains of what was once the biggest building in Australia (the complex stretched across a whole block and remained intact until the 1960s) and takes in the courtrooms, the chapel with its subterranean cells and the gallows, where 32 unfortunates were hanged. (Tours daily 10am, 11.30am, 1pm, 2.30pm; ghost tour 8pm; admission charge; tel: 6231 0911.)

Tracking back down the hill, turn left at Collins Street and go to the end where the **Wapping History Wall** is an interesting sculptural display which maps the development of the first area of settlement at Sullivan's Cove. Not only did it adopt the name of one of London's better-known slums, it also appears to have taken on many of its characteristics. Dock workers and seafarers lived cheek by jowl in conditions where disease was rife, floods frequent and the brothels and gaming houses did little to contribute to good order. Naturally, the area is now dotted with exclusive inner-city apartments and boutique hotels.

Winding round towards the water,

a quick detour up the hill to the east, taking care to avoid traffic steaming down from the Tasman Bridge, is rewarded with the tranquillity of the **Cenotaph** ❶ on the Queen's Domain. The monolith itself is undistinguished but either side of the approach to it there are new triangular concrete and glass constructions to salute Australian winners of the Victoria Cross. Walking around the base of either one of them triggers audio extracts describing the recipients' exploits or re-enacting historic scenes, such as the departure of troop ships from Hobart docks. There are good views out across the bay as well.

Returning to the hurly burly of the city, the Gasworks complex presents a rather sorry picture of failed enterprise. The working distillery, which was supposed to establish itself on the tourist circuit, has moved out of the city and all that's left is a chain restaurant and a bottle shop (liquor store). The redbrick Victorian industrial architecture is still attractive, however, and there may be somebody, even now,

poised with the next "big idea".

Across the road is the rear of the **Federation Concert Hall** ❷, a sleek modern auditorium that is home to the Tasmanian Symphony Orchestra. The dynamic geometric shapes of the hall abut the altogether more pedestrian Hotel Grand Chancellor with which it shares a foyer. This appears to be an uncomfortable arrangement. The main orchestral concert season runs from March to November.

Around the docks

Across Davey Street, **Hunter Street** ❸ runs alongside **Victoria Dock** and accounts for some of the most picturesque of the city's old maritime buildings which have been extensively, if controversially, renovated in recent years. The old Henry Jones & Co. IXL jam factory has been divided up into a number of operations, the first of which is the **Henry Jones Art Hotel**. It claims to be "Australia's first and only dedicated art hotel". In practice this means that over 250 works by Tasmanian artists are exhibited

Map on page 72

BELOW LEFT: old and new structures at the Cenotaph. **BELOW:** a performance of *Louisa's Walk* at the Female Factory.

The Bernacchi Tribute – tourists just out of shot.

RIGHT: Errol Flynn.

throughout the building and most are available for sale. Visitors are free to wander around the public areas to inspect the work and there are guided tours on Friday afternoons (5.30pm; free).

Further along Hunter Street is the **Centre for the Arts**, a department of the University of Tasmania. This section of the old jam factory has been imaginatively converted into a series of open-plan studios, workshops and galleries. Light floods in through the roof and the picture windows overlooking the harbour. Visitors, once they've checked in at the security desk, can stroll along the paint-spattered walkways and look at work in progress. The students appear not to mind.

Just past a bridge across the entrance to Victoria Dock, look out for a group of bronze figures, which constitute **The Bernacchi Tribute** ❶. Tasmanian Louis Bernacchi was a scientist, photographer and writer, and the first Australian to winter in the Antarctic. He went on to become Scott's chief scientist. Sculptor Stephen Walker has depicted him with his favourite husky and posing for a photo. The representation of a camera on its tripod triggers a reflex response in the majority of passing tourists, who whip out their own equipment and insist on being photographed with the figures. Resist.

In the dock itself the fishing boats can often be seen unloading their catch, crayfish pots full to bursting. And along the edge of **Constitution Dock** punts are moored selling fish fresh or cooked up with chips. On the outer side of the docks kiosks sell tickets for everything from 20-minute harbour tours to full-day excursions to Bruny Island (*see pages 105–8*).

Another few yards further on and it's back to Salamanca Place.

Out of town

For the other highlights of Hobart, some form of transport is required, especially when it comes to visiting the viewpoints on the surrounding hills. Admittedly there are those who choose to cycle or walk up to the summits, but such errant

Errol Flynn

Tasmania's most famous export, the dashing romantic hero with wicked, wicked ways, Errol Flynn, made it big in Hollywood as the king of the swashbucklers, shooting to fame in *Captain Blood* in 1935 and consolidating his status in *The Adventures of Robin Hood* three years later. "In like Flynn", an affectionate homage to the lovable rogue's womanising ways, has entered the lexicon in Australia and overseas.

Tasmanians are generally quick to claim as their own anyone successful who has even the remotest links with the state. Indeed, Flynn has been so celebrated that tours have traced his childhood and youth in Hobart (he left for Sydney when he was 15), including the Town Hall where he reputedly lost his virginity.

However, some are ambiguous about him. Marlene Dietrich is said to have called him "Satan's Angel", and his close friend, David Niven observed: "you know where you stood with Errol: he would always let you down." This, combined with the womanising and assault cases, have left locals unsure as to how they might appropriately celebrate his birthplace. After a lengthy debate, Hobart City Council has agreed to rename a small reserve in Battery Point in his honour.

behaviour diminishes the time available to take in the vistas at the top.

Mount Nelson  to the south is the first stop. There is a bus service and plenty of room to park. Along with the sweeping views across the city and the Derwent, there is another staging post in the chain of semaphore signal stations to Port Arthur. This was also the point from which first news of visiting ships would be relayed. There is a restaurant in the old signalman's house.

For an even loftier view of the city, take the long winding road to the top of **Mount Wellington** ❷, 1,270 metres (4,170 ft) high. This is the peak that dominates the city from every perspective. It acts as a weather gauge: dusted with snow for weeks at a time in winter; clear or hazy in the summer depending on how the heat is stirring the air; or hidden from view as clouds move in with yet another band of rain. There's a bus from downtown Hobart to Fern Tree and then a shuttle bus for the final run to the summit. If the view isn't thrilling enough then there is an outfit which organises bike runs all the way back down to sea level. Or you can explore a network of walking tracks.

On the way down indulge in a tour of the **Cascade Brewery** ❸. The grand stone facing, which looks so impressive offset by the foothills of Mount Wellington behind it, was commenced in 1824, eight years before the first beer was brewed. Behind the facade, shining modern equipment pumps out six different ales along with seasonal specials. Guided tours take an hour and a half and end in the plush modern tasting room where vouchers, included in the price, allow for three different samples. After this it would seem churlish not to try the other three. (Cascade Road, South Hobart; daily, times vary; bookings essential; admission charge; tel: 6224 1117.)

Around the corner at the end of Cascade Gardens is the **Female Factory** ❹, or what's left of it. The outer walls give an idea of the scale of this workhouse/prison and interpretive boards explain how the female inmates manufactured soap and blankets or took in sewing and

Maps: pages 72, 82

Students get the benefit of the beautifully renovated Centre for the Arts.

BELOW: the view down from Mount Nelson.

Time for a tiger. Find a Tasmanian tiger at the Cascade Brewery and in bars all over the city.

washing. To one side is a small fudge factory from where guided tours of the site run weekdays at 10.30am (charge; tel: 6223 1559). A new theatrical interpretation gives a more vibrant and moving introduction to the story: *Louisa's Walk* is a promenade production that processes from outside the brewery to the Female Factory, vividly breathing life into the story of a typical deportee (daily Oct–Apr 2.15pm, 5pm; winter by arrangement; charge; booking essential; tel: 6230 8233.) The site is also open all day without a tour (free).

Before returning to the city centre, a turn off to the south leads to **Sandy Bay** ❺. This is a salubrious suburb with appeal to sailors – the Royal Tasmanian Yacht Club is based here – and to gamblers, who can get their fix in Australia's first (1973) casino, situated beneath the landmark tower of the Wrest Point Hotel.

Back through the city, past the waterfront, the road heads east across the **Tasman Bridge** (*see panel, page 85*). Nestling alongside it is another viewpoint across Hobart, although this one is only 95 metres (310 ft) high. **Rosny Hill** is close to the first point of settlement

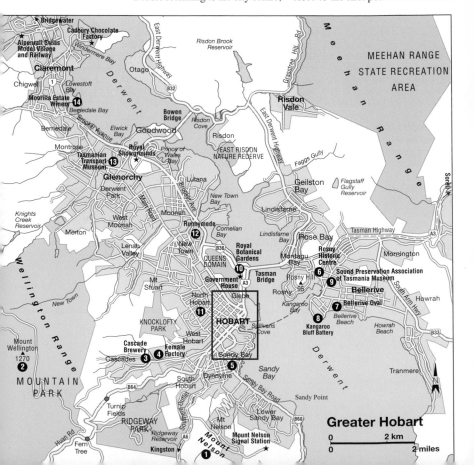

and the **Rosny Historic Centre** ❻ is the place to go to learn all about it. There are three buildings: the Schoolhouse Gallery, Rosny Cottage and the 1820 Rosny Barn. (Rosny Hill Road; Tue–Fri 11am–4pm, Sat–Sun noon–4pm; free; tel: 6245 8740.)

South around Kangaroo Bay lies the attractive marina and waterfront of **Bellerive** with its modern boardwalk. The suburb is known to cricket fans for the **Bellerive Oval** ❼ where the state team is based and international one-dayers and test matches are played, although there can be a four-year gap between tests. On a summer day, with Mount Wellington looming in the background, there is something incongruous about sitting on the grass nursing a drink and seeing some of the best players in the world in an atmosphere reminiscent of a village green. If there is no match on, there's always the **Tasmanian Cricket Museum** (Tue–Thur 10am–3pm, Fri 10am– noon, match days 1–3pm; tel: 6211 4206).

The year-round attraction in Bellerive is **Kangaroo Bluff Battery** ❽, a companion installation to the one at Battery Point in an equally picturesque setting. There are ramparts to climb, cannons to straddle and trenches to hide in – and the children will probably enjoy it, too.

An obscure gem is the **Sound Preservation Association of Tasmania Museum** ❾, where a collection of old gramophones and radios is lovingly nurtured. There is an amazing hand-powered record player for use in the bush made from an artfully folded sheet of cardboard and a needle – ask for a demonstration (19 Cambridge Road, Bellerive; Mon, Wed–Fri 11am–3pm; donation; tel: 6245 1153).

It is worth turning right off the road back to the city, once over Tasman Bridge, to visit the **Royal Botanical Gardens** ❿ in the Queen's Domain just north of Government House. Walk through the grandiose maroon and gold wrought-iron gates into this quiet idyll, first established in 1828. Wander between formal flowerbeds and immaculately groomed hedges

Map on page 82

TIPS

Tasmanian cricket tends to punch above its weight in Australia. It has produced some noteworthy internationals, including long-serving and highly successful test captain Ricky Ponting. The state team has enjoyed success too but without the silverware to go with it until 2005's one-day trophy triumph. However, only lesser test matches are played here.

BELOW: testing times, but not very often. Locals pitch for more.

BELOW: the Sunday market in Glenorchy.

and trees, perhaps visit the old conservatory or enjoy the restrained pleasures of the Japanese Garden. The Sub-Antarctic Plant House recreates a tiny part of Macquarie Island *(see margin, left)*, while the Arthur Wall, built in 1829 is internally heated for growing exotic fruits. There are plenty of interactive games to be found in the Botanical Discovery Centre as well as exhibitions, a restaurant and shop. The gardens are open daily Oct–Mar 8am–6.30pm, Apr 8am–5.30pm, May–Aug 8am–5pm, Sept 8am–5.30pm; free; tel: 6236 3050; www.rtbg.tas.gov.au.

North Hobart

North Hobart ⑪ has built a reputation for fine food and a buzzing nightlife. In a short suburban strip can be found cuisines from around the globe in everything from garishly lit dim-sum palaces to elegant gourmet dining rooms. The pubs have to produce good counter meals to keep up and some, such as the Republic Bar, throw in leading Australian and international bands as well. Most evenings there will be a mix of students, besuited conference-goers, tourists and local bon viveurs, all happily intermingling.

Just to the north is **New Town**. **Runnymede** ⑫ is the main attraction here, a National Trust-maintained Georgian-style homestead built *c.*1836 for Robert Pitcairn, Tasmania's first home-grown lawyer. There are attractive gardens (61 Bay Road, New Town; daily Aug–June 10am–4.30pm; admission charge; tel: 6278 1269).

A little further north is a collection of old railway buildings and sheds chock full of locomotives, carriages, trams, trolley buses, coaches and other vehicles which fill the **Tasmanian Transport Museum** ⑬. It is staffed by volunteers who will regale you with every last detail of each exhibit. Trains are fired up for rides on the first and third Sundays of the month (Anfield St, Glenorchy; Sat–Sun, public hols 1–4.30pm; admission charge; tel: 6272 7721). A visit can be tied in with the nearby Sunday market at the **Royal Showgrounds** in Glenorchy, home of the

Map on page 82

Royal Hobart Show, the agricultural show which takes place each October.

Head for the **Moorilla Estate Winery** ⓴ in its glorious riverside setting. There are tasting rooms, an upmarket restaurant and a **Museum of Antiquities**. Far from merely being a lure to attract customers to the winery, this is a serious collection of artefacts from ancient Egypt, Central America, Africa and the Roman Empire, all housed in a purpose-built, light-filled pavilion (Main Rd, Berrie-dale; daily 10am–4pm; free; tel: 6277 9900; www.moorilla.com.au).

A little further on in the suburb of Claremont is the **Cadbury Chocolate Factory**. There are those who visit to garner a deeper appreciation of the Quaker principles which informed the establishment of the factory in the early 1920s, where the wellbeing of the workers was paramount and manifested in the provision of affordable housing, quality recreational facilities and a supportive environment. There are others who go for the free tastings. Indeed, much of the tour does consist of tast-

ings. The latter group is particularly appreciative of the big bags of "seconds" which are sold off cheaply in the shop at the tour's end. (Guided tours; Mon–Fri 8am–2.30 pm, half-hourly; admission charge; bookings essential; tel. 1800 627 367.)

The **Alpenrail Swiss Model Village and Railway** is a quirky enterprise in a quiet suburban street. Rudi Jenni migrated to Australia from Switzerland with his family when he was 12 and set about building a model railway. Somehow, with the indulgence and assistance of his father, it got completely out of hand and became this astonishing 200 sq. metre (2,150 sq. ft) representation of a corner of the Bernese Oberland. The main station is modelled on the one in Spiez and there are many other identifiable landmarks. The trains operate with Swiss precision to a computer-controlled timetable; each cycle runs for over 20 minutes and includes a storm, nightfall and dawn, with mist rising over the lake (82 Abbotsfield Rd, West Claremont; daily 9.30am–4.30pm, admission charge; tel: 6249 3748). ❏

An African figure made from beads at the Museum of Antiquities, part of Moorilla Estate Winery.

BELOW: the Cadbury factory.

The Tasman Bridge

In 1964 the new four-lane Tasman Bridge across the Derwent River east of Hobart city centre was opened to ease congestion in and out of the city. It did so until 5 January 1975 when a bulk ore carrier crashed into one of the supporting pylons. A section of bridge crashed down, sinking the ship and killing seven of its crew. A further five people died when their cars crashed into the water. It wasn't until October 1977 that the rebuilt bridge, almost 1.4 km (0.9 miles) in length and complete with a new fifth lane and improved safety measures, opened and saved residents of the eastern suburbs a 50-km (31-mile) drive into the city.

RESTAURANTS, PUBS, CAFÉS AND BARS

Restaurants

Amulet
333 Elizabeth St,
North Hobart
Tel: 6234 8113
Open: L & D daily. **$$**
Considering the quality of the produce and the complexity of some of the dishes, Amulet is one of the most reasonably priced dining rooms in town and supported by a good wine list. Chef Lisa Thorsen is strongly committed to sourcing local organic produce.

Annapurna
305 Elizabeth St,
North Hobart
Tel: 6236 9500
Open: L Mon-Fri, D daily. **$**
It helps to be very hungry or with a group if you're going to do justice to the generous servings in this Indian restaurant. The masala dosa is particularly good.

Ball and Chain
87 Salamanca Place
Tel: 6223 2655
www.ballandchain.com.au
Open: L Mon-Fri, D daily. **$$**
The Ball and Chain is recommended for its chargrilled steaks, which are served with oven roasted potatoes and self-serve salads, and its selection of red wines.

Blue Skies
Murray St Pier
Tel: 6224 3759
www.blueskiesdining.com
Open: L & D daily. **$$**
Popular, informal, reasonably-priced waterside restaurant with an eclectic menu.

Choux Shop
4 Victoria St
Tel: 6231 0601
Open: L Tues-Fri,
D Tues-Sat. **$$$**
Casual by day and dressed up at night, Choux Shop is the latest venture for Chris Jackman, one of Tasmania's most thoughtful chefs. Some dishes feature produce he grows or breeds on his own farm.

Cornelian Bay Boat House
Queens Walk, Cornelian Bay
Tel: 6228 9289
www.theboathouse.com.au
Open: L daily, D Mon-Sat. **$$**
The inspiration for the Boat House's fusion menu comes from every continent but belongs to none.

Da Angelo
47 Hampden Rd,
Battery Point
Tel: 6223 7011
Open: D daily. **$$**
One of the best of Hobart's Italian restaurants, Da Angelo serves good pasta and makes a mean pizza.

Drunken Admiral
17 Hunter St
Tel: 6234 1903
Open: D daily. **$$**
This long-established

seafood themed waterfront dining room is very popular, especially the eat-all-you-want salad bar.

Fish 349
349 Elizabeth St,
North Hobart
Tel: 6234 7788
Open: L & D daily. **$**
This is the sort of place that gives fish and chips a great name. It's very casual – order and pay at the bar – but the fish is fresh and cooked to order.

Fish Frenzy
Elizabeth St Pier
Tel: 6231 2134
Open: L & D daily. **$**
This casual, waterfront restaurant does a roaring trade in fish and chips. It pays to eat very early, especially if you want an outside, dockside table.

Flathead
4 Cascade Rd, South Hobart
Tel: 6224 3194
Open: L Tues-Sat, D daily. **$**
This tiny, informal restaurant, which locals would prefer to keep a secret, serves up some of the best seafood in town. The menu changes daily depending on what's available but if the chargrilled octopus is on, it's a must. The fish and chips are good too.

LEFT: sozzled sailor in Hunter Street

Francisco's
60 Hampden Rd,
Battery Point
Tel: 6224 7258
Open: L & D Wed-Sun. $$$
This is a good venue if
you feel like grazing. The
best dishes are to be
found amongst the
selection of Spanish
inspired tapas.

Gondwana
22 Francis St, Battery Point
Tel: 6224 9900
Open: L Tues-Fri,
D Mon-Sat. $$$
The Battery Point
cottage might be old but
the dining concept is
thoroughly modern.
Local produce is
thoughtfully teamed
with complex sides.

Henry's (Henry Jones Art Hotel)
25 Hunter St
Tel: 6210 7700
Open: L & D daily. $$$
There's some interesting
food to be had in this
hotel dining room, that's
best enjoyed in the
annex in the beautiful
Henry Jones atrium. The
menu pays more than lip
service to vegetarians.

Kelley's Seafood
5 Knopwood St,
Battery Point
Tel: 6224 7225
Open: L Mon-Fri, D daily. $$$
Picturesquely located in
a cottage in Hobart's
historic Battery Point,
Kelly's is especially
recommended for its
famous octopus, mus-
sels, and its freshly-
cooked local fish.

Khaow Thai
85 Harrington St
Tel: 6234 1013
Open: L & D Mon-Sat. $
Simple freshly-cooked
Thai dishes that are sat-
isfying for a quick lunch
or early dinner. BYO.

Le Provencal
417 Macquarie St,
South Hobart
Tel: 6224 2526
Open: D Tues-Sat $$
As close to a French
dining experience as
you'll get in Hobart, La
Provencal is recom-
mended for its steak
with béarnaise.

Lebrina
155 New Town Rd
Tel: 6228 7775
Open: D Tues-Sat. $$$
One of Tasmania's
great dining rooms. Each
dish from chef Scott
Minervini's small,
seasonal menu is likely
to be memorable. Highly
recommended.

Magic Curries
41 Hampden Rd,
Battery Point
Tel: 6223 4500
Open: D daily. $
Conveniently-located,
Magic Curries hits the
mark when you're ready
for a little spice.

Mai Ake Thai Takeaway
277 Elizabeth St,
North Hobart
Tel: 6231 5557
Open: L & D daily. $
This elegant little Thai
restaurant is well-
regarded for its freshly-
cooked dishes.

Maldini
47 Salamanca Place
Tel: 6223 4460
Open: L & D daily. $$
Maldini is one of the few
Italian restaurants around
that takes advantage of
Tasmania's seasons. The
specials menu offers
some of the best options.

Marque iv
Elizabeth St Pier
Tel: 6224 4428
www.marqueiv.com.au
Open: L & D daily. $$$
Clean contemporary
lines, one of Hobart's
most comfortable dining
rooms, great food, and
a great waterfront
location, make this a
good choice for a big
night out.

Mures
Victoria Dock
Tel: 6231 1999
Open: L & D daily. $$$
One of Tasmania's most
famous restaurants,
Mures is renowned for
its shellfish and fish
such as trevalla and
stripey trumpeter. Much
of the fish comes from
the Mures' own boats
that berth beside the
restaurant to unload.

Orizuru
Victoria Dock
Tel: 6231 1790
Open: L & D Mon-Sat. $$
The premium seating at
Orizuru is one of the few
stools at the bar from
where you have a birds-
eye view of the intricate
preparation required to
produce Hobart's best
sashimi and sushi. BYO.

Paesano Pizza & Pasta
28 Lower Jordan Hill Rd,
West Hobart
Tel: 6234 2111
Open: D Tues-Sun. $
It's tricky to get a table
at this much-loved
neighbourhood
restaurant but well
worth the effort for the
excellent pizza. BYO.

Prosser's on the Beach
Sandy Bay Regatta Pavilion
Tel: 6225 2276
Open: L Wed-Fri, D daily. $$
Stuart Prosser sources
some of the state's best
fresh seafood and cooks
it with commendable
restraint.

The Quarry
27 Salamanca Place
Tel: 6223 6552
www.thequarry.com.au
Open: L & D daily. $$
Part lounge, part bar and
a menu that's designed
for grazing, this is the
newest hot spot in
Salamanca Place in the
heart of Hobart.

Rockerfellers
11 Morrison St
Tel: 6234 3490
www.rockerfellers.com.au
Open: L Mon-Fri, D daily. $$
Well known for its gener-
ous burgers and over the
top desserts.

PRICE CATEGORIES
Prices for a three-course
dinner per person with a
half-bottle of house wine:
$ = under A$50
$$ = A$50–A$75
$$$ = over A$75
L = lunch, D = dinner, BYO
= bring your own alcohol.

Sen's Asian Sensation
345 Elizabeth St,
North Hobart
Tel: 6236 9345
Open: L & D daily. **$**
If you order small dishes from the selection of dim sum followed by a platter of roasted meats you'll enjoy some of Hobart's best Chinese food.

Sirens
6 Victoria St
Tel: 6234 2634
Open: L Mon-Fri,
D Tues-Sat. **$$**
Sirens' vegetarian menu is so sophisticated that you hardly notice the lack of meat. This food's good enough to tempt carnivores as well.

Sisco's on the Pier
Upper Level, Murray St Pier
Tel: 6223 2059
Open: D Mon-Sat. **$$$**
Sisco's is justly famous for its lobster, crab, mussels and other shellfish, but Ramona's Spanish desserts are possibly even more memorable.

Sugo
9 Salamanca Square
Tel: 6224 5690
Open: L & D daily. **$$**
As well as making excellent coffee, this Salamanca Square café has

---

PRICE CATEGORIES

Prices for a three-course dinner per person with a half-bottle of house wine:
$ = under A$50
$$ = A$50–A$75
$$$ = over A$75
L = lunch, D = dinner, BYO = bring your own alcohol.

---

good pizza, pasta and other largely Italian-inspired dishes. Ideal for an informal lunch. BYO.

T42
Elizabeth St Pier
Tel: 6224 7742
www.tav42.com.au
Open: L & D daily. **$**
One of the best bars in town, T42's waterfront location also makes it a popular casual dining option, albeit a noisy one. There's an interesting wine list.

The Point
410 Sandy Bay Rd
Tel: 6211 1750
www.wrestpoint.com.au
Open: L Fri, D daily. **$$$**
This revolving restaurant at the top of Wrest Point Casino is an institution. It's a great location for getting your bearings, and has an excellent wine list.

The Source
Moorilla Estate, 655 Main Rd, Berriedale
Tel: 6277 9900
www.moorilla.com.au
Open: L daily, D Wed-Sat. **$$**
Set amongst vineyards, this relatively new first-floor dining room is one of Hobart's most spectacular. Chef Justin North is a strong supporter of local producers.

Vanidol's
353 Elizabeth St,
North Hobart
Tel: 6234 9307
Open: D Tues-Sun. **$**
Vanidol's eclectic menu includes the cuisines of

Thailand, Indonesia and India. It's BYO, which makes for a good-value night out.

Pubs, cafés and bars

Afterword Café
140 Collins St
Tel: 6224 2488
www.fullersbookshop.com.au
Open: L daily. **$**
This mezzanine above the busy Fullers Bookshop is a popular meeting place for locals deal-making or just soaking up the atmosphere over a good coffee or a real tea.

Bar Celona
45 Salamanca Place
Tel: 6224 7557
Open: L & D daily. **$**
As popular late at night as it is on a warm summer's day, this is a relaxing bar in Salamanca Square.

Criterion Street Café
10 Criterion St
Tel: 6234 5858
Open: L Mon-Fri. **$**
Many Hobartians start their day with breakfast at the communal table here.

Dukkah
112 Elizabeth St
Tel: 6234 6131
Open: L Mon-Sat. **$**
This is a popular, central place for snacks and very good coffee. Sit on stools. BYO.

Grape Bar Bottleshop
55 Salamanca Place
Tel: 6224 0611

Open: L & D daily. **$$**
A shiny new venue that has immediately been adopted by locals as a pleasant place to sit and enjoy a snack and some very smart wines by the glass.

Halo
37a Elizabeth St
Tel: 6234 6669
Open Thur–Sun. **$**
Secret night-time venue reached by a secret lane where you approach a secret door with a not-so-secret guard. It opens at the secret time of 10pm.

Hope & Anchor
65 Macquarie St
Tel: 6236 9982
www.hopeandanchor.com.au
Open: L & D daily. **$**
Old-fashioned pub with a wonderfully idiosyncratic upstairs bar.

Irish Murphy's
21 Salamanca Place
Tel: 6223 1119
Open: L & D daily. **$**
Popular waterfront hotel where you can sit and admire the beautiful gardens in front of Tasmania's Parliament House.

Jackman & McRoss
59 Hampden Road,
Battery Point
Tel: 6223 3186
Open L daily. **$**
One of the most popular meet-and-greet venues in Hobart and the source of some of the best bread and best pastries around.

RIGHT: dining al fresco in Salamanca Place.

IXL Long Bar
Henry Jones Art Hotel,
25 Hunter St
Tel: 6210 7700
Open: L & D daily. **$**
One of the most relaxed
bars in Hobart set within
the wonderful Henry
Jones waterfront devel-
opment in Hobart's
Hunter Street.

Knopwood's Retreat
39 Salamanca Place
Tel: 6223 5808
Open: L & D daily. **$**
Hobart's traditional
Friday-night watering hole
which sees hundreds of
locals spilling onto the
nearby Salamanca lawns
to enjoy the drinks and
the locale.

Lark Distillery Café
14 Davey St
Tel: 6231 9088
Open: L Mon-Sat. **$**
Which one of the 76
local or Scottish whisky
varieties will you try?
Whether your tipple is
Springbank, Laphroaig,
Highland Park or
Lagavulin this is the
place for you.

Lizbon
217 Elizabeth St, North
Hobart
Tel: 6234 9133
Open: D Mon-Sat. **$$**
Choose from the wide
selection of wines by the
glass or something more
exotic, but enjoy one of
Hobart's most sophisti-
cated venues.

Machine Café and Laundry
12 Salamanca Square
Tel: 6224 9922
Open: L & D daily. **$**
People queue here for
breakfast in Hobart's
Salamanca Square. If you
have been travelling you
can launder your clothes
while enjoying your food.

Macquarie St Food Store
356 Macquarie St
Tel: 6224 6862
Open: L daily. **$**
This inner-city gem has
been a magnet attracting
locals for many years.
Good coffee and snacks.

New Sydney Hotel
87 Bathurst St
Tel: 6234 4516
Open: L Mon-Sat, D daily. **$**
If you are a beer drinker
then this is one of the
places to consider.
British specialities.

Nourish
129 Elizabeth St
Tel: 6234 5674
Open L Mon-Sat,
D Thurs-Fri. **$**
For serious vegetarians,
Nourish provides a bet-
ter-than-average selec-
tion of dishes that cater
for a wide variety of
dietary needs.

Republic Bar and Café
299 Elizabeth St,
North Hobart
Tel: 6234 6954
Open: L & D daily. **$**
The music, poetry, and
politics are just as
important as the beer,
and they do an excellent
steak marinated in Jack
Daniels.

Retro Café
31 Salamanca Place
Tel: 6223 3073
Open: L daily. **$**
This has been Hobart's
gathering place of choice
for the past 15 years,
and is still going strong.
Great coffee. BYO.

Syrup
39 Salamanca Place
Tel: 6224 8249
Open: D Wed-Sat. **$**
A good venue for late-
night music above
popular Knopwoods in
Salamanca Place.

EAST OF HOBART AND THE TASMAN PENINSULA

The convict route from Hobart to the prison at Port Arthur takes in a scenic time capsule, Richmond, and a selection of natural attractions on and around the Tasman Peninsula

Map on page 92

This chapter follows the route from Hobart to the notorious penal settlement at Port Arthur (the most visited tourist site in Tasmania). It was the only route available prior to 1872; after that date, the completion of the Sorell causeway cut **Richmond ❶** out of the loop. In retrospect, this is one of the best things that could have happened to the town. It entered a period of economic inertia which prevented the destruction of what is now one of the very best preserved Georgian towns in all of Australia.

Richmond

The route, which goes under the badge of the "Convict Trail" in Tourism Tasmania's parcelling up of the state into marketable chunks, crosses the Tasman Bridge out of Hobart and follows the A3 to Cambridge where the B31 leads off to the north and Richmond. The town is only 25 km (15 miles) from the city, which accounts for its popularity for day trips.

Whichever direction you enter from, it is the preservation of so many buildings of the same era that seems so remarkable. The area was settled very early in the colony's history and the town itself, founded in 1824, became a key point on the route to the east coast once the Coal

River was bridged. When Port Arthur opened in 1830, it became a staging post for the movement of convicts, troops and supplies. Most of Richmond was built in this period through to the mid-1840s, and much remains intact to this day.

It makes sense to start at one of the earlier structures: **Richmond Bridge**, completed in 1825, is the oldest bridge in Tasmania. If you can put to one side the fact that it was constructed by convicts under extremely harsh conditions, the

LEFT the bridge at Richmond.
BELOW: craft shop in one of Richmond's many historic buildings.

The War Memorial outside Richmond Town Hall.

BELOW: Luke warm. St Luke's Anglican Church in the Richmond sun.

structure has a simple elegance to it, and if you see it glowing with the late afternoon sun on its sandstone blocks, and **St John's** church rising above the lawns behind it, the word "idyllic" really isn't good enough.

St John's is the oldest operating Catholic church in Australia, although mass is now held only every other week. The font and main stained-glass window were designed by Augustus Pugin, who was responsible for the Houses of Parliament in London. The church has an interesting cemetery, not to mention fine views down to the bridge.

Walk back down, being wary of the rather territorial geese, cross the bridge and follow the river bank to the left for a delightful walk up the hill to the village green. Set back from this is the old **Gaol** (daily 9am–5pm; admission charge; tel: 6260 2127), built in 1825 and used until 1928. Its inmates included one Ikey

Solomon, reputedly the model for Fagin in *Oliver Twist*. It's relatively small, yet a peek at the flogging yard or solitary confinement cells suggests it was just as fearsome as larger institutions elsewhere.

Bridge Street, aside from some nasty later additions like the supermarket, contains many of Richmond's best buildings. Several of these are now antique shops or venues for a cream tea (or Devonshire tea as they're known locally). This is also where you can find the **Old Hobart Town Model Village**, which recreates the place as it would have looked in 1820 (21 Bridge St; daily 9am–5pm; admission charge; tel: 6260 2502). The display includes hundreds of models of people getting up to all sorts, and there is a spotter sheet to keep the kids amused.

Just down the street is **Richmond Maze** (13 Bridge St; daily 9am–5pm; admission charge; tel: 6260

2709) or rather mazes, since there are two – of differing complexity – linked to each other. They are made with wooden fencing and the aim is to reach the centre of each and then get out again. Allow twice as long as you think you will need.

Coal Valley

Some 6 km (3½ miles) out of town on the C322 is **Richmond ZooDoo Wildlife Fun Park**, which is about as entertaining as it sounds (daily 9am–5pm; admission charge; tel: 6260 2444; www.zoodoo.com.au). There are plenty of native animals and birds, including Tasmanian devils, and some domesticated ones as well. If that weren't enough, three times a day four miniature ponies, mounted by soft toys, are set to race against each other round a track.

A highlight of the Coal Valley is the plethora of vineyards, all offering tasting opportunities. There are a good half dozen of them on the road back to Cambridge, where, eventually, you turn left for **Sorell** ❷, reached after crossing the eponymous causeway.

The town's own promoters exhort visitors to "explore the streets behind the busy main road to uncover treasures of history" – but you need to be very selective about which streets. Walker Street has the Bluebell Inn and the Barracks; there are a couple of old pubs elsewhere and three churches. After the riches of Richmond, however, it's a rather sorry place. Best to get onto the Arthur Highway (A9) and keep going.

Copping is a tiny huddle of buildings, and so you notice the rather primitively modelled mechanical policeman waving at you from the side of the road. It is there to promote the **Copping Colonial and Convict Collection** (daily Sept–May 9am 5pm; June–Aug 9am–4pm; admission charge; tel: 6253 5373; www.coppingmuseum.com.au), which proclaims itself to be "one of the largest collections of convict and colonial artefacts in Australia". Inside there's a vast room full of stuff that people have hung on to without really knowing why. A previous owner constructed crude motorised figures from some of the material and they clank away

Map on page 92

A walking map of Richmond is available at the Gaol, but there's no need to follow it slavishly. Stroll down almost any street in town and there is something interesting – churches, the old Richmond Arms Hotel, St Luke's Church, or perhaps the Old Schoolhouse of 1834.

BELOW: Old Hobart Town Model Village.

TIPS

The Cascades Colonial Accommodation at **Koonya** was originally a probation station for Port Arthur. The old convict workshop is now "perfect for a romantic getaway" apparently. Guests have access to a private museum, cells and a mess hall, and other sites in the grounds (tel: 6250 3873).

BELOW: the Dog Line at Eaglehawk Neck.

when a switch is thrown. There's a wall full of calling cards, another of photos of every coach that's ever stopped there. It's all quite overwhelming and unfocused. "A wonderful living museum of fabulous junk", says the sign by the policeman, with only partial accuracy.

Dunalley has a monument to Abel Tasman and a good fish market and then you're on to the **Forestier Peninsula** at the bottom of which is a sign to the **Tessellated Pavement**. A walking track leads down to this strange rock formation on the seashore where peculiar symmetrical erosion patterns have created the impression of a spread of paving stones. At low tide you can walk across it and investigate some good rockpools.

The Forestier is joined to the **Tasman Peninsula** by a narrow isthmus, the infamous **Eaglehawk Neck ❸**. It is here that the "Dog Line" was set up. Ferocious guard dogs were chained to a row of posts at the narrowest point in such a way that they could intercept anyone trying to escape. There is a lifelike

sculpture of one of these fearsome brutes showing it tethered to the barrel which acted as its kennel. There is also a good free explanatory display in the old Officers' Quarters, possibly the oldest timber military building in the country.

Onto the Tasman Peninsula

Crossing over the Neck, there are a few natural phenomena to discover before reaching the penal settlement. A road off to the left takes you up to the **Tasman Arch and Devil's Kitchen ❹**, both within the Tasman National Park. Each has its own car park but it's only a five-minute walk between the two so cover them both in one stop.

The Tasman Arch comes first. The sea has worn through weaker strata of cliff rock until this massive arch was created. Eventually the top will collapse, but for now you can walk round and over it in order to reach the viewpoint above the Devil's Kitchen. Here a narrow gash has been carved into the cliff – the top must have collapsed a long time ago – and you look down at the

seething water 60 metres (200 ft) below. It is not a large viewing platform and can get busy when the coach parties on their way to Port Arthur stop by.

On the way back to the highway, there's a turnoff to a **Blowhole**. This is coastal erosion in a different form with waves forcing water down a tunnel and compressing air in a side cave until it blasts out again in a powerful spray. This is a lateral eruption and, while not as dramatic as the one at Bicheno *(see page 144)*, you can still get soaked.

Elsewhere in Tasman National Park many walks make the most of the stunning coastal scenery, so if you can spare a few hours make for Bivouac Bay, Cape Hauy or maybe Cape Raoul. The *Tasmania's Great Short Walks* booklet has details (free from information centres).

The settlement just before the blowhole is known as **Doo Town** as all the dwellers there have given their houses names such as Doodle-Doo, Thistle-Doo-Me and Wattle-I-Doo. While you ponder this one, enjoy the fine seafood snacks or

fresh berries at the "Doolicious" trailer in the car park.

At Taranna the **Tasmanian Devil Park** (daily 9am–6pm; admission charge; book for Devils in the Dark tour by 5pm; tel. 6250 3230; www.tasmaniandevilpark.com) has several feeding sessions each day as well as raptor displays. Particularly noteworthy is the Devils in the Dark tour when a guide leads you on a prowl, taking in all the nocturnal activity you don't normally see.

Port Arthur

Another few minutes down the road, possibly after a detour to the pretty **Stewart's Beach** for a spot of kayaking, you reach **Port Arthur** ❺ (daily 8.30am–dusk; admission charge; tel. 1800 659 101; www.portarthur.org.au). This is where it gets busy. You will be directed to one of several car parks and then on to the visitor centre. As you buy your ticket to the Penal Settlement you are allocated a time for a boat cruise and another for the guided tour, ensuring that the constant flow of visitors is fed through

Map
on page
92

Coastal erosion has created interesting phenomena such as Remarkable Cave.

BELOW: the dramatic coastline of the Tasman National Park.

Lucky devil. This inmate of the Tasmanian Devil Park has a better chance than its wild cousins of avoiding the epidemic of mouth cancer which is decimating the species.

BELOW: the Commandant's House provided a fine view over the Port Arthur site.

as comfortably as possible. You can easily spend a whole day here and, since the ticket lasts for 48 hours, you may well want to return on the next day as well. Children are kept engaged with a free 20-page activity book which refers to the key features around the site.

A random playing card is handed out with each ticket and you need this downstairs in the Interpretation Gallery for the "Lottery of Life" exhibition. Each card corresponds to an inmate whose history you then follow through the display. You may have been transported for stealing a handkerchief but worked your way through the system to attain the prized ticket of leave. Alternatively, you may be a recidivist who meets a sticky end. It's a clever idea, which seems to work for all ages.

At the end of this you come out onto the site and can start exploring. The guidebook, which is also included in the entrance fee, gives comprehensive information about the different areas and is a useful addendum to the guided walking tour. In peak season actors perform short plays at various spots, and there are usually other special activities. In January archaeologists encourage children to help with the digging and sifting, for instance.

The warehouse-like **Penitentiary** stands out when you first look across the site – this is the building which features most often on postcards. It was originally a flour mill but problems with powering it, firstly by water wheel and then with convicts in a kind of giant hamster wheel, led to its abandonment. In 1848 it was converted into a 136-cell prison for the worst offenders. On other floors were a dining room, library, Catholic chapel and dormitory. It was burnt out in 1897 and now there is just the shell, although enough remains of the cells to give an idea of the deprivations endured.

The turreted building visible on the hill behind was the **Barracks**. Overcrowding was a problem for the soldiery with each man only having half as much space as that allocated to each convict and the building had to be extended several times. Only part of it remains.

The white-painted **Commandant's House** is perched up on the hill to allow a clear view across the settlement and harbour befitting the man who had to oversee all aspects of Port Arthur except for the garrison, which came under the authority of the Senior Military Officer. The latter's dwelling enjoyed similar pre-eminence until it burned down in 1897. The semaphore pole, first in the series linking the site to Hobart, was further up the hill.

Staying on the hill but moving away from the water you come to the ruins of the **Hospital**, which had a reputation for being a staging post to the Isle of the Dead cemetery out in the bay. Skeletal steel beds give an idea of how a ward would once have looked.

A short way up the hill behind it sits the distinctive yellow-painted **Smith O'Brien's Cottage**, where the eponymous Irish nationalist lived a solitary life in rather better conditions than other inmates. He had been transported for his part in a failed uprising in Ireland in 1848 and was moved to Port Arthur from Maria Island in 1850. He only stayed for four months before being granted a ticket of leave.

The Asylum, down the hill to the west, was capable of housing 100 patients from all over Van Diemen's Land. The emphasis was on cure as much as containment – an improvement on the corresponding 'madhouses' in Britain. The building now houses a museum and café.

Beyond it, the **Separate Prison**, built in 1849, also reflected new thinking. Convicts were to be isolated to reflect on their misdeeds and to this end would spend 23 hours a day in solitary confinement. Masks were worn to prevent contact with others when out of the cell and, as can be seen, attendance in chapel saw each individual being allocated a separate stall with a view of the celebrant and nothing else.

From the back of the Separate Prison a path winds past a handful of cottages towards the **Church**. Attendance at mass was compulsory for all prisoners until a virulently anti-Catholic prelate antagonised members of that order who, thereafter, worshipped separately. Fire gutted the building, but the shell is well maintained.

A stroll through the Government Gardens leads down to the cove where the *Marana* cruises out to The Isle of the Dead and Point Puer. The 40-minute voyage is open to all but to be set down at either point requires additional tickets.

The Isle of the Dead contains the remains of over a thousand people and their location depends on social status; the toffs are at the top of the hill, the convicts and paupers at the bottom, mostly in unmarked graves.

There is not a lot left of **Point Puer Boys' Prison** beyond a few foundations but it's an interesting place nonetheless. It was the first

Map on page 92

TIPS

The quieter times at Port Arthur are first thing in the morning before the coach tours arrive from Hobart, and mid-afternoon onwards when most of them have departed. It is, however, a huge site and so even in the summer peak season it is possible to find a secluded spot in which to avoid the throng.

BELOW: Coal Mines Historic Site commemorates another convict labour site.

A grim reputation

Port Arthur has come to represent the worst of the convict system. Its eerie landscape, dominated by the grim modus operandi and architecture of penal slavery, ensured its status as the enduring relic of Tasmania's convict past.

Marcus Clarke's Gothic novel *For the Term of his Natural Life* (1847) has contributed to its notoriety. Clarke's innocent hero, Rufus Dawes, was subjected to all manner of violent acts and injustices as he was shuffled around the worst corners of the British penal system, none apparently more wicked than Port Arthur. In practice, other locations, such as Sarah Island, witnessed far greater brutality.

Old-fashioned post box at Port Arthur.

BELOW: the Barracks at Port Arthur.

boys' prison in the British Empire, aimed at isolating the inmates from the older, hardened criminals and, at the same time, giving them a rough education and teaching them a trade. It was, though, a harsh regime and in its 15 years of operation, with up to 800 boys at a time, the results were mixed.

Back on the main site, a few minutes' walk around the headland from the jetty lie the remains of the **Dockyard** where convicts were employed in ship building.

On the way back to the visitor centre, the shell of the Broad Arrow Café is part of a **Memorial Garden** to the victims of a gunman who massacred 35 people in and around the site in April 1996. His name is mentioned in none of the plaques or literature. Visitors are asked not to broach the subject with staff.

After doing the rounds of Port Arthur, a break is in order at the visitor centre café. Once refreshed, you may consider returning for the popular lantern-lit ghost tour at dusk.

Take the road from Port Arthur and drive south 6 km (4 miles) to **Remarkable Cave** ❻. Wooden steps lead down from the car park to a viewpoint at sea level revealing that erosion here has created more of a tunnel than a cave. At the top Maingon Bay lookout provides views of dramatic cliffs and pounding seas.

Coal Mines Historic Site

Now return towards Port Arthur and follow the sign to **Nubeena**, with its few shops, plenty of boating and pair of surf beaches. Carry on through to Premaydena, take a left and follow the road, which becomes a track, to the **Coal Mines Historic Site** ❼ (daily 24 hours; free). This recently developed but under-publicised site, overseen by the Parks and Wildlife Service, contains the remains of Tasmania's first mine. Coal was discovered here in 1833 and a party of convict labourers was immediately despatched to set up a mine. Conditions faced by the "most refractory convicts" employed underground were appalling.

There are eight different walks taking between 10 minutes (to the main settlement) and three hours return. The remnants of stone buildings include the prisoners' barracks, complete with punishment cells in the basement, the solitary cells and separate apartments. The latter were the authorities' attempt to counter the rampant homosexuality that had developed in these "sinkholes of vice and infamy". It didn't work, and this, combined with the poor quality of the coal and consistent mismanagement, led to the selling off of the enterprise in 1848.

The mines were finally abandoned 30 years later. The irony, as with Port Arthur, is that the grim history of the site is hard to reconcile with the strikingly beautiful setting. There are glorious views across Norfolk Bay and it is only a short walk down to the beach. ❑

RESTAURANTS, PUBS, CAFÉS AND BARS

Restaurants

Cambridge

Barilla Bay
1388 Tasman Highway,
Cambridge
Tel: 6248 5454
www.barillabay.com.au
Open: L & D daily. **$$**
Barilla Bay is one of
Tasmania's premium
oyster suppliers and this
restaurant exists to
showcase them –
heaven for oyster lovers.

**Coal Valley Vineyard
Restaurant**
257 Richmond Road,
Cambridge
Tel: 6248 5367
www.coalvalley.com.au
Open: L Thurs-Mon,
D Oct-Mar Fri **$$$**
The restaurant serves
delicious, rustic food
and there's also a tapas-
style menu if you only
want to graze and taste
the wine.

Meadowbank Estate
699 Richmond Road,
Cambridge
Tel: 6248 4484
www.meadowbankwines.com.au
Open: L daily. **$$**
This beautiful, lunchtime-
only dining room is the
must-visit venue for food
lovers in this part of the
state. The menu is truly
seasonal and the cook-
ing delicious. There's
also a wine-tasting room.

Richmond

Prospect House
1384 Richmond Road,
Richmond
Tel: 6260 2207
www.prospect-house.com.au
Open: D daily. **$$**
Dining in this splendid
Georgian guesthouse is
at its best on a winter's
night, with an open fire
and game on the menu.

Tasman Peninsula

Dunalley Hotel
Arthur Highway, Dunalley
Tel: 6253 5101
Open: L & D daily. **$**
The steak and seafood
are recommended here.

Felons
Port Arthur Historic Site
Tel: 1800 659 101
www.portarthur.org.au
Open: D daily. **$$**
Within the historic site's
visitor centre, dinner can
be frenzied if you eat
prior to the ghost tour
start – book later for a
leisurely meal.

The Mussel Boys
5927 Arthur Highway,
Taranna
Tel: 6250 3088
Open: L & D daily. **$$**
The best food on the
Tasman Peninsula,
making the most of
what's available locally –
and not just the mussels.
The degustation menu is
a regional showcase.

Pubs, cafés and bars

Dodges Ferry

Mullet Café Park Beach
2 Payeena St, Park Beach,
Dodges Ferry. Tel: 6265 7971
Open: L Wed-Mon Sept-May. **$**
An unlikely place to find
middle-eastern-inspired
dishes, but good. BYO.

Richmond

**Ashmore on
Bridge Street**
34 Bridge Street, Richmond
Tel: 6260 2238
www.ashmoreonbridge.com.au
Open: L daily. **$**
Classic Devonshire tea
territory, with more sub-
stantial dishes too. BYO.

Tasman Peninsula

Dunalley Waterfront Café
4 Imlay St, Dunalley

Tel: 6253 5122
Open: L daily. **$**
Café with great views,
perfect for a lazy brunch.

**Eaglehawk Café &
Guest house**
5131 Arthur Highway,
Eaglehawk Neck
Tel: 6250 3331
www.theneck.com.au
Open: L daily summer,
Fri-Mon winter.
Wonderful breakfasts,
home-style dishes and
sunny aspect.

PRICE CATEGORIES

Prices for a three-course
dinner per person with a
half-bottle of house wine:
$ = under A$50
$$ = A$50–A$75
$$$ = over A$75
L = lunch, D = dinner, BYO
= bring your own alcohol.

RIGHT: plenty of options at the Richmond Arms.

PORT ARTHUR

It attracts more tourists than any other site in Tasmania, and yet Port Arthur is sizeable enough to allow visitors to reflect in peace on the traumas endured in both the 19th and 20th centuries

The first impression on most visitors to the Port Arthur Historic Site is of the attractiveness of the setting. Lawns stretch across a kind of natural amphitheatre framed by mature trees and lapped down to the left by the placid waters of Mason Cove. In favourable weather the sun imparts a warm, welcoming glow to the picturesque sandstone ruins. It takes some leap of the imagination to envisage this as a penal settlement whose fearsome reputation stretched to the furthest corners of the British Empire.

The sheer size of the place is remarkable. This is prison on an industrial scale. It's not basket weaving for the inmates (or picking oakum as it would have been then), but ship-building and timber felling, with enough agriculture and animal husbandry to keep a community afloat. The punishment cells and some of the experimental treatments in the Separate Prison are gruesome but, under the harsh light of historical revisionism, it is mooted that conditions in the slums of London's East End or some of the industrialised cities in 19th-century Britain were as bad, if not worse. But, before subscribing to the "hard but fair" theory, imagine being a convict on a cold winter's day, knowing you'll never see your home country again...

ABOVE: as part of the "enlightened" punishment regime in the Separate Prison, convicts were kept apart at all times. Even during the mandatory attendance at chapel, screens prevented contact with other prisoners but allowed a view of the minister.

BELOW: on Sundays upwards of 1,000 people – convicts and garrison – worshipped in the church.

LEFT: in a corner of the reflecting pool that makes up part of the memorial to the 1996 massacre are 35 bronze leaves; one for each of the gunman's victims.

VISITOR EXPERIENCE

A lot of thought has gone into making a visit memorable and from the very first point of contact, where the tickets are bought, a sense of involvement with the site is engendered. The playing card that comes with the ticket gives each person the name of a real convict to identify with. It's then a matter of finding snippets of that convict's story at various points in the Interpretation gallery so that by the time a visitor comes out into the site proper, they will have some grasp of the sort of people who would have been sent to Port Arthur in the early days. Guides – some quite flamboyant – then add colour during the introductory walking tour. In peak season extra activities are programmed, such as short site-specific plays in which performers re-enact stories culled from the memoirs of the original inmates and their gaolers.

ABOVE: bushfires ravaged the site in 1897, destroying some buildings Including the Senior Military Officer's House, and leaving others, like the Penitentiary, as shells.

RIGHT: for the soldiers set to guard the convicts, conditions were testing. The barracks were overcrowded and some of the men had to sleep on the floor.

LEFT: children are given a *Port Arthur Journey* activity book with their tickets and encouraged to use all their senses in a series of exercises. One task is to find four posts with convict love tokens on them and, with a pencil, rub the images into their books.

BELOW: the Penitentiary was originally the settlement's flour mill. Built in 1845, it was never a success and was soon converted into a detention block, with 136 cells on the first two floors for "prisoners of bad character under heavy sentence".

RIGHT: it was in the Broad Arrow Café on Sunday 28 April 1996 that the first shots were fired, or at least the first in the historic site, during what became known as the Port Arthur Massacre. Some time later the café was stripped back to a shell and a reflecting pool installed in front of it to create a place of quiet contemplation. It was formally dedicated on 28 April 2000.

THE HUON VALLEY

South of Hobart the landscape becomes thoroughly rural as the road winds down to the southern tip of the state. With estuarine coast to the east and the beginnings of the wilderness to the west, it's one beautiful area

The area to the south of Hobart has always been important to the economy of Tasmania, with a robust maritime tradition of fishing and boat-building combined with the exploitation of the extensive wilderness forests for logging. Above all, though, it was fruit-growing which established the Huon Valley in the popular imagination. In particular it was the success of the apple orchards, which generated substantial export income and was responsible for the soubriquet, "The Apple Isle".

Apples are still important to the area, but nowadays many of the orchards have been given over to berries and other fruit as tastes have changed along with global trading conditions. As with other elements of Australia's export industries, the traditional colonial trade links have been severely tested by the barriers resulting from the United Kingdom's membership of the European Union.

For the visitor there are still heritage centres and roadside stalls dedicated to the apple. However, the main appeal lies in the sheer beauty of the area, whether it be the meandering coastal scenery, the cave systems, the forests, or the plethora of walking tracks in the national parks. These provide opportunities to reach the country's southernmost

tip or to explore the edges of the vast southwestern wilderness.

The Channel Highway

It's only a short hop out of Hobart, past Sandy Bay, along the Channel Highway to the beginning of what the tourist authorities have proclaimed "The Huon Trail". Branded interpretive signs, as we're supposed to call them, are dotted throughout the region, and the first is found at **Taroona ❶** beside the impressively large **Shot Tower**

LEFT: the Tahune Forest Airwalk.
BELOW: the Shot Tower at Taroona.

The Huon Valley was the heartland of the apple industry that helped to define Tasmania.

(daily 9am–6pm, admission charge; tel: 6227 8885). The structure – carefully qualified as the "only remaining circular sandstone shot tower left in the world" – provides extensive views across the Derwent River estuary and Storm Bay for those fit enough to climb the stairs to the top, and one of Tasmania's better cream teas (or Devonshire teas as they're known locally) for those content to sit it out on the stone terrace or in the tearoom at the bottom. The tower was built 58 metres (190 ft) high to allow enough time and distance for the molten lead, poured down the middle from the top, to form into perfect spheres and then solidify by the time it reached the bottom, producing shot for guns in the process.

Taroona has taken on new notoriety in recent years as the birthplace of Mary Donaldson, or Princess Mary of Denmark as she is now better known outside the village. She met Crown Prince Frederik in a pub in Sydney in 2000, went on to marry him and has now provided the next heir to the Danish throne.

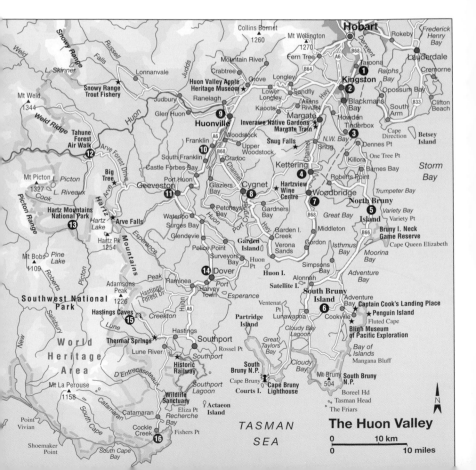

The Huon Valley

The apparent absence of people in Taroona suggests that Mary's peers may well have upped sticks in search of similar good fortune in the drinking dens of Sydney.

Busier by far is **Kingston ②**. The town doesn't offer a great deal except for the Australian Federal Government's **Antarctic Division Headquarters** (Mon–Fri 9am–5pm, free; tel: 6232 3516) on the road south from the centre. Visitors can peruse displays detailing some of the expeditions and research projects undertaken by scientists. There's a café as well. Kingston itself has a good sheltered beach with safe swimming, about a kilometre east of the town centre. **Blackmans Bay**, another 3 km (2 miles) south, also has good sand and swimming.

Keep going south along the sweeping coast road and at the tip of the peninsula pause at the delightful **Tinderbox ③**. Vineyards slope down to a small sheltered bay where swimmers can follow the underwater snorkel trail – a series of information boards on plates on the seabed explaining the marine life of the Tinderbox Marine Nature Reserve. The trail begins on the right of the beach.

The road now winds up via Howden and rejoins the Channel Highway which proceeds south to **Margate**. Parked at the side of the road on the outskirts there's an old steam locomotive with all its carriages lined up behind it. This was the last passenger train to run in Tasmania, and it now houses an information office, a bookshop, craft shops and draws people to the nearby antique store.

On the road behind the train is the entrance to the attractive **Inverawe Native Gardens** (daily Sept–May 9.30am–5pm; admission charge; tel: 6267 2020; www.inverawe.com.au), where over 4,000 native trees and shrubs cover 9.5 hectares (24 acres) overlooking North West Bay. Birdwatchers may spot up to 70 different species here.

Onto Bruny Island

A further 13 km (8 miles) down the road, past the pleasingly-named small town of **Snug** (so-called

The Antarctic Division Headquarters has a free exhibition.

BELOW: vineyards roll down the hill to the beach at Tinderbox.

The ferry to Bruny Island, the *Mirambeena*, runs 10 return trips a day with an extra one on Fridays (from Kettering (6.50am–6.30pm, Fri 7.30pm, from Bruny 7.15am–7pm, Fri 7.50pm; tel: 6272 3277).

BELOW: stairway to haven. The beach on the Neck has protected areas for penguins and mutton birds.

because of the sheltered merits of its harbour), lies the town of **Kettering** ④. Oyster Cove is an ideal destination for kayakers who can rent boats by the hour or join organised tours out into the cove and beyond. Most visitors, however, are making for the ferry, which will transport them and their vehicles over to **Bruny Island**.

It's 63 km (39 miles) from the top of Bruny Island to the bottom, but that includes a narrow sand isthmus which effectively divides it into two: North Bruny and South Bruny. The ferry lands at Roberts Point which is in **North Bruny** ⑤, where the more benign landscape is to be found. There are gently rolling hills largely given over to agriculture and a few beautiful bays dotted with holiday homes. For secluded breathtaking bathing or boating spots there's little to choose between Barnes Bay, Great Bay and Nebraska Beach which leads up to Dennes Point on the northern tip. From the latter there are marvellous views back to the mainland all the way round to the Tasman Peninsula.

The Neck, as the isthmus is known, is a highlight of the island. In the middle there's a passage through to a long deserted beach and a hide from which penguins can be seen waddling up to their nests in the dunes at dusk or mutton birds flying down to theirs. There is also a set of steps running high up to a viewing platform with spectacular views across the island and beyond. Here there is a simple memorial stone to Truganini, arguably one of the few Tasmanian Aboriginals most locals could name (*see panel on page 107*).

South Bruny ⑥ has more for the visitor and is more populous than the north, but it still feels empty most of the time. **Adventure Bay** is as busy as it gets, with a general store, a café, a scattering of houses and the **Bligh Museum of Pacific Exploration** (daily 10am–3pm; unofficially 8.30am–late; admission charge; tel: 6293 1117). It's a single room, little bigger than a garage, and illustrates the fascinating story of the early explorers who landed here. Abel Tasman was the first

European to spot the island in 1642, and subsequent visitors included Tobias Furneaux, James Cook and William Bligh. However, the key figure is French Rear Admiral Bruni d'Entrecasteaux, who conducted the first survey of the area in 1792 and after whom the island is named – albeit erroneously.

He is also remembered by the D'Entrecasteaux Channel between the island and the mainland. It was, though, after Furneaux's ship that Adventure Bay was named.

At the furthest extreme of Adventure Bay there's a sometimes challenging trail to the dramatic **Fluted Cape**, with the optional extra of walking across to Penguin Island when the tide is out. For nature in a more controlled state there are, just north of Adventure Bay, formal gardens at **Morells** as well as a gallery and café, while over the road **Hiba**'s fine gardens surround a modern ersatz chateau complete with turrets, and a fudge factory.

The road up across the island to the west features a couple of good viewpoints, and then there are two options if you want to take in either of the separate wings of **South Bruny National Park**. One runs down to **Cloudy Bay** where you can settle for some surfing or fishing, or hike along a track to the viewpoint at East Cloudy Head.

The second option is to continue to Lunawanna and then drive south to **Cape Bruny Lighthouse**, the second oldest in Australia, built in 1836. It's not open for inspection but there's enough to look at with the panoramic views and lots more dramatic fluted rock cliffs. For serious walkers there's a seven-hour trek around the **Labillardiere Peninsula**, featuring beaches, forests and open grassland.

The road back to the Neck passes through the administrative centre, **Alonnah**. It has a school, hotel, council office with history room (a couple of folders of cuttings) and a police station. The police force can sometimes be found positioned at the edge of the settlement with his radar gun in hand, waiting for speeding malefactors. Be warned.

Fearsome weapons are on display at the Bligh Museum of Pacific Exploration.

Map on page 104

BELOW: the memorial to Truganini at the viewpoint on the Neck.

THIS MEMORIAL IS DEDICATED TO THE MEMORY OF TRUGANINI 1812 - 1876

Truganini

There are a number of conflicting accounts of Truganini's life, death and status, but her main legacy is symbolic. She may or may not have been the last pure-bred Aboriginal from Tasmania when she died in 1876. She very probably wasn't, but her history and the possibility that her people died with her, represents a sorry indictment of the worst policies of the colonial establishment.

Truganini was born around 1812 on Bruny Island and in short order saw her mother killed by whalers, her two sisters abducted and sold into slavery, and her fiancée killed as he tried to save her from her sisters' fate. In 1830 she, with her husband, was one of a group of, allegedly, the last Aboriginals rounded up and shipped to Wybalenna on Flinders Island under the "protection" of George Augustus Robinson. In 1856, the few who had survived on the island were relocated to Oyster Cove on the mainland. Truganini, the last of this group, died in Hobart in 1876. She was buried at the Female Factory but exhumed two years later and her remains put on display in a Hobart museum. It wasn't until 1976 that she was finally cremated and her ashes scattered in the sea off Bruny Island.

TIPS

Another way to appreciate Bruny Island's rock formations, with a special emphasis on the wildlife, is to take the Bruny Island Charters Eco Cruise and check out a seal colony, dolphins, seabirds and, sometimes, whales. The boat operates from Adventure Bay and can also be boarded in Hobart. Tel: 6293 1465; www.brunycharters. com.au

BELOW: batik work is one of many skills on offer at Geeveston's Southern Forest Working Craft and Furniture Centre.

Woodbridge

Having returned to the mainland, it's not far down to **Woodbridge** ❼, a township featuring some beautifully preserved weatherboard buildings. This is another place which attracts direct boat trips from Hobart, this time with underwater cameras relaying scenes of life below the keel to the passengers above. The bait here is **Peppermint Bay**, a sleek new restaurant/bar complex with smashing views of the water.

Gourmands who still have a corner to fill can visit **Grandvewe Cheesery**, which produces a whole range of cheeses, with a tasting room for testing the results (Birch's Bay; tel: 6267 4099; www.grandview.au.com).

At **Fleurtys** farm and distillery there's less to be seen in the way of production but this hardly matters considering the views from the onsite café. The shop sells a whole range of home-produced essential oils under the Diemen Pepper label (Birch's Bay; tel: 6267 4078).

The options now are to drive around the coast and enjoy more fine views, or take the short cut inland, maybe dropping into the **Hartzview Wine Centre** en route. Either way, the next destination is **Cygnet** ❽. This is an attractive town featuring lots of red brick in its historic buildings. There's a hefty church on a rise from the main street with an austere nunnery to one side and a sumptuous priest's house on the other. Elsewhere there are some interesting shops, cosy eateries, and a couple of small museums: the **Cygnet Living History Museum** (Thurs–Sun 12.30–3pm; donation; tel: 6295 1602) and the **Living History Museum of Aboriginal Cultural Heritage** in a converted church (daily 10.30am–2.30pm; admission charge; tel: 6295 0004).

Cygnet is central to the apple industry as is the next stop, **Huonville** ❾, the bustling commercial heart of the region. The Huon River runs through the town and is likely to feature in a visit, whether it be a gentle stroll along the banks looking at the wooden sculpted figures outside the well-preserved weatherboard houses, or

the altogether more dynamic experience of the Huon Jet. This is adrenaline on the water, a jet boat which roars along between the trees before turning on a sixpence and reducing the passengers to gibbering wrecks – an exciting way to uncover any dormant cardiac conditions. The same company also runs sedate two-hour cruises to Franklin and back.

The Parks and Wildlife Service has an information centre in town and it's worth stopping to pick up permits or maps if you're planning to visit any of the national parks in the area (22 Main Rd; Mon–Fri 9am–4.30pm; tel: 6264 8460).

Six km (4 miles) up the road in Grove an unprepossessing shed houses the surprisingly interesting **Huon Valley Apple and Heritage Museum** (daily 9am–5pm Sept–May, 10am–4pm June–Aug; entrance fee). There's a complete history of the apple industry in the area, as well as a blacksmith's forge and carpenter's shop. It's not to be confused with the Apple Valley Centre on the Huon Highway, which promises a German Model Train World and a Tudor Court Model Village in an attempt to draw tourists into an arts and crafts world.

Better to spend a few moments in **Ranelagh**, host to the **Home Hill Winery**. It combines modern architecture with a mountain backdrop, making the 200-seat restaurant a popular attraction.

Along the river

It's now time to turn back to the south, through Huonville, and on to **Franklin ⑩**. Stroll along the banks of the river and it's hardly a surprise to find the **Wooden Boat Centre** taking pride of place as the main tourist attraction. Students of all ages embark on an 18-month boat-building course here, at the end of which they will have built a wooden

vessel from scratch. The finished product is then sold. Visitors look around a display of boat-building history and techniques and then watch the work in progress in the workshop (daily 9.30am–5pm; admission charge; tel: 6266 3586).

Elsewhere, there is some attractive Federation, and earlier, architecture, particularly the Palais Theatre and the Franklin Tavern, while on the foreshore the former courthouse has been converted into the appealing Petty Sessions café.

There are some beautiful views on the road south along the river. The **Kermandie Hotel** in Port Huon is worth a stop for adventurous pub food, before the next stop at **Geeveston ⑪**, where two huge logs either side of the road as you arrive give a solid clue to the main local industry.

The **Forest and Heritage Centre** (daily 9am–5pm, gold coin donation) in the Town Hall takes up the theme and provides a comprehensive overview of forestry and logging since the early days of settlement. Upstairs there's a gallery

Tasmania's apple industry may be smaller than it once was, but visitors can still enjoy the fruits of its labours.

BELOW: hard work at Franklin's Wooden Boat Centre.

Waratahs beside the path to Waratah Lookout in Hartz Mountains National Park.

BELOW: chiselled good looks in Geeveston.

of works in wood by local artists. The zealous visitor can even take lessons in woodturning.

Staying with the wood theme, there's a trail to follow around town of Huon pine sculptures of local characters and historical figures in a style familiar from Huonville.The **Southern Forest Working Craft and Furniture Centre** spreads its net a little wider by incorporating weavers, batik makers, jewellers, painters and silversmiths in its workshops, but the woodworkers are there, too, to keep an eye on things. All kinds of products are available for sale and at prices rather more competitive than some found in the busier tourist centres.

Many people make a stop in Geeveston simply to break the journey out to the spectacular **Tahune Forest Air Walk** ⑫, which has rapidly become the region's biggest tourist draw. It's a 28-km (17-mile) drive west along the Arve Road; if you have time on your hands, it's worthwhile picking up a leaflet in Geeveston pinpointing the various lookouts and walks on the way.

The Forest Air Walk itself (daily 9am–5pm, later in summer peak time; admission charge; tel: 6297 0068) is a 600-metre (1,970-ft) long anodised steel walkway sitting on huge pylons and averaging over 20 metres (65 ft) above the ground through the forest canopy.

At the far end there's a section cantilevered out towards the Huon River giving terrific views down to where the Huon and Picton rivers merge. Those who fear heights may find the swaying disconcerting, especially when undisciplined children jump up and down in a, to date, doomed attempt to bring the whole structure crashing to the ground. Abseiling down is an option for those with no such worries.

There are good walks at ground level through the pines, and opportunities to go rafting. Just upriver is **Eagle Gliding**, which provides a hang-gliding experience without the danger or unpredictability; you strap yourself in and then fly down over the river suspended from a wire. Twice.

Travel back towards Geeveston for 15 km (9 miles) to the turnoff to the **Hartz Mountains National Park** . Suddenly you're away from the crowds and free to explore beautiful alpine countryside. There are several marked trails, some on boardwalks, ranging from 10 minutes to four hours taking in waterfalls, glacial lakes and steep mountain climbs.

The shortest walk to Waratah lookout is well worth it for the view across the serated Hartz peaks and beyond. It's a tantalising glimpse of the largely inaccessible Tasmanian Wilderness World Heritage Area. In season the red blooms of the waratahs add to the splendour. Some of the longer walks are only for the fit and experienced and, as always, be prepared for sudden changes in weather conditions.

Dover and beyond

Dover lies 22 km (14 miles) south and sits prettily on Port Esperance where the fishing fleet comes in past the three islands known as Faith, Hope and Charity. Dover was a probation station, then a timber town, and now relies on fruit and fish, whether from the ships or the local salmon farms. Besides some walks around the bay and a "gourmet tour" involving a boat trip and lunch at the Dover Hotel (tel: 6298 1210), there is not a great deal to detain a non-fishing visitor. Being described as "the southernmost town of some importance in Australia" doesn't exactly set the pulse racing.

The Huon Highway runs out of steam at **Southport**. This is another small fishing port, this time with a beach as well, which accounts for the few basic holiday homes scattered along the road. When you drive through everybody waves at you, which suggests they don't see a lot of visitors (or there's something wrong with the car).

Just before Southport the C636 leads through Hastings to the **Hastings Caves and Thermal Springs** . You come first to the visitor centre at **Thermal Springs State Reserve**, where tickets must be purchased for the guided tour of the cave and they include admission to

Map on page 104

TIPS

A joint venture between various agencies has seen the publication of a free booklet, *Great Short Walks*, which outlines 60 treks in some of the most beautiful areas in the state. The walks range from just a few minutes long to several hours. There are information boards at the start of each route co-ordinated with the design of the booklet.

BELOW:
Port Esperance shoreline at Dover.

Map on page 104

The whaling industry was responsible for the first settlement at Cockle Creek

BELOW: Newdegate Cave at Hastings Caves and Thermal Springs.

the springs. There is a small display area and behind the centre a path leads down to the thermal springs, or rather open-air pools filled with hot water piped from the springs. It feels like a resort swimming area but in its rural setting is a pleasant place to relax.

For the cave tour it's necessary to drive another 5 km (3 miles) up the road and then walk for five minutes through old forest to the entrance; leave enough time for this when contemplating a dip before a tour. **Newdegate Cave** was first revealed in 1917 by a group of woodcutters but, since they were trespassing on someone else's land at the time, it was only formally discovered once they had disingenuously established a legal right to be there.

A complex trail of steps and walkways leads through the subtly lit chambers (daily Jan–Feb 9am–6pm, Mar–Apr & Sep–Dec 9am–5pm, May–Aug 10am–4pm; admission charge; tel: 6298 3209). Inside it's always a chilly 9°C (48°F). Well-informed guides explain the processes behind the growth of intri-

cate stalactite formations. Longer and more rigorous tours of other caves can be booked at least a day in advance.

The southern tip

The road south passes through Lune River and Ida Bay and is then unmade but well maintained, mostly through forest, all the way down to **Cockle Creek** ⑯. There are immaculate beaches facing out to Recherche Bay (or *Research* as the locals insist on calling it). It was named after his ship by French navigator Bruni D'Entrecasteaux when he explored the area in 1792.

Cockle Creek was originally a sizeable whaling station, which became a victim of its own success when all the whales were killed. It then became a centre for logging and, when coal was discovered, plans were made for an expansive town to be called Ramsgate. But when the coal ran out sooner than expected, people drifted away and the place has been a somnolent backwater ever since.

Just past the bridge over the creek, signs announce the start of **Southwest National Park**, which extends for miles into the wilderness to the west and the north. This is the start of the **South Coast Track** to Port Davey, which will take experienced walkers several days. Flights back can be arranged.

Many visitors will follow the first section of the South Coast Track across to South Cape Bay on the other side of the peninsula and just about the most southerly point you can get to in Australia. It's around two hours each way on a boardwalk and the reward is beautiful scenery and another wonderful beach.

For those pressed for time, or if the weather's closing in, there's a five minute stroll to a bronze sculpture of a whale set on a point facing across the bay and out to sea. ❏

RESTAURANTS, CAFÉS AND BARS

Restaurants

Franklin

Melaka
3422 Huon Highway,
Franklin. Tel: 6266 3328
Open: D Sat. $
Only open one night a
week, Melaka's
Malaysian dishes have
injected some spice into
the Huon dining scene.

Pear Ridge
1683 Channel Highway,
Margate. Tel: 6267 1811
Open: Wed-Mon $
Surrounded by its own
vegetable garden, the
chefs at Pear Ridge have
access to a fabulous
array of produce.

Huonville

Huon Manor
1 Short St, Huonville
Tel: 6264 1311
Open: L & D daily. $$
Serves local favourites
such as oysters, salmon
and mussels.

Ranelagh

Home Hill Vineyard
38 Nairn St, Ranelagh
Tel: 6264 1200
www.homehillwines.com.au
Open: L daily, D Fri-Sat. $$
A beautiful dining room
in a contemporary build-
ing that also houses a
tasting room for Home
Hill's wines.

Woodbridge

Peppermint Bay
3435 Channel Highway,

Woodbridge. Tel: 6267 4088
www.peppermintbay.com.au
Open: L daily, D Sat. $$$
One of Australia's best
regional dining experi-
ences, Peppermint Bay
also has one of the most
beautiful aspects. Chef
Steve Cumper has culti-
vated an impressive array
of local suppliers, and he
creates distinctive, sea-
sonal dishes. A great way
to get a feel for the
breadth of the Huon and
Channel food basket.

Pubs, cafés and bars

Birchs Bay

Fleurtys Café
3866 Channel Highway,
Birchs Bay. Tel: 6267 4078
Open: L daily. $
This delightful modern
café and spacious ter-
race is perched above a
market garden and a
farm growing plants for
distillation into essential
oils. There are also walk-
ing trails around the farm.

Bruny Island

Hothouse Café
46 Adventure Bay Road,
Bruny Island
Tel: 6293 1131
Open: L & D daily. $$
Set in delightful gardens
with great views, this is
perfect for slow
brunches.

**Lunawanna
Licensed Café**
10 Cloudy Bay Rd,
Lunawanna, Bruny Island

Tel: 6293 1173
Open: L & D Mon-Sat. $$
The food's delicious in
this little café and
restaurant near the
southern tip of Bruny
Island. The local oysters
are especially good.

Cygnet

Cygnet Conservatory
20 Mary's St, Cygnet
Tel: 6295 1414
Open: L Thurs-Mon,
D Fri-Sun. $
Although it's open all day
for cake and coffee, the
Cygnet Conservatory's
menu has much more
than just café fare, with
a selection of lunchtime
dishes that make full
use of local produce.

Red Velvet Lounge Café
87 Mary St, Cygnet
Tel: 6295 0466
Open: L daily, D Thurs-Sat.$
If it was any more laid
back here you'd never be
served, but somehow
things do happen in this
well-loved local institution.

Dover

**Gingerbread House
Bakery & Café**
Main Road, Dover
Tel: 6298 1502
Open: L daily. $
A bakery that also
serves light lunches and
tea and coffee.

Franklin

**Petty Sessions
Gourmet Café**
3445 Huon Highway,

Franklin. Tel: 6266 3488
Open: L daily, D Wed-Sun.
$$
A comfortable riverside
dining room that's
equally famous for its
abalone soup and an
impressive display of
desserts and cakes.

Geeveston

Kyari
13 Church St, Geeveston
Tel: 6297 1601
Open: L Wed-Mon, D Fri-Sat. $
An ideal location for
brunch on the way to or
lunch on the way back
from Tahune Airwalk, the
food is freshly cooked,
the bread good, and the
staff welcoming and
enthusiastic. It's open
for dinner on Friday and
Saturday night. BYO.

Kettering

Oyster Cove Inn
1 Ferry Road, Kettering
Tel: 6267 4446
Open: L & D daily. $
This grand old pub, once
a private house, over-
looks the picturesque
marina at Kettering. Its
gardens encourage
exploration – great for
lively children.

THE DERWENT VALLEY AND THE WILDERNESS

The focal point for much of the environmental debate that has gripped Tasmania for decades, this is the area to get to grips with the ancient forests and the modern dams

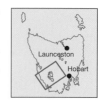

A massive parcel of southwestern Tasmania is almost inaccessible to man. It is a World Heritage Area that the world never gets to see. There are a handful of walking routes, several days long, which the serious hiker can undertake with a bit of preparation, and there is always the option of a scenic flight over the region (*see margin tips pages 76 and 122*) if you can afford it. On the whole, though, it is off the radar for most visitors.

This chapter looks at how to nibble at the edges of this remarkable area and enjoy one of the great under-developed visitor routes. And do it now, because plans are afoot to develop some serious tourism projects along the Gordon River Road.

New Norfolk

The region is accessed from Hobart via the Derwent Valley. The pleasant town of **New Norfolk** ❶, 38 km (24 miles) northwest of Hobart, was first established in 1811 and called Elizabeth Town after Governor Lachlan Macquarie's wife, setting a pattern that will become familiar. The name was changed in 1825 in recognition of the influx of several hundred convicts, soldiers and free settlers from Norfolk Island.

The big paper mill is a dominant presence on the approach to town

and this is the main economic driving force locally, but there are also several pointers to the other industry on which New Norfolk has built its reputation: hop growing.

Start your orientation at **Pulpit Rock**, a lookout on the north bank of the river which affords views across the town and surrounding countryside. From here it's easy to pick out the towers of the oast houses where the hops were hung to dry. Combine these with the many National Trust-listed colonial buildings redolent of

Map on page 116

LEFT giant of the Styx Valley.
BELOW: playground in Mount Field National Park.

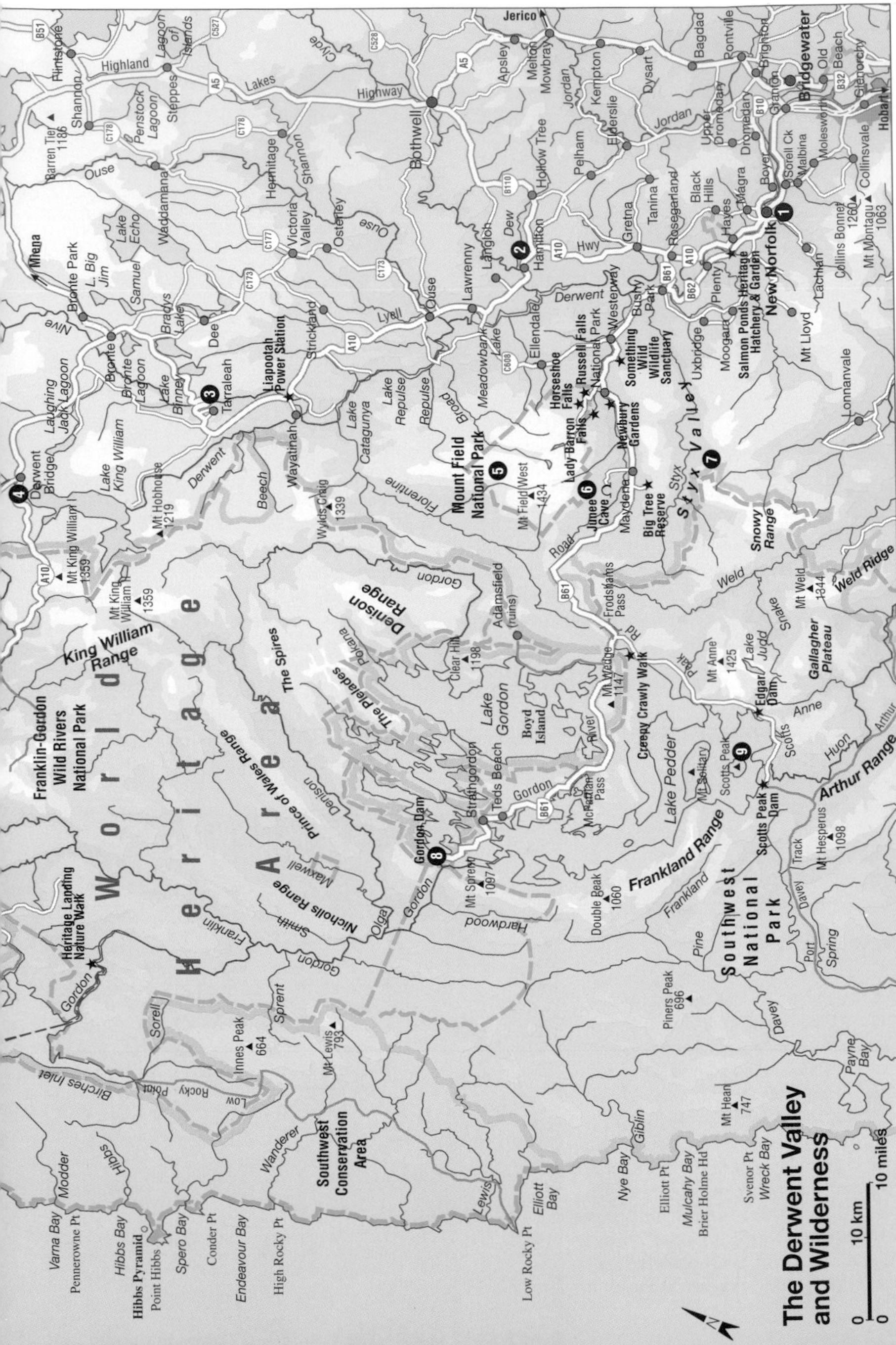

The Derwent Valley and Wilderness

0   10 km
0   10 miles

N

old England and it is easy to see why comparisons have been made with rural Kent.

To learn more about hop processing, cross over the river, turn left into Montagu Street and follow it round to the Lyell Highway where **Tynwald Park** on the left accommodates **The Oast House**. It was in operation for 100 years before being turned into a museum (daily 9am–6pm; admission charge; tel: 6261 2067) and tearooms where the history of hop farming is explained on a self-guided tour downstairs around the old kilns. The fancifully named Beer Experience is simply an opportunity to indulge in some tasting.

Just along the riverbank and originally part of the same estate as the Oast House is **Tynwald**, a pristine three-storey Victorian mansion with exquisite ironwork on its verandas. It is now upmarket accommodation.

Further exposure to hops can be had by returning along Montagu Street and having a look at two ancient hotels. The first, the **Old Colony Inn**, is not actually a licensed premises any more but runs as a bed and breakfast outfit incorporating a small museum of colonial artefacts and a large antique dolls house (daily 10am–5pm; admission charge; tel: 6261 2731). The distinctive black and white building was constructed in 1815 along rather unconvincing mock-Tudor lines. Westwards along the same street, the **Bush Inn** of 1815 has been continuously licensed since 1825.

At the bottom of the High Street **St Matthew's** Anglican Church is the oldest church in the state although it has been so altered over the years that it is a somewhat hollow claim. The stained-glass windows are noteworthy.

Head along the High Street and turn left on Charles Street. At the end you will find **Willow Court**, the old Asylum. Colonial architect John Lee Archer was commissioned to design a unit for sick and invalid convicts in 1832 and facilities for the insane were added four years later. In 1848 it was reclassified as a lunatic asylum and remained as such, albeit with adjustments to the terminology, for the next 150 years. It closed in 2000 and the site is now under development. It is a mess at the moment but some fine stone and brick buildings remain and it occupies an attractive position.

Along the Derwent Valley

Unless you want to hurl yourself up and down the Derwent on a speedboat, it's time to move on to the altogether more tranquil surroundings of the **Salmon Ponds Heritage Hatchery and Garden** (daily 9am–5pm; admission charge; tel: 6261 5663), which is 9 km (5½ miles) out of town on the road to Plenty.

Salmon and trout eggs were carefully transported from England and placed in purpose-built ponds. The trout thrived, the salmon did not. The ponds are still operational and

An attractive garden square faces St Matthew's Anglican Church in New Norfolk.

BELOW: the Old Colony Inn harks back to another age.

White fish. One of the tanks at the Salmon Ponds.

BELOW: Salmon Ponds Heritage Hatchery and Garden.

surrounded by well-kept lawns under the shadow of mature English trees. It is a beautiful place to visit. You can feed the fish and generate a seething flurry of splashing mayhem or you can leave that to passing children and just settle back with a picnic or a snack from the café, maybe puzzling on the reasons behind maintaining a whole pond full of albino trout. Or maybe not. The committed might dally in the **Museum of Trout Fishing and Tasmanian Angling Hall of Fame**.

Drive on through Plenty and the hop fields on the way to Bushy Park before turning right on the B61 and joining the Lyell Highway (A10) to **Hamilton ❷**. The common epithet for Hamilton is "sleepy" and, apart from the sound of laughter coming from the churchyard, there's little here to contradict it.

The setting is lush rolling countryside and it appears as if somebody has come along and plonked down one perfect stone colonial structure after another, with random gaps between them. This gives a somewhat disjointed air to the place.

Part of the reason for this is that the expectation, when the settlement was founded, was that it was going to develop into a sizeable town and, to a degree, it did with around 800 inhabitants through the 19th century. There were two breweries, six inns, a convict probation facility and a police station with 11 officers and a dedicated flagellator. It didn't last though. Some buildings have disappeared, while others never got built.

What remains is a pretty National Trust-classified town. The highlights include the **Hamilton Inn** of 1830; the **Warders Cottage**, which now houses the Hamilton Heritage Centre; **Jackson's Emporium**, an old store with an eclectic stock; and the **Old School House**, which had separate doors for boys and girls in a building barely big enough to support one entrance.

There are attractive cottages galore, most of which appear to be available for rent, and then there's **St Peter's** church. It has only one door and the assumption is that this was in order to hinder escape attempts by convicts, who would

Map on page 116

have made up a large proportion of the congregation in the early days. The graveyard has several interesting tombstones, including that for 8-year old Sarah Lane, who died in 1844 and rests beneath the epitaph:

> *This little inoffensive child*
> *To Sunday school had trod*
> *But sad to tell was burnt to death*
> *Within the house of God*

Into the hills

Carry on to Ouse (pronounced *ooze*) along the Lyell Highway and, as the road climbs, you come to your first power station at Liapootah. This is hydro country. The Tarraleah hydro-electric scheme was set up to channel water from the upper Derwent River and Lake St Clair.

It took hundreds of workers several years to build and maintain the dams, pipelines and power stations and so a residential village was set up at **Tarraleah ❸**. It sits on top of a hill with dramatic views of vast pipes pouring down into the valley. There are still some workers living in a collection of portable huts and prefabs, but the village is now in private hands and rooms are available for tourists. It's oddly quiet, like a deserted holiday camp, but fascinating nonetheless and the 1930s Art Deco chalet is well worth a look.

The highway continues on past the end of Lake Binney and at Bronte you can turn off for a quick detour to **Bronte Park** and a look at an alternative approach to revamping hydro huts. This settlement was used in the 1950s, largely by recent migrants from overseas and, as testament to this, each cabin is named after a different country. Most occupants today are here for the fishing, which is superlative in the surrounding lakes.

Return to the highway and note a stone trig point marking the geographical centre of Tasmania and commemorating the achievements of early surveyors. Another 26 km (16 miles) further on is **Derwent Bridge ❹**. For years there has been little here of note apart from a pretty good pub and a few places to stay. Its main claim to fame was as a jumping-off point for Lake St Clair and the Overland Track (see *page 206*) or as a stop on the way to the

BELOW: scenery around Norfolk.

Rumoured sightings of the officially extinct thylacine in the south-western forests have become fewer and fewer. Slim hopes that a few individuals may survive are fading (see page 41).

BELOW: Greg Duncan at work.

west coast (see *page 213*). Now, however, there is **The Wall**.

The Wall in the Wilderness, to give it its full title, is sculptor Greg Duncan's ambitious project to produce a relief measuring 100 metres (330 ft) long by 3 metres (10 ft) high. In a purpose-built extendable gallery, he works on metre-wide panels of Huon pine, to portray the history and development of the people and environment of the Central Highlands.

The square-jawed, great-coated axeman used on the publicity material suggests a harking back to socialist realism but that would be to devalue a complex and sophisticated work. Duncan anticipates that it will take 10 years so there are plenty of opportunities to drop in and check on the progress of the sculpture and of the building (daily Sept–Apr 9am-5pm; May–Aug 9–4pm; admission charge; tel: 6289 1134), which will be enlarged as more panels are added.

The Mount Field route

For those not jumping to another chapter at this point (*see page 213*), there is a further arm to this route. It is a matter of returning down the Lyell Highway, not quite as far as Hamilton, and turning onto the C608 after Ouse. Cross Meadowbank Lake and pass through the quiet village of **Ellendale** and then at Westerway turn right onto the Gordon River Road.

The **Something Wild Wildlife Sanctuary** (daily 10am–5pm; admission charge; tel: 6288 1013; www.somethingwild.com.au) looms up on the right with its garish signage. It takes in orphaned and abandoned wildlife and there is the standard collection of devils, wombats, quolls, koalas and possums.

The big draw in the area is **Mount Field National Park ⑤**. This is one of the busier parks, being within such easy reach of Hobart, so in peak season and at weekends patience may be needed for parking. The visitor centre, however, besides being both architecturally imaginative and in tune with its surroundings, is capable of dealing with crowds of customers with aplomb.

Mount Field has stands of massive swamp gum; sections of rainforest where myrtle, sassafras

and tree fern dominate; and, if you drive up higher, there is the alpine climate to be expected in one of only two winter ski fields in the state.

The question is where to begin. There are five nature walks rated as easy, including the 25-minute return trek to **Russell Falls**, the signature dish of the park. The path is suitable for prams and wheelchairs and there is a sizeable viewing platform at the base of the falls. You get a clear view of the falls flowing down tiers of rock in picture-postcard manner. You can climb a few steps to the top platform and, since you've got this far, why not carry on up to **Horseshoe Falls** as well? Make sure you take the side track beyond the bridge and don't mistake the bubbling waters lower down for the falls. Horseshoe Falls, although not as hefty as Russell, doesn't attract the same crowds and is more atmospheric in consequence.

It is relatively easy walking from here to the **Tall Trees** loop where you can have your first clear view of the mighty *Eucalyptus regnans* or swamp gum or mountain ash,

according to taste. This is the highest species of tree in Australia and the highest in the world after the sequoia or Californian redwood. It is distinctive for its broad trunk with rough bark for the first few metres before it becomes smooth all the way up to the rather stunted-looking branches that wave down at you from near the top. There are even bigger examples than these to come further along this route.

The tall trees walk ends on a roadway, which leads down to the visitor centre. (It's possible to drive up to just do that loop in half an hour or less.) Or you can keep going for another hour or so and take in **Lady Barron Falls**.

For all other walks it is a drive further into the park and, with a couple of exceptions, they get longer and more arduous. It is a winding 16 km (10 miles) to Lake Dobson but worth it for some terrific views and a variety of walks. Really, you could spend several days in the park without ever repeating yourself.

Just beyond the settlement of National Park, pause to have a look

Map on page 116

BELOW: Horseshoe Falls in Mount Field National Park.

TIPS

Scotts Peak is a popular access point for the Southwest National Park. Alternative access is by the Gordon River Road to Strathgordon, Cockle Creek (near the South East Cape – *see page 112*). Scenic flight options are offered by Par Avion Wilderness Tours: bushwalker flights to Maleleuca, half-day scenic flights over the wilderness, or 3-day fly-cruise trips to Port Davey – tel: 1800 144 460, for tour maps and other details see www.paravion.com.au.

BELOW: fallen giant in the Big Tree Reserve.

at the splash of colour in **Newbury Gardens** in front of a cottage on the left. Visitors are welcome in return for a donation.

Maydena is the last service centre on the road to the west and has attractions of its own. Turn right down Junee Road and follow it for about 4 km (2½ miles) to the beginning of a path to the entrance of **Junee Cave** ❻. There is a walk of a few minutes through forest with a chance of spotting platypus before coming to an entrance in a cliff from which water is gushing out into a stream. Cave divers can take it further from here through a karst system of more than 30 km (19 miles).

The other key sight in the area is the **Styx Valley** ❼, just beyond Maydena. Cross a bridge over a track, take the first right and then wind round under the road and keep going for several minutes until you see a sign for the **Big Tree Reserve**. You are in the midst of the "Valley of the Giants". The land is managed by Forestry Tasmania, who have been having a few PR problems recently and have started to encour-

age more people to go and have a look at the biggest trees in the state, all swamp gums. For now there is just a short boardwalk loop, which takes in the famed **Big Tree** and, because the original has actually lost a few of its 97 metres (320 ft) since being first measured, the new **Bigger Tree**. There are interpretive signs putting the reserve into the wider context of forestry across the state, and there are strident rebuttals scrawled by activists at ever increasing length as the trail progresses.

The Wilderness Society publishes a leaflet, which directs you to several other tall trees in the area, including "Gandalf's Staff", which was the subject of a well-publicised sit-in in 2004 (*Styx Valley of the Giants Self-Drive and Walking Guide*, downloadable from www.wilderness.org.au). Oh, and word has it that a new Even Bigger Tree has been discovered.

West to Strathgordon

There is now a long drive west through the wild mountain scenery of the **Southwest National Park** until you finally pull into **Strathgordon**.

This is another encampment built for hydro workers which now doubles as comfortable accommodation for tourists. The restaurant overlooks **Lake Pedder**, a glacial lake considerably enlarged by the controversial hydroelectric schemes. The lake is popular with fishermen.

Carry on for another 12 km (7½ miles) and you reach the end of the road at the **Gordon Dam ❽**. You can climb down flights of metal steps to get to the top of the dam and walk around it, enjoying views across the water on one side or down a deep gorge on the other. And you can just gawp at the scale of this massive, double-curvature concrete structure.

This is the end of the road – beyond lies a vast untouched wilderness extending to the stormy southwestern coast, Macquarie Harbour and north to Cradle Mountain. To properly experience the rainforest and mountains involves a lot of walking – for details of adventure tour operators specialising in walks and tours of the region, *see page 256*.

Some 53 km (33 miles) into the return trip east, take a right turn and follow the gravel road south to the comparatively compact **Edgar Dam**, followed shortly by **Scotts Peak Dam**. It is just a short run up a hill to get to the viewpoint across Lake Pedder to **Scotts Peak ❾** itself. Even in bad weather – and with over 300 days of rain each year, that's most of the time – this is a view to die for. It's peak, lake, peak, lake ad infinitum, and wilderness in every direction.

Many of those who do make it this far will be fishing or bush walking. The Port Davey Track to **Melaleuca** in the far southwest starts from this spot. However if that is too daunting, stop a couple of kilometres before rejoining the Gordon River Road and tackle the **Creepy Crawly Walk**. This is an excellent boardwalk trail in which walkers are invited to follow a series of boards and be the gumshoe who solves a murder in the forest. Flushed with this small success, it is time to face the long haul back. ❑

The Gordon Dam is spectacular to look at – and for the adventurous/ foolhardy there are abseiling trips off the top.

RESTAURANTS AND BARS

Bush Inn
49-51 Montagu St,
New Norfolk
Tel: 6261 2256
www.thebushinn.com.au
Open: L & D daily. **$**
Lays claim to being the oldest continually licensed hotel operating on the same site and in the same building in Australia. Decent pub grub.

Giants Table
Junee Rd, Maydena
Tel: 6288 2293
www.giantstable.com
Open: D Tues-Sat
(summer only). **$**

Fresh soup and lamb shanks with mash make a satisfying meal after exploring the breathtaking forests in the area.

Glen Clyde House
22 Grace St, Hamilton
Tel: 6286 3276
Open: L daily. **$**
Dine in front of a roaring open fire at this 1840's coaching inn in the historic town of Hamilton. Devonshire teas and light lunches.

Lake Pedder Chalet
Strathgordon

Tel: 6280 1166
Open: L & D daily. **$**
Don't expect haute cuisine when you dine here, but the food is hearty and satisfying.

Pancakes at the Ponds
70 Salmon Ponds Rd, Plenty
Tel: 6261 5663
Open L daily. **$**
Simple dining (obviously including pancakes) looking out over the beautiful salmon ponds.

Tynwald Willow Bend Estate
Hobart Rd, New Norfolk
Tel: 6261 2667
www.tynwaldtasmania.com
Open: D daily. **$$**

Excellent food in an historic house on the edge of the Derwent River.

Verandahs in the Valley
21 Burnett St, New Norfolk
Tel: 6261 4461
www.verandahsvalley.com.au
Open: L Tues-Sun,
D Tues-Sat. **$$**
One of the best options in the valley for modern, well-cooked food in pleasant surroundings.

● ● ● ● ● ● ● ● ● ● ● ●
Prices for a three-course dinner per person with a half-bottle of house wine.
$ = under A$50
$$ = A$50–A$75
$$$ = over A$75
L=lunch, D=dinner

THE MIDLANDS AND THE LAKES

Some of Tasmania's earliest and most
picturesque colonial settlements are strung
along the Midland Highway, while in the hills to
the west a scattering of lakes provides superb fishing

The Midland Highway is the spine of Tasmania linking Hobart and the south with Launceston and the north coast. It is probably the busiest road in the state and yet, this being Tasmania, it is rarely very crowded, always manages to provide a section of attractive countryside to keep you interested and allows for constant rest stops in astoundingly well preserved historic villages. This is the "Heritage Highway". Being one of the first routes to be established in the new colony, it has more than its fair share of the oldest colonial buildings and, by extension, appears to be the most "English" in character.

Pontville

Very early on, heading north from Hobart, the road passes through the curving high street of a settlement rich in early sandstone cottages, shops and, of course, the obligatory churches. One of these differs from the run-of-the-mill Georgian or Gothic models by displaying distinctly Romanesque tendencies. This is **Pontville ❶**, just 32 km (20 miles) from the city and already a world away.

This was a garrison town in the 19th century, much of it built by convict labour, as indeed was the highway itself in the early 1800s. It looks

picturesque as you drive through. When you stop, though, the road which gave it its lifeblood now becomes a barrier to its chances of becoming a popular tourist destination. Further up the road, many of the towns benefit from by-passes, clearing them of traffic, but this is not the case here. The buildings are quite spread out and walking between them is hazardous. Logging rigs and other traffic bear down on the pedestrian who is searching in vain for the sanctuary of a pavement.

**Map
on page
126**

LEFT: St Andrew's Uniting Church in Evandale.
BELOW: old traction engine in Kempton.

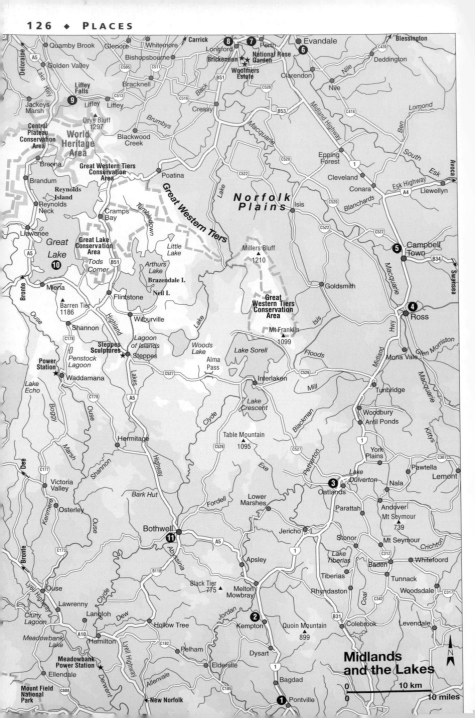

Midlands and the Lakes

The **Crown Inn** is worth a look, as are the two churches: one Catholic, one Church of England. Paradoxically, it is the latter, **St Mark's**, which is Romanesque, built in 1839 to a design by James Blackburn, a convict architect.

This is good agricultural country and many of the early settlers who were granted land here prospered with wheat and apples enough to build themselves grand houses. Some of these are in evidence as the road passes through exotically-named **Mangalore** and **Bagdad**.

Kempton and Oatlands

Kempton ❷ was named after one of the more colourful characters in local history: Anthony Fenn Kemp. He has been called the "Father of Tasmania" and is considered at some length in Nicholas Shakespeare's *In Tasmania*. In essence, Kemp was an entrepreneurial army officer who, with some ruthlessness and a touch of the larrikin spirit, contrived to acquire an estate and respectability. Kempton was the site of that estate.

This is a settlement which does have a by-pass so you can safely wander along the main street looking at the lovely old houses – some of them quite substantial. There are old coaching inns to investigate and **St Mary's** church, which is first glimpsed down a long avenue of trees. This church was also designed by James Blackburn (*see above*) and its graveyard contains the remains of one Elizabeth Flexmore, a member of the First Fleet. Don't be surprised to hear the sound of hooves coming down the high street as a local drives his gig along to the store to pick up supplies.

Stay with the A1 as it passes Melton Mowbray and consider the option of making a brief detour through **Jericho**, a small settlement on the upper reaches of the Jordan River. This may appeal to those wishing to send postcards imbued with biblical portents, but there is little to see on the ground beyond the remains of a couple of rammed mud walls from an 1840s probation station. It is in a shelter a little way to the north of the settlement with the customary interpretive sign.

Better to stay on the highway and keep your eyes peeled for a series of rusting steel silhouettes of figures pertinent to the history of the area. There are soldiers, highwaymen, a stagecoach and more, all listed in a leaflet available at the visitor centre, or "Heritage Highway Centre", as it is known, in **Oatlands ❸**.

"A very eligible situation for a town, being well watered and in the midst of rich fertile country", was the verdict of Governor Lachlan Macquarie when he named the district in 1821. It was also designated one of four sites to have a military post along the main north-south highway. So it was that in the 1820s and 1830s plans were laid out for what some envisaged would eventually become the state capital.

St Mark's church in Pontville has an unusual Romanesque facade.

BELOW: one of a series of steel cutouts along the Midland Highway.

Sculpture

While Tasmania may not have the population or clout to attract the major arts events that are a feature of life on the Australian mainland, there is a thriving arts scene when it comes to the visual disciplines, with several painters and photographers making the island their home. The most ready manifestation of this phenomenon is in the amount of public sculpture that can be seen on travels through the state.

Deloraine has made much of the sculpture trail down its main street and the large and colourful works that dot the parkland by the banks of the Meander River, while Greg Duncan has dedicated the next few years of his life to the massive Wall in the Wilderness project at Derwent Bridge (see page 120).

Wood carver Bernie Tarr has created a series of life-size figures based on local personalities, which loiter, apparently at random, around the centre of Geeveston. For this project, completed over five years, the council had been keen to incorporate a forest and timber theme into its public art to reflect the predominant local industry, so all the figures are made from Celery Top or King Billy pine (see picture, page 110). Similarly,

local pine is the material used for the collection of carvings by Roland Gabatel of Boer War-era soldiers in Ladysmith Park by the river in Huonville.

However, the doyen of public art in Tasmania is Stephen Walker. Originally from Victoria, Walker's work can be found all over Australia and in some very prominent locations. His Tank Stream is a large work apparently flowing down the pavement outside the terminal at Sydney's Circular Quay, and the Petrie Tableau depicts a pioneer explorer on a plinth beside Brisbane's City Hall. He's been living in Tasmania for several years now, working out of a studio in Campania, north of Richmond.

He works in clay, cast in bronze, and the pieces have an organic feel to them that makes them look as if they have just emerged from the earth and could be subsumed back into it at any moment. This reaches its apogee in the Steppes sculptures, a collection of 12 pieces arranged in a loose circle in a forest glade just off the Lake Highway on the way up to Miena from Bothwell. They represent pioneer settlers in the highlands (see page 136).

Elsewhere it seems that every piece of bronze you set eyes on bears the legend, "sculptor: Stephen Walker". In the far south he was responsible for Whale on the edge of the bay at Cockle Creek (see page 112); in Hobart he has a number of works around the waterfront, including the Bernacchi Tribute (see page 80) and the seals lurking on the rocks just beneath, while the façade of the Supreme Court bears an expressionistic interpretation of the scales of justice. In the centre of Queenstown, Miner's Siding features a large-scale work telling the story of the opening up of the west and the development of mining in a series of tableaux (see page 216). There are several other smaller Walker sculptures, some in the most out of the way places.

There's plenty to take home too. Each village seems to have its own gallery selling everything from the frankly puzzling efforts of edgy young artists to the often more sedate, sometimes expensive, works of established practitioners. ❑

LEFT: Stephen Walker in Oatlands.

History dictated otherwise, but it still became a sizeable township and now boasts the "largest collection of colonial sandstone buildings in a village in Australia". There are 138 of them, 87 in the High Street alone. Convicts dug out the stone for construction from the edge of Lake Dulverton nearby and work gangs built everything from the old gaol (of which only the gaoler's residence survives) to the humblest cottage.

These days it is an important centre for the local farming industry and derives much of the rest of its living from tourism. You can take a walk around the village aided by a sheaf of papers from the visitor centre detailing the histories of each building. Alternatively there is a local, Peter Fielding, to take you on a guided tour by day and a ghost tour at night (tel: 6254 1135).

The focal point for many visits, and even more photographs, is **Callington Mill**, which spent much of the 20th century in a state of ruin but has been steadily restored, along with the surrounding buildings, since 1978 (daily 9am–4pm; free). Less enticing is **Dolls at the Mill**, in the old mill residence – a rather disorganised jumble of over 2,000 dolls (daily 10am–4pm; admission charge; tel: 6254 0039.

Elsewhere, there is another sculpture trail to follow, this time of topiary figures designed by local artist Stephen Walker; a Catholic church by Pugin; antique shops; tearooms; and, when the water level is high enough, extensive bird life down at **Lake Dulverton**.

Perfectly preserved Ross

Return to the highway and, keeping a look out for more of the steel sculptures, make for **Ross ❹**. This village is also by-passed and so there is little traffic to spoil your enjoyment of one of the prettiest settlements in Australia. It vies with Richmond for the title of most perfectly preserved Georgian town, sharing with its southern neighbour such features as the convict-built stone bridge across a dawdling river, complete with church on the hill behind; a landmark pub; numerous well-preserved shops; and plenty of greenery to offset the golden stone. In that there is no jarring modern supermarket in the main street, Ross may just shade it. Still, it's not a competition so just settle back in one of the tearooms and contemplate the delights on offer.

The **Tasmanian Wool Centre** is first stop, not so much because of its exhibition on the history of one of the area's major industries, but because it also houses the visitor centre where you may want to join a (pre-booked) tour or pick up a map to help you do it yourself. There is a small museum for which a donation is requested (daily Oct–Mar 9am–6pm; Apr–Oct 9am–5.30pm; free; tel. 6381 5466).

Turn left outside and begin a stroll down one of the most attractive streets in the country. With elms

Map on page 126

Church Street in Ross is one of the best preserved colonial thoroughfares in Australia.

BELOW: Callington Mill.

shading the pavement and the matchless Georgian buildings, **Church Street** is a paean to England. The rich, rolling countryside must have reminded the early settlers of their homeland so why not set about recreating a typical Cotswold village? Indeed, now that elms have more or less disappeared from England, this is perhaps more authentic than the originals.

At the crossroads with Bridge Street, be careful to avoid tour guides who will be regaling their charges with the tired old story of the "four corners of Ross": the buildings on each corner, representing temptation (the pub), recreation (the town hall), salvation (The church) and damnation (the gaol – now a house).

Go instead down to the **Bridge.** Walk over it and then down the steps to the banks of the river in order to appreciate the pleasing proportions, courtesy of government architect John Lee Archer, and the carvings, all 186 of them, which are the remarkable achievement of convicted highwayman Daniel Herbert.

He received a pardon for his efforts.

There is a "heritage walkway" along the riverbank which threads past the Uniting Church, with its clean lines and soaring spire, to the site of the **Female Factory** (daily 9am–5pm; free). There is only one building left standing, but a display inside gives an idea of how it operated. Anyone who has visited the similar operation in Hobart will have an idea of the scale of the original complex. The walkway continues on to the graveyard where more of Daniel Herbert's carving can be seen on some of the stones, including his own.

Ross Village Bakery awaits you back in Church Street where, on the pretext of having a look at one of the last few working wood-fired ovens left in the state, you can settle down with a cream tea or some other hard-earned treat, such as Tasmanian speciality, the scallop pie. If it's too busy there, plenty of alternatives can be found. The town has many antiques shops and, less predictably, the Tasmanian Scottish Centre, for tartan and tat.

BELOW:
the bridge at Ross.

Map on page 126

Campbell Town to Evandale

Macquarie's devotion to all things Scottish (and to perpetuating his own or his family's memory) accounts for the naming of Ross and of the next stop to the north. **Campbell Town ⑤** feels like more of a working town; the highway goes through, not around it; the heritage buildings are interspersed with more modern utilitarian ones; and the original structures have less chocolate-box homogeneity.

The old courthouse houses both the visitor centre and the **Heritage Highway Museum** (Mon–Fri 10am–3pm; free; tel: 6381 1353). The latter is in the courtroom itself and provides an overview of local characters from history and displays the familiar artefacts of colonial life.

The bridge here over the Elizabeth River (named after Macquarie's wife, whose maiden name had been Campbell) was built in 1838, also by convicts, and is only two years younger than the one in Ross. However, because it is made largely of brick – over a million of them – it appears to date from much later and has a more utilitarian appearance than its glamorous southern counterpart. It is known as the **Red Bridge**. The brick motif is picked up in a much more recent enterprise, the **Convict Brick Trail** *(see margin, right)*.

It is worth wandering around town and taking in **Bridge Street**, the original main thoroughfare leading to the first bridge of 1822. The Red Bridge was in fact part of a plan to create an early by-pass and channel traffic away from the centre. Also of note is another fine red-brick structure, **St Luke's Church**, opposite the hospital, also from the drawing board of John Lee Archer.

The land north of Campbell Town flattens out into the Norfolk Plains and it's an uneventful 50 km (31 miles) before you come to another beautifully restored heritage town, which is listed by the National Trust: **Evandale ⑥**.

It is little surprise that this site too, or at least one a short distance away, was first selected by Macquarie and the town was originally to be called Morven, presumably after another of his relatives or possibly a pet. If you need an excuse to enter the atmospheric **Clarendon Arms Hotel**, there are murals inside portraying Macquarie's early expeditions and a whole host of other historically significant occasions.

The current site was chosen because it was to be the starting point of an, as it transpired, over-ambitious plan to channel the waters of the South Esk River through to Launceston via a series of canals and tunnels. The **Water Tower** north of the centre was to be part of the scheme and sits over the remains of a tunnel. Although this venture failed, the largely convict-built town (including a contribution from John Kelly, father of Ned) managed to thrive on sheep and cattle farming.

It is rewarding simply to amble

A line of bricks is set in the pavement on both sides of the road from Campbell Town's Red Bridge to the hospital. Each has a convict's name, age, crime committed, punishment and name of their transport ship. The project will one day extend to accommodate all 68,000 transportees.

BELOW: grand house in Campbell Town.

through the streets, uncovering architectural gems, with or without a guide map from the visitor centre in High Street. If time is limited, have a look for the two **Churches to St Andrew**; the Gothic one on the right side of High Street is Church of England and the more unusual Greek Revival example facing it is the Uniting Church, built in 1839. In Russell Street pop into **Brown's Village Store** and have a look at the old wooden counter and shelving.

On Sundays there's a huge market in **Logan Park** (8am–2pm) featuring a healthy mix of produce, craftwork and bric-a-brac. And if you happen to be around at the end of February, the **National Penny Farthing Championships** take place. Year round you can learn how to ride a penny farthing and then tour Evandale on it (tel: 6391 9101).

Take a quick side trip 10 km (6 miles) down the C416 to **Clarendon Homestead** (daily Sept–May 10am–5pm, Jun–Aug 10am–4pm; admission charge; tel: 6398 6220), a large country house built between 1830 and 1838 for James Cox, who had made his money in the wool trade by pioneering the introduction of the merino to Van Diemen's Land, before going into politics. Clarendon is set on the banks of the South Esk River and has 3.6 hectares (9 acres) of gardens as well as farm and service buildings. The house is one of the finest in Australia with beautifully proportioned rooms and a sumptuous conservatory. It is now run by the National Trust.

West to Longford

Retrace your steps to Evandale and cut across to **Perth ❼** which lies on the A1. A name like that has Macquarie's fingerprints all over it and, sure enough, he came up with it in 1821. While there are some interesting buildings to be found, preferably with the help of the *Path of History Walk through Perth*, it is not a cohesive Georgian town and, with such fierce competition for the tourist dollar, it will never feature high on most people's schedules. Worth a glance is the **Leather Bottell Inn** of 1830 as an early

BELOW: Evandale is home to annual penny farthing races.

Map on page 126

example of a hotel. The **Baptist Tabernacle** (1889) is unusual.

Longford 8, by contrast, is well worth inspection, especially around the so-called "village precinct" where there are numerous listed buildings. A group of premises along Wellington Street, including the Victorian **Library** and the **Queen's Arms Hotel** of 1837, is just exquisite in the afternoon sun.

And only a little further along the street, **Brown's Big Store** is a fine late-Victorian example of shop design. There are many other listed premises around town with several dwellings turned into holiday lets or bed and breakfast outfits, and the usual number of shops given over to antiques. The dominant edifice in town is the heavy sandstone **Christ Church** set back from Wellington Street. It hosts representatives from many of the leading local dynasties in its graveyard.

Grand estates

One such is the Archer clan, who were responsible for four of the great country estates in the area.

Two of these are now major attractions. **Woolmers Estate** (daily 10am–4.30pm; regular guided tours of the house, admission charge, www.woolmers.com.au; tel. 6391 2230) was founded by Thomas Archer and occupied by the family from 1819 to 1994. It is situated 5 km (3 miles) southeast of Longford on the C520. The interior of the house has been maintained in immaculate condition and gives a comprehensive insight into how a prosperous settler family could live. The dining room is spectacular.

The grounds are extensive and, as well as the formal gardens surrounding the main house, you can explore the coach house and stables, various workers' cottages (some available for accommodation), the oldest working woolshed in Australia, a cider house and several other structures. You can easily spend a few hours here, if only to picnic in the grounds and enjoy the grand views. To cap it all, on the eastern side of the estate you will find the **National Rose Garden**. It is planted over old orchards and the

TIPS

If you are driving in Tasmania, the RACT has reciprocal arrangements with similar organisations in other states in mainland Australia as well as overseas operations such as AAA in the US and RAC in the UK. Have your card handy in case you need assistance. It may qualify you for discounts on accommodation as well. *See pages 233–4.*

BELOW:
Longford's Big Store.

Dutch treat. The old barn at Brickendon is still in use.

BELOW: fishing is a popular pastime.

plan is to display over 500 varieties of rose. Even with current numbers, it is still an impressive collection, at its peak in spring and early summer.

Thomas Archer's brother, William, established **Brickendon** in 1824 and it is still in the hands of his descendents. The house here is plain Georgian, without the Italianate embellishments of Woolmers, and smaller in scale. It is not open to the public but the gardens are and they feature 180 varieties of roses.

The point of difference at Brick-endon is the **Historic Farming Village** (Tues–Sun 9.30am–5pm; admission charge; accommodation available; www.brickendon.com.au; tel. 6391 1383). William Archer set out to build a model English farm, complete with hedgerows, and much of it survives today. The farm buildings are set over a relatively small area, weathered and quaint, and instantly transport you back to the 19th century. The Dutch Barn is still in use; the 1830s poultry shed is not, although it is of immeasurable value, being one of the earliest in existance. The tiny brick church is a

reminder that the Archer family would have been responsible for the spiritual welfare of their convict workers.

Into the Lakes region

Part company with the "Heritage Highway" and follow some winding narrower roads to the west through Bishopsbourne and Bracknell to **Liffey Falls** ⑨. The countryside changes quickly to become wooded and hilly now that you are on the lower slopes of the Great Western Tiers. It's time to tackle a few inclines after the easy sightseeing through the Midlands.

There are two options with Liffey Falls: the easier one is a 45-minute return walk from the upper car park off the C513; otherwise you have a two-hour plus excursion on a lesser track from the lower car park. The Liffey cascades down rock steps, beautifully framed by the surrounding sassafras and myrtle of the rainforest. When the river's in full flood, which is often, these falls vie to be the most beautiful in Tasmania.

Carry on westward on the C513,

Fishing

While brown and rainbow trout are plentiful in the central lakes, there are strict conditions on how and when you can go about catching them. The season runs from August to May, although a few places have year-round opening, and you will need a license, available from agents. Information on where to find these, and on the various regulations, can all be found at www.fishonline.gov.au. Of course, the best way to pick up information is to find a fellow enthusiast, preferably a local, who will tell you all you need to know as long as you nod respectfully while they insert a few whoppers about what they've caught.

climbing all the while, to join the A5 Lake Highway. Turn to the south and continue the winding climb up the Western Tiers and onto the Central Plateau. You are around 1,000 metres (3,300 ft) above sea level now and in bleaker, rockier country where the harshness of the winter can drive out all but the hardiest of locals. In the warmer months, however, although never busy, the area attracts visitors and many of these come for the fish. There are literally thousands of lakes across the plateau; admittedly, many of them are completely inaccessible but that still leaves more than enough.

The A5 leads straight to **Great Lake ❿**, the biggest of the lot at 40 km (25 miles) long. There are some good lookout stops to give you an idea of its scale and setting. The dolorite rock outcrops give a roughness to this glacial landscape. As you continue around the western shore it's something of a shock to find evidence of whole communities living in crude fibro shacks, many of which look as if they've just been plonked down on the bare ground

with no thought to permanence. It is somehow paradoxical to find real estate signs offering them for sale. In fact, many of these are holiday shelters for keen anglers. In the 1860s and 1870s trout were introduced into the lakes and they have been multiplying ever since. It is a woeful fisherman who comes away with nothing round these parts.

At Liawenee the road to the west provides access to the **Central Plateau Conservation Area**. You need a commitment to desolate barren landscapes and a 4WD vehicle.

The more benign Lake Highway winds around the southern end of the water to the only serious settlement, **Miena**, where a few substantial buildings provide services for yet more shacks. Every other vehicle has a boat in tow or awaits the return of one from the lake

Proceed down the highway and, depending on time, decide whether to take in a lengthy detour to a power station museum or stay on the highway and take in an idyllic woodland setting filled with sculpture. Power station enthusiasts should turn right

Map on page 126

The right stuff. Every angler's need is catered for.

BELOW: rough and ready shacks around the shores of the Great Lake.

Map
on page
126

Exclusive club. Some of the rare exhibits at the Australasian Golf Museum in Bothwell

BELOW: the sculptures at Steppes.

down the C178 and follow the signs towards **Waddamana** where you can learn about one of the earliest hydroelectric schemes, commenced in 1910 (daily 10am–4pm; free). The C178 rejoins the highway 27 km (17 miles) later.

If you have stayed with the highway, (or even if you've returned from the power station detour) continue south for a dozen kilometres and look for the sign to the **Steppes Sculptures**. Down a short path into the trees there is a clearing in which sculptor Stephen Walker has set the *Circle of Life*; there are 12 lumps of stone, each adorned with cast-bronze figures representing pioneer and Aboriginal life in the highlands. You don't necessarily need to like the works to appreciate the magical setting. And it's very likely that you will have the place to yourself.

It is plain sailing now down to **Bothwell ⓫**. There were a lot of Scots involved in the establishment of Bothwell in 1824 which accounts for its name, its setting on the River Clyde and it may well also explain why it is the site of Australia's first

golf course. Capitalising on this is the **Australasian Golf Museum** (daily; Sept–May 10am–4pm; Jun–Aug 11am–3pm; admission charge; tel: 6259 4033) in the old schoolhouse. It has a rather old-fashioned feel to it in these days of multimedia dynamic hands-on interactive experiences but enthusiasts seem quite content with row upon row of old clubs and trophies.

The museum doubles as the visitor centre and the staff will supply the customary self-guiding tour map. One of the highlights is right next door in the shape of **St Luke's Presbyterian Church**, where the Ross Bridge double act of John Lee Archer (architect) and Daniel Herbert (sculptor) have worked their alchemy again. Elsewhere, down the extraordinarily wide streets out of all proportion to the placid little town, can be found another 52 buildings classified or registered by the National Trust.

It is only another 20 km (12½ miles) down the Lake Highway to Melton Mowbray and the junction with the Midland Highway, which runs back down to Hobart. ❑

RESTAURANTS, CAFÉS AND BARS

Restaurants

Longford

Racecourse Inn
114 Marlborough St,
Longford
Tel: 6391 2352
www.racecourseinn.com
Open: D daily, bookings
essential. **$$$**
If you're staying in Long-
ford, this is your best
bet. There's an excellent
menu, largely French in
inspiration but with a few
Asian influenced dishes,
good wines, and some of
the food is grown in the
inn's garden.

Miena

Central Highlands Lodge
Haddens Bay, Miena
Tel: 6259 8179
Open: L & D daily Sept-Apr. **$$**
Trout is the speciality
here. They'll even cook
one you've caught
yourself.

Oatlands

Blossoms
116-118 High St, Oatlands
Tel: 6254 1516
Open: L Thurs-Mon. **$**
Worth a stop for morning
or afternoon tea – the
scones are freshly made.

Mishka at Kentish Hotel
60 High St, Oatlands
Tel: 6254 1119
Open: L daily, D Wed-Sun. **$**
Mishka has a more
interesting menu than
your average pub and a
dedicated dining room.

Ross

Man O' Ross Hotel
35 Church St, Ross
Tel: 6381 5445
Open: L & D daily. **$$**
This historic hotel, which
has been a coaching inn
since 1835, has a
pleasant restaurant.

Pubs, cafés and bars

Campbell Town

Zeps
92 High St, Campbell Town
Tel: 6381 1344
Open: L & D daily. **$**
The most popular
stopping point on the
Midland Highway, either
for coffee and cake or,
at night, a good pizza.

Evandale

Clarendon Arms Hotel
11 Russell St, Evandale
Tel: 6391 8181
Open: L & D daily. **$**
A good pub meal and
there's also a beer gar-
den for hot summer days.

The Muse Café
14 Russell St, Evandale
Tel: 6391 8554
Open: L daily. **$**
Excellent coffee and
tempting morsels.

Longford

Woolmers Estate
Woolmers Lane, Longford
Tel: 6391 2230
Open: L daily. **$**

This café, which serves
light meals, is part of a
complex that includes
one of Tasmania's most
impressive colonial
houses and a national
rose garden.

Oatlands

Casaveen
44 High St, Oatlands
Tel: 6254 0044
Open: L daily. **$**
Enjoy a coffee while
shopping for beautiful
Tasmanian knitwear
where it is made.

Ross

That Place In Ross
34 Church St, Ross
Tel: 6381 5413
Open: L & D daily. **$**
Lively café and tea
rooms, with house made
specialties. BYO.

Ross Bakery Inn
15 Church St, Ross
Tel: 6381 5246
Open: L daily. **$**
Delectable home-made
pies, breads and pas-
tries are cooked in a
wood fired oven.

**The Old Ross General
Store**
31 Church St, Ross
Tel: 6381 5422
Open: L daily. **$**
Justly famous for its
scallop pies.

PRICE CATEGORIES

Prices for a three-course
dinner per person with a
half-bottle of house wine:
$ = under A$50
$$ = A$50–A$75
$$$ = over A$75
L = lunch, D = dinner, BYO
= bring your own alcohol.

RIGHT: a filling meal.

THE EAST COAST

Beaches, fishing and some outstanding National Parks keep the emphasis firmly on the outdoors in an area that's perhaps the closest that Tasmania comes to a holiday playground.

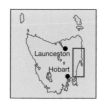

There are no guarantees in Tasmania but if it's time on a beach you're after, with some prospect of reasonable weather, then the east coast is usually the best bet. And what beaches! Perhaps the finest of them all, The Bay of Fires, will be dealt with in a subsequent chapter *(see page 154)*. That still leaves some of the most beautiful, and surely the emptiest, stretches of sand in Australia. There are none of the palm trees of the tropics, just those pristine granules, close to white at times, and beautifully offset by surrounding rocks aglow with a vibrant orange lichen.

When it's too wet or blustery, there are three national parks to explore, food and wine producers to visit, more relics of the Island's convict past to ponder, and, by way of variety, the state's second-highest mountain just a short drive inland.

Orford and Maria Island

The Tasman Highway, once it joins the coast, provides one stupendous view after another as it winds its way northwards. It is at this point, as the sea first hoves into view, that you find the small resort of **Orford ❶**. It's sited at the mouth of the **Prosser** River which spills forth from the same dramatic gorge that the highway has been following. Fishing is a core activity and numerous patient exponents will be found along the river banks and around into the estuary, trying to ignore the adolescents hurling themselves off the bridge into the water. Some will escape by taking their rods out on one of the boats that dots the bay. Others might head for the sheltered Orford or Shelly beaches. Prettiest of the lot is **Spring Beach**, a short drive to the south.

Were you to continue south, a reasonably good dirt road zig-zags its way through the **Wielangta Forest**,

Map on page 140

LEFT: the blowhole at Bicheno.
BELOW: boats moored along the Prosser River at Orford.

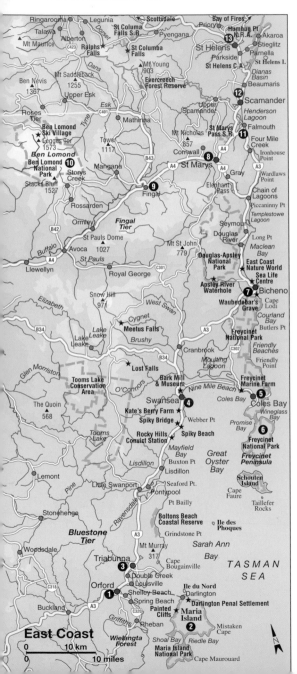

offering great ocean views through the towering blue gums. It can be slow at times but offers a quicker way through to the Tasman Penisula and Port Arthur.

Clearly visible from the beaches at Orford is the home to another of Tasmania's penal settlements: **Maria Island ②**. Access is by ferry from a jetty at the grim Eastcoaster Resort at Louisville Point, 4 km (2½ miles) north of Orford, and takes about 25 minutes (departures at 9.30am, 1.30pm, 3.15pm; tel: 6257 1589).

Maria Island was named by Abel Tasman after Van Diemen's wife in 1642. The French produced the first charts in 1802 and the echo of their presence is to be found in the place names, such as Cape Boullanger. However, its colonial history dates from 1825 when it became a British penal settlement. Even then it was only used as such for seven years before the inmates were removed to Port Arthur. It later housed convicts during a spell as a probation station.

The island is vehicle-free, so pack walking boots or a mountain bike. Bikes can be hired from On-Ya-Bike Bike Hire (tel: 6257 4086), but have to be booked in advance and taken over with you. The Parks and Wildlife Service provide a very useful brochure with a map of **Darlington** – the only settlement as well as the set-down point for the ferry. It includes a series of different walking routes with historical notes. For riders, there's a whole-island map available at the **Commissariat Store**, which houses a small information centre and is also the place to pay park fees.

A visitor can wander through cottages, administrative buildings, the old penitentiary (now a bunk room for over-nighters) and a significant later addition, the Coffee Palace. The latter was built in 1888 to serve tourists who, even then, were fascinated by Tasmania's convict past. It now houses displays illustrating the island's subsequent roles as host to a silk industry, to vineyards, and farming. Then there was the cement works, the ugly remnants of which can be found by the jetty.

After a few minutes in Darlington, it's time to seek out the island's natural attractions. A series of walks takes in the **Fossil Cliffs** (fossils can be readily found in the abandoned limestone quarry), the **Painted Cliffs** (layers of different coloured sandstone best seen at low tide), and the more challenging route to the **Bishop and Clerk Peaks**. Cyclists can venture further afield on gently undulating tracks to deserted beaches and the remains of other settlements at the other end of the island. Even at peak season there are only ever a few dozen people on Maria Island, making it a superb destination for a genuine getaway.

Back on the mainland, it's only a short distance north to **Triabunna** ❸, where there is another ferry to Maria Island (although there have been spells when it's been out of service; check on 0427 100 104). There is a scattering of old colonial buildings in town and the interesting **Seafarers' Memorial**, which features plaques commemorating various maritime disasters, both military and civil, including the 1998 Sydney to Hobart yacht race.

The central east coast

As the highway continues north the seaward views come to be dominated by first Schouten Island and then the Freycinet Peninsula until, around Swansea, the distinctive peaks of The Hazards contribute to what the writer Nicholas Shakespeare, a little further round the bay in his house on Nine Mile Beach, regards almost with reverence: "I knew that I was gazing at the most beautiful place I had seen on earth, a conviction that all subsequent experience has served to deepen."

But we're getting ahead of ourselves. A few minutes before arriving in Swansea, one of the brown heritage signs on the roadside tips you off to **Spiky Bridge**, a convict-built construction, which takes its name from the jagged shards of rock lodged in its parapet. It's worth a

Map on page 140

The old Morris General Store in Swansea.

BELOW: Fossil Cliffs on Maria Island.

quick look, but the serendipitous delight is to be had by crossing the road and popping down to the tiny **Spiky Beach**.

If not delayed further by the scrumptious pleasures of **Kate's Berry Farm**, you soon come to **Swansea ④**. This is a good base for exploring the local area – usually a euphemism for a dull spot with no attractions of its own, but Swansea has quiet charms, including a reasonable beach, more heritage architecture (much of it for rent as holiday accommodation), and **Glamorgan War Memorial Museum** (Mon–Sat 9am–5pm, Tues 9am–4pm; admission charge), featuring a historic billiards room where you can play for AD$2 per game. On the northern edge of town is a rather larger museum complex, the **Swansea Bark Mill**. This long-established collection of accoutrements from the local farming and coastal communities, along with a restored and working mill, reopened in 2006 after a makeover to bring it blinking into the 21st century. There's a new pub for the less historically minded.

Swansea's Glamorgan War Memorial Museum.

BELOW:
vivid orange lichen on rocks above one of the beaches at Coles Bay.

The Freycinet Peninsula

The route is now drawing closer to the Freycinet Peninsula. A drive down the road to **Nine Mile Beach** reveals a few rooftops in the dunes and the odd pathway down towards the sea. Take any of these and you'll find yourself, predictably, on a limitless stretch of sand. Perhaps there will be the odd windsurfer swooping across Great Oyster Bay, maybe somebody walking a dog, but the odds are you'll have it to yourself. Carry on further and it can be frustrating that this is a spit of land (the main route to Freycinet loops north of Moulting Lagoon via Cranbrook). You have to turn back and drive a long 60 km (37 miles) just to face the end of the spit from the other side of the channel. But, of course, if the beach were on the main route to the peninsula, it probably would have been developed years ago.

Coles Bay ⑤ is to some extent a service centre for the neighbouring National Park, but that is to overlook the expansive **Muirs Beach**. It is just down from the bakery and pub, and purchases from either or both can be enjoyed while watching a game of beach cricket or a grumbling parent retrieving a kite from the sea. Around the other side of the headland lie wispier sands where boats bob offshore and the craggy pink granite Hazards dominate the view. Boats and kayaks can be rented or there are cruises to Schouten Island or Wineglass Bay (Freycinet Sea Charters; tel. 6257 0355).

Freycinet National Park ⑥ (*see also pages 150–151*) is one of the defining destinations of Tasmania. In consequence it's also one of the most popular and can get very busy in the peak months after Christmas. A modern **visitor centre** just past the park entrance (daily 9am–4.30pm; tel: 6256 7000; www.parks.tas.gov.au) helps plan your stay and offers walking

routes ranging from 10 minutes return to upwards of five hours. The shortest of these is a wheelchair-accessible path behind the centre to **Richardsons Beach**.

The most popular walk is the fairly stiff climb up to the saddle between two of the Hazards: Mount Amos and Mount Mayson. This houses the **Wineglass Bay** lookout. Even for regulars, the view down can take you aback; there's the fault-less symmetry of the curve that gives the bay its name and, if you're lucky and the sun's out, the impossible azure of the sea. For the first-time visitor, it is just breathtaking. It is not unusual to find groups of people settled on the benches or clumped on nearby rocks, gazing down in silence, lost in contemplation. Of course, some are simply getting their breath back. It will be little consolation to them that the Parks Service is replacing the irregular wooden boardwalk and worn rock path with stone steps and constant risers.

It's a fairly easy scramble down the hill to set foot on the beach and a good 20-minute walk round the curve to the far end, rewarded by good views back to the Hazards. For hardy walkers there is a path continuing southwards up to Mount Graham and even more dramatic vistas. For the rest it's a choice of returning up the steep hill to the lookout or taking the less strenuous but much longer route across the isthmus track, on to Hazards Beach and then round the promontory at Fleurieu Point. The visitor centre carries advice on conditions and requirements for the longer and overnight walks.

For those with young children or otherwise unable to tackle challenging walks, there are shorter strolls: the **Cape Tourville Walk** is generously estimated at 20 minutes, and offers a partial view of Wineglass Bay as well as a look at a lighthouse; nearby, a track provides views over **Sleepy Bay** with the option of a climb down to **Little Gravelly Beach**. Whichever walk you choose, it would take a melancholic bent of the highest order not to be swept away by the beauty and grandeur of Freycinet.

Map on page 140

TIPS

Day entry to National Parks in Tasmania costs A$20 per vehicle and can be purchased upon arrival with cash to be left in envelopes provided. For multiple visits a two-month pass costs A$50 but it can only be bought from staffed National Park offices or visitor centres, as well as some state Visitor Information Centres, so plan ahead. *See also page 257.*

BELOW: admiring the view across Wineglass Bay.

Fishermen can often be seen unloading their catches at harbours all along the east coast.

BELOW: fresh crayfish feature on menus throughout the state.
RIGHT: the waterhole in Douglas-Apsley National Park.

The sea has been a provider since the original inhabitants, the Great Oyster Bay tribe, were consuming the crustaceans whose discarded shells form the middens which can be found behind Richardson Beach if you look carefully enough. The sea is still teaming with food and you only have to tie a bit of prawn to a piece of string and throw it in the waters of Honeymoon Bay to guarantee a fish for dinner. People with boats can catch tuna or marlin, while those with cars can visit **Freycinet Marine Farm** and sample the oysters (tours 10am daily; admission charge; tel: 6257 0140).

Bicheno to St Marys

It's a 27-km (17-mile) drive back to the Tasman Highway, where the next stop is a further 11 km (7 miles) to the north at **Bicheno ❼**. This is a relaxed family resort with a couple of beaches, handy facilities and splendid natural attractions, including tours to see the incoming fairy penguins (daily at dusk all year; admission charge; tel: 6375 1333; www.bichenopenguintours.com.au).

Waubs Bay is a protected, safe stretch of sand, ideal for young children, while **Redbill Beach** is a more picturesque strand, sweeping round to **Diamond Island** – a short amble across the sand at low tide. This is the place to come for surfing or body-boarding.

To the east of town is **The Gulch**, a sheltered channel where the fishing fleet rests up, and a little to the south of that is the **Blow Hole**. Here, depending on the tides and the swell, a vast spout or a desultory spurt of water is forced up through a hole in the rocks. Hours of fun can be had watching over-confident children prove their parents right yet again; yes, they were too close. There's a footpath around the coastline linking all these features.

The **Sea Life Centre** (daily 9am–5pm; admission charge; tel: 6375 1121) has a small aquarium and some marine detritus. A few kilometres further on, **East Coast Nature World** (daily 9am–5pm; admission charge; tel: 6375 1311; www.natureworld.com.au) is part animal refuge and part wildlife park, which also

features a good restaurant with cream teas. But before that is the turnoff to the **Douglas-Apsley National Park**. A relatively new park, it was set up at the end of the 1980s to preserve an area of dry sclerophyll forest (trees with thick evergreen leaves designed to reduce moisture loss – this is one of the driest parts of Tasmania) with uniquely diverse plant and animal life. There are few facilities and many of the longer walking tracks are only accessible from an unmade loggers' track. However, from the Tasman Highway it's not too far to the car park, which acts as a starting point to a short walk to a lookout over the Apsley River. Directly below, specks can be seen bobbing in a waterhole and you can join them by clambering down a marked path. It's a good place for a picnic and a soak on a hot day. In dry weather there's a good walk to the impressive Apsley Gorge, about an hour upstream.

Inland to Ben Lomond

The road continues to hug the coast until the turnoff up into the hills through **Elephant Pass** and on to **St Marys 8**. This is a quiet hill town, founded on farming, and now developing a reputation for its arts and crafts. Nearby are Irish Town, German Town and Dublin Town, reflecting the area's immigrant past. Many visitors are attracted by the prospect of climbing the nearby peaks of **St Patricks Head** (2–3 hours return), **North Sister** (40 minutes, some climbing) and **South Sister** (10 minutes up steps). The road to the latter through state forest is not well signed but the views are worth the effort.

Were you to carry on inland from St Marys, the small town of **Fingal 9** has some attractive colonial edifices, including the well-preserved Victorian Holder Brothers Store building, one of Tasmania's oldest schools, St Peter's Church, the Fingal Hotel with a collection of hundreds of scotch whiskys, and two grand old houses: Malahide and Tullochgoram.

From Fingal there's a road which follows the South Esk River up into the hills past Mathinna. Much of the route is through forest until it opens

Map on page 140

Elephant Pass is named after nearby Mount Elephant, which reputedly has an elephantine form. Or, as a local tall-story has it, the name commemorates a circus elephant who died from heat exhaustion here after being forced to free a trapped circus cart. The pachyderm connection is well in evidence at the Mount Elephant Pancake restaurant nearby (see page 148).

BELOW: on the waterfront at St Helens.

A detail from the war memorial in Cecilia Street, St Helens.

BELOW: end of the line. Fishing from the old railway bridge in Scamander.

out into true alpine scenery with lush meadows surrounded by steep wooded hills. The road off to **Ben Lomond National Park ❿** runs for 8 km (5 miles) before the park entrance, from where it's an increasingly steep ride up an unmade road until the beginning of the notorious **Jacob's Ladder**, a series of sharp hairpin bends which provides stunning views and difficult moments for nervous passengers. There are a couple of viewing points, but drivers are not encouraged to stop elsewhere – tempting though it is to grab the camera and shoot the jagged dolerite columns which drop down to the crumbling scree below.

At the top of the Ladder is a plateau and a scattering of grey wooden buildings which constitute the **Alpine Village**. In winter, for a short season (July–September), this is Tasmania's ski centre, offering both downhill and cross-country. There is some accommodation at the Ben Lomond Creek Inn, and more in the various ski-club chalets, but many skiers travel up for the day from Launceston – a mere hour or so

away. For the rest of the year there are opportunities for rock climbing or walks across the bleak lunar landscape, perhaps up to the highpoint of **Legges Tor** (at 1,573 metres/5,161 ft, Tasmania's second-highest peak), with wallabies the only company, and a carpet of alpine flowers in the summer. There's comfort to be found round the fire in the bar of the pub in the village all year round.

Falmouth to St Helens

Back on the east coast, the small settlement of **Falmouth ⓫** has just a few holiday houses and no shops, but basks in a spectacular setting with every one of those houses afforded a dramatic view to the north, the east or the south. Beach access is at Henderson Point at the mouth of Henderson Lagoon, a tranquil spot ideal for youngsters to cavort in the water and try out canoeing.

If Falmouth is something of a secret, the opposite can be said of **Scamander ⓬**, a resort developed at a time of architectural impoverishment. The brick holiday homes are in just the wrong shade of

Map on page 140

municipal-toilet-yellow, and the Chancellor Inn hotel, sitting high above the river, is pure Gold Coast 1974, but without the style. The beach, while clean and quiet, can never make up for its surroundings.

Beaumaris, the next township along, is another mishmash of holiday homes and motels with a pristine beach hiding behind the dunes.

St Helens ⑬, at the heart of the absurdly named Break O'Day municipality, is the largest town on the east coast. The road in winds around the bottom of the attractive Georges Bay past jetties, as likely to be occupied by fishermen as boats. The serious vessels – this is a busy fishing port, Tasmania's biggest – are to be found just over the Golden Fleece Bridge on the edge of the town centre.

Much of the town's growth came with the discovery of tin in the surrounding hills. St Helens became a key shipping hub and continued to hold its own even after the mines closed down. These days tourism is a major contributor to the local economy. Ironically, it is one of the few places on the east coast without

a spectacular beach, but it's not far to the Bay of Fires to the north, or **Beer Barrel Beach** at St Helens Point – only half an hour's walk away. Just a bit further and you come to the extensive **Peron Dunes**.

Many visitors come for the fishing and with the sheltered waters of Georges Bay; while game fishing is for those who want to test themselves against various tuna, marlin and sharks. There's a useful brochure available at the tourist office (daily; tel: 6376 1329).

In the same building is one of St Helens few indoor attractions, a new **History Room** with special emphasis on the impact of World War II on the area. A colourful memorial nearby reinforces the war's significance to locals.

Just along the road is the site of the town's old pub, which burned down in 2005 and will be rebuilt at some point, but for now the nightlife options are limited unless you're around from Thursday to Saturday, when the atmospheric boutique cinema, The Forum, shows up to four films a day (tel: 6376 1000). ❏

Georges Bay has plenty of variety on offer for anglers. Estuary and bay fishing offers bream, garfish, salmon, flathead and trevally; deep-sea fishing adds trevalla, gemfish, blue grenadier and others; offshore reef options include stripy trumpeter, silver morwong, cod, perch and squid; from rock or beach you can expect to find bream, mullet, salmon, skate, gummy shark and flathead.

BELOW: the beach at St Helens.

RESTAURANTS, CAFÉS AND BARS

Restaurants

Bicheno

Facets
Diamond Island Resort, 69
Tasman Highway, Bicheno
Tel: 6375 0100
Open: D daily. **$$**
Local produce features
on the seasonal menu of
this restaurant that's
part of the Diamond
Island resort.

Coles Bay

Iluka Tavern
Esplanade, Coles Bay
Tel: 6257 0429
Open: L & D daily. **$**
Casual pub dining that
does a good trade with
locals as well as
tourists.

Madge Malloy's
3 Garnet Ave, Coles Bay
Tel: 6257 0399
Open: D Tues-Sat. **$$**
Take the advice from
your waiter as to what
fish is fresh then ask
them to match it with
one of the region's fabu-
lous wines. Much of the
fish served here is
caught by the restaurant
owners.

PRICE CATEGORIES

Prices for a three-course
dinner per person with a
half-bottle of house wine:
$ = under A$50
$$ = A$50–A$75
$$$ = over A$75
L = lunch, D = dinner, BYO
= bring your own alcohol.

The Edge
Edge of the Bay, 2308 Main
Rd, Coles Bay
Tel: 6257 0102
www.edgeofthebay.com
Open: D daily. **$$**
Enjoy resort dining with
a magnificent view. The
menu is innovative and
eclectic, with local
scallops a speciality.

The Bay
Freycinet Lodge, Freycinet
National Park, Coles Bay
Tel: 6257 0101
Open: L & D daily. **$$**
This spacious, light and
comfortable dining room
has a picture-perfect
location. It's an ideal
place for enjoying local
oysters and seafood,
and more besides.

Orford

**Scorchers by the River
Gallery Cafe**
1 Esplanade, Orford
Tel: 6257 1033
Open: L & D daily. **$**
Excellent pizzas are
cooked in a wood-fired
oven. The menu includes
some unusual
combinations of ingredi-
ents, including some
Tasmanian specialities.

Just Hooked
Tasman Highway, Orford
Tel: 6257 1549
Open: L & D daily. **$**
Impeccably cooked fish
and chips and good
oysters make this well
worth a stop. There's a
fishmonger as well.

St Helens

Fidlers on the Bay
2 Jason St, St Helens
Tel: 6376 2444
Open: L & D daily. **$$**
The founding chef may
have moved on, but Terry
Fidler left a competent
team behind. Still the
best dining in St Helens.

Swansea

Kabuki by the Sea
Rocky Hills, Tasman High-
way, Swansea (12 km south)
Tel: 6257 8588
www.kabukibythesea.com.au
Open: L daily, D Dec-Apr Tues-
Sat, May-Nov Fri-Sat. **$$**
There are few better
locations than this eyrie
perched on the side of a
cliff with magical views
of Freycinet. The menu
ranges from Devonshire
tea to sashimi.

Schouten House
1 Waterloo Rd, Swansea
Tel: 6257 8564
Open: D daily. **$$**
A relatively formal dining
room, located in one of
Swansea's oldest build-
ings, now a guest house.

Pubs, cafés and bars

Bicheno

Cod Rock Café
34 Foster St, Bicheno
Tel: 6375 1340
Open: L & D daily. **$**
A crayfish sandwich is an

unusual option in this
little café in the centre
of Bicheno.

Freycinet Bakery & Café
55 Burgess St, Bicheno
Tel: 6375 1972
Open: L daily. **$**
Big breakfasts and all-
day snacks and coffee
ensure a roaring trade in
summer.

St Helens

Captain's Catch
The Wharf, St Helens
Tel: 6376 1170
Open: L daily. **$**
Possibly the best fish
and chips in Tasmania.
This is a big claim for a
boat moored in the
St Helens Harbour, but
ask the locals and they
will confirm that only
the freshest fish are
used here.

Deck on the Bay
1 Quail St, St Helens
Tel: 6376 1999
Open: L & D daily. **$$**
A smart venue in the
Doherty resort where the
comfort of the location
and the views across the
bay make it a good place
for a coffee or evening
drink.

St Marys

Mt Elephant Pancakes
Elephant Pass,
(east of) St Marys
Tel: 6372 2263
Open: L daily. **$**

RIGHT: gourmet options at the wharf in St Helens.

Something of an institution, partly because it's such an unlikely place to find a pancake parlour, a stopover here will reward you with beautiful views across the valley as well as a huge range of European-style savoury and sweet pancakes.

E.Scape Tasmanian Wilderness Café and Gallery
Main St, St Marys
Tel: 6372 2444
Open: L & D daily. $
Plenty of reading material, a wood heater, TV, couches, a pool table, and a gallery means you get more than just coffee and cakes here.

Purple Possum Wholefoods and Café
5 Story St, St Marys
Tel: 6372 2655
Open: L Mon-Fri. $
There are plenty of healthy dining options in this alternative café.

Scamander
Scamander News and Mouth Café
167 Scamander Ave, Scamander
Tel: 6372 5275
Open: L & D daily. $
Good, well-cooked fish and chips that taste even better when sitting on the deck looking out over the mouth of the Scamander River.

Eureka Farm
Upper Scamander Rd
(2 km south of Scamander)
Tel: 6372 5500
Open: L Oct-June daily. $
Drive up a narrow road to this food-lovers' haven. Great coffee, beautiful Italian-style ice creams, great preserves and wonderful desserts based on the farm's produce all feature here.

Swansea
Left Bank
7 Maria St, Swansea
Tol: 6257 0090
Open: L Sept-Apr Wed-Mon, May-July Thurs-Mon. $
Serving the best coffee on the east coast, great breakfasts, and an interesting lunch menu, Left Bank is reason enough on its own to make Swansea a base. BYO.

Kate's Berry Farm
Addison St, Swansea
(3 km south)
Tel: 6257 8428
Open: L daily. $
Most tourists take the time to stop here, even if it's out of season. The berry ice creams, Devonshire teas, breathtaking views, and friendly welcome explain why and, in season, there are fresh berries available too.

Ugly Duck Out
2 Franklin St, Swansea
Open: L & D daily. $
A huge menu that caters for just about every fast food mood – pasta, curries, salads, burgers, grills, and fish and chips.

Swansea Bark Mill Tavern
96 Tasman Highway, Swansea
Tel: 6257 8094
Open: L & D daily. $
One of Swansea's main attractions, it's worth a visit to check out the Tasmanian wines, beers and other specialities.

Triabunna
Girraween Gardens and Tearooms
4 Henry St, Triabunna
Tel: 6257 3458
Open: L daily, closed Sat June-Aug. $
Old-fashioned hospitality amid pretty gardens. BYO.

FREYCINET

Wineglass Bay is the headline attraction in Freycinet National Park, but there is plenty more to see and keen walkers could easily spend a few days here

Without overstating it, the Freycinet Peninsula must be one of the most beautiful places in the world. The combination of mountains, forest, beaches and blisteringly blue sea, not to mention the abundant wildlife, is hard to match and impossible to beat. Best just to surrender to it and allow as much time as possible to take it all in. Pitch a tent just back from the beach and get close to nature (but not too close; secure food from inquisitive wallabies and wombats who can sniff a bonanza every time they hear a tent peg being hammered in). Alternatively, follow the path to luxury and book into the Freycinet Lodge, inside the Park boundary, for a couple of nights of hedonism. Settle on the balcony of your cabin and watch the scurrying animals in the undergrowth below.

In summer there is good swimming to be had, while fishermen are spoilt for choice. Above all, though, this is a place for walking. The Wineglass Bay Track is a must, whether it's just a climb up to the saddle for the view, or perhaps as part of a longer trek which could take in Mount Graham or Mount Freycinet. People with mobility problems or young children can still take on the shorter walks, some with views of Wineglass Bay. Another option is to join one of the boat trips around the peninsula which embark from Coles Bay.

ABOVE: they're cute and friendly but visitors are warned not to feed the wallabies in Freycinet because some processed foods can cause a fatal bony growth called lumpy jaw.

LEFT: the waters around the Freycinet peninsula are rich in marine life so fishing is popular. However, it tends to be the professionals who procure giant crabs like this.

BELOW: the bright orange deposits on boulders along the shoreline in Freycinet and all along the east coast are in fact a type of rock lichen. They are a complex mixture of fungi and algae which extract nutrients from the rocks they're attached to.

LEFT: the Cape Tourville walk, which affords partial views of Wineglass Bay, is an easy 20-minute stroll around the lighthouse. The walk is accessible to wheelchair users.

ABOVE: nothing beats that first view of Wineglass Bay which, for most people, comes as a generous reward for the steep climb up to the saddle between Mount Amos and Mount Mason.

VISITOR FACILITIES

The Visitor Centre is just a few hundred metres inside the park on the right hand side. This is where park permits can be purchased and maps and guides picked up. Even those who have already paid their park fees should find a stop rewarding as there are displays about many aspects of the park's history and geology, as well as useful pointers towards the weather and the state of the various walks.

One of the walks starts immediately behind the Visitor Centre. The Great Oyster Bay walk is a 5-minute amble down to Richardsons Beach where the cormorants play, and the Hazards loom above. The Centre is also the place to register for the campsites, which need to be booked in advance at all times. Indeed some, such as those at Honeymoon Bay (open only at Easter and in the summer) are so popular that a ballot system is used to allocate spaces. There are powered sites for caravans and RVs, and unpowered for tents. Electric barbecue facilities are provided at various points as all camp fires are banned, although portable fuel stoves are allowed.

RIGHT: Sleepy Bay is one of many blissful spots in the park and can be accessed just five minutes from the car park. The way down to the beach is a bit of a scramble but more than worth the effort.

RIGHT: it can take a good 15 to 20 minutes to walk to the end of the beach at Wineglass Bay, and then the choice must be made whether to return via the saddle or take the longer, less steep route via Hazards Beach.

LEFT: a ranger from the Parks and Wildlife Service promotes the campaign to keep foxes out of Tasmania and increase awareness of the devastating consequences for indigenous animal and birdlife if this predator were to gain a toehold in the state. Several species, already wiped out on the Australian mainland, would be endangered, including quolls and bandicoots.

THE NORTHEAST

Often overlooked by visitors, the
sunny northeastern corner of Tasmania has
some delightful villages, attractive low-key resorts
and one of the most beautiful beaches in the world

Sometimes in Tasmania it can seem that you're the only person for miles around. It's a common phenomenon in the northeast where the only way to see all of the Bay of Fires is on a four-day walk, or where some historic settlements are now just a few piles of stones, unvisited and well off the beaten track. Busy it's not, but worth investigating it certainly is.

St Helens made a natural end point to the previous chapter's trip up the east coast. It can also lay a claim to be the launchpad for travel into the northeast. It is a junction for roads both to the southern end of the Bay of Fires, and also up into the hills to farming and tin-mining country. The History Room (*see page 147*) at the visitor centre devotes space to many of the areas described in this chapter. So bone up and prepare to begin by travelling the short distance up the coast towards Binalong Bay.

Binalong Bay

The St Helens–Binalong Bay road clings to the side of Georges Bay before climbing up towards Humbug Hill. There is an unmade road off to the right into the **Humbug Point State Recreation Area**, and it isn't far to the top of **Humbug Hill** where the views both to the south and the north reveal endless prospects of unspoilt coastline. The track continues on to picnic spots and viewpoints at either **Little Elephant**, looking south, or **Humbug Point** itself, on the edge of Skeleton Bay, looking north.

Returning to, or sticking with, the main road brings visitors round the side of the hill, past the doubtful charms of a busty nymph, or at least a crude statue of one, into **Binalong Bay ❶** itself. This is a small holiday resort, which just happens to be at

Map on page 154

LEFT: sculpted rock formations on the edge of Binalong Bay.
BELOW: cheese from the Pyengana Dairy Company.

Milking it. Souvenirs at the Holy Cow Café.

the southern end of one of the world's great beaches. Anywhere else and it would have become a huge holiday resort by now. Yet, this being Tasmania, there are just a few dozen holiday cottages rising up the steep sides of Humbug Hill, ensuring magnificent views for each and every one of them. There is an excellent café and beyond that, it's just you and the beach.

But this is no ordinary beach. At first sight it repeats the formula found along the rest of the east coast. The sand is crystalline and almost pure white. The sea picks up the colour from the sky and distils it into brilliant azure and cobalt, with the usual rider of the sun needing to shine unobscured by cloud. And the rocks are flecked with the same deep-orange lichen that does so much to give this coast its identity. The formula may be the same, then, but the scale is quite different. This

beach runs northward for another 30 km (19 miles).

This coast was dubbed the **Bay of Fires ❷** by Tobias Furneaux in 1773 when he remarked on the many Aboriginal campfires spotted along the shoreline as he surveyed the area. There were probably more people found on the beach then than now, since great stretches of it are still inaccessible by road. There is a four-day guided walk from top to bottom (Bay of Fires Walk; tel: 6391 9339; www.bayoffires.com.au), including an overnight stop in a luxurious and architecturally distinguished lodge, but otherwise pick your spot in the south, or visit Mount William National Park in the north (see page 157).

Binalong Bay, then, is as busy as this beach ever gets. There is good surf, although the currents have to be watched. And there is the bonus of the placid **Grants Lagoon**

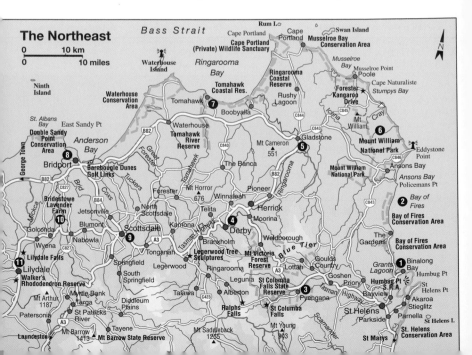

stretching away behind the dunes, which is perfect for children, kayaks and the odd jet-ski.

On the way out of Binalong there is a road off to the right after 2 km (1¼ miles) which joins the bay a bit further north and runs along the edge of the coast for about 8 km (5 miles) until arriving at **The Gardens**. There must have been some here when Lady Jane Franklin (the wife of Governor Franklin; see margin opposite) came up with the name in 1840. Now it's just more perfect sand and surf, with a couple more lagoons en route.

Along the Tasman Highway

The other route north from St Helens is the Tasman Highway. This makes its way inland and climbs steadily into the hills. A short distance past Goshen there is a road off on the right to **Goulds Country**. This is the only township in Tasmania where all the structures were made of wood, but there is surprisingly little of it left today, especially considering that it was big enough to accommodate over 400 residents in 1900 and could claim a bank, a school, churches, council chambers and a telegraph office, as well as the usual residential buildings.

That was in the bygone days of tin mining, when **Blue Tier** – the mountain looming up in the north – was yielding up to 60 tons of ore each year and men flocked to the area. A short distance north, some of the remains of the mine at **Lottah** are visible.

Pyengana ❸ is just off the highway to the south. The pasture here is ideal for dairy herds, but in the early 1900s it wasn't practical to transport milk to the coast. Cheese, however, proved a viable alternative, and it has been produced here ever since. The **Pyengana Dairy Company** and the attached **Holy Cow Café** cater to tourists with free tastings and the opportunity to watch production going on behind glass (daily 9am–5pm, winter 10am–4pm; free; tel: 6373 6157). Have a snack on the café terrace for that authentic whiff of cow.

Down the road is the St Columba Falls Hotel, better known as **The Pub in the Paddock**. The spirit of the original interior (*c*.1880) has

Map on page 154

As well as naming The Gardens north of Binalong Bay, Lady Jane Franklin was a major influence in the renaming of Van Diemen's Land to Tasmania.

BELOW: Priscilla enjoys a cold one at the Pub in the Paddock.

The Weldborough Hotel prides itself on being the "worst pub in the world".

BELOW: the old National Bank of Tasmania building at Derby now houses an art gallery.

been preserved giving it a cosy old English pub feel. But surely only an Australian establishment would have Priscilla the beer-drinking pig. In her pen in the garden, she'll knock back a stubbie in three seconds flat. Priscilla has become something of an attraction but she's getting old so a successor is being quietly groomed behind the scenes.

Follow the road to **St Columba Falls State Reserve**. The falls can be seen from the road but the best way to appreciate the full grandeur of the 90-metre (300-ft) drop is to walk for 10 minutes to the base. Falls fans may want to take the turn-off just before St Columba and go to **Ralphs Falls**. They are less dramatic in themselves but have more extensive views.

The Tasman Highway twists and turns through some tight hairpin bends to the **Weldborough Pass**, where wonderful views and the 15-minute Weldborough Pass Rainforest Walk are tantalising distractions. So too is the historic hotel at **Weldborough**. This is another atmospheric Victorian pub, which has been operating since 1886.

Moorina has a Chinese altar in its old cemetery as well as Chinese graves, reflecting the influx during the tin mining days. Another memento of the Chinese presence, the old Weldborough Joss House, is now on display in the Queen Victoria Museum in Launceston (*see page 170*).

At this point there are two options: divert through to beautiful Mount William National Park in the far northeast of Tasmania, then head across to Bridport; alternatively, stay on the Tasman Highway through some more mining and farming country. Both routes end up at Scottsdale.

The Derby route

The Tasman Highway route has its next stop in **Derby ❹**, pronounced the American way. Another mining town that boomed for several years before falling on hard times, Derby turned its attention to agriculture and, latterly, tourism. Perhaps it was appropriate for an industry so subject to the cavalier dispensations of fortune that the town's Briseis Mine

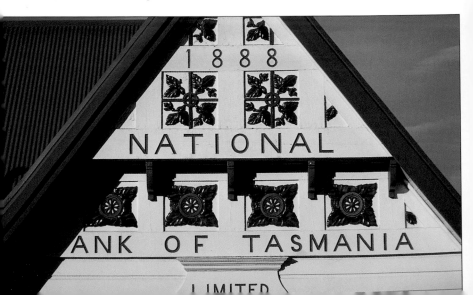

1888
NATIONAL
ANK OF TASMANIA
LIMITED

was named after a horse that won the Melbourne Cup.

Main Street is perched on the side of a hill above the Ringarooma River and holds the major points of interest. The **Derby Tin Mine Centre** (daily 9.30am–4.30pm; admission charge; tel: 6354 2262) occupies an old school and, while the exhibition of old implements, documents and photos is quite interesting, the real appeal lies outside. A shanty town has been reconstructed with shops, a Briseis Mine office, a printing press, a couple of cells from the old town gaol and even an old 1930s radio station. Further down Main Street an old wooden National Bank of Tasmania building has been restored to gleaming perfection. It is now the **Bank House Manor Gallery**.

In nearby **Branxholm** there are more Chinese graves in the cemetery, while the **Red Bridge** project commemorates a clash between Chinese and European miners in 1877. Today timber and hops dominate both the landscape and the economy.

A side trip off the highway to the **Legerwood Tree Sculptures** is worthwhile. Eight trees were planted after World War I in memory of fallen locals. When these became dangerous and were earmarked for felling, it was agreed that the stumps would be retained and carved into representations of soldiers. This is the result.

The Tasman Highway continues to Scottsdale (see page 159).

Mt William National Park

The northeastern route means taking the B82 to **Gladstone ❺** (the turning is roughly halfway between Moorina and Derby). The mine at Gladstone didn't close down until 1982, and the torpor suggests that nothing much has happened here since. There are more Chinese gravestones, some eccentric dwellings and not much else.

Immeasurably more rewarding is time spent in **Mount William National Park ❻**, which extends from the top end of the Bay of Fires to Musselroe Bay in the far northeast. The C843 road from Gladstone forks after 8 km (5 miles) – take the

Map on page 154

TIPS

Watch out for snakes when out in the wilds of Tasmania. There are four species on the island, all of them venomous. However, sightings are rare and bitings even rarer. If bitten stay calm and seek help.

BELOW: camping just behind the beach in Mount William National Park.

BELOW: an artist at work at Tomahawk on the north coast.

left fork for the northern section of the park (the right fork leads to Ansons Bay, *see below*).

The terrain is open, with heath and occasional stands of trees. In the early morning or late afternoon onwards, take the **Forester Kangaroo Drive** for almost guaranteed sightings of these marsupials, also known as eastern greys. This is the only species of kangaroo in Tasmania. Look out too for Bennetts wallabies, pademelons (a small marsupial closely related to the rock wallaby), wombats and echidnas, as well as the odd snake. (Bear in mind that all four species of snake found in Tasmania are venomous.) There are also over 100 species of birds and, occasionally, you might be lucky enough to spot a sea eagle or a wedge-tailed eagle.

A walking track runs to the top of **Mount William** which takes an hour or so there and back. It's worth it for views across miles of sweeping countryside and down the coastline. On clear days you can even see Flinders Island across Bass Strait. There are basic campsites just behind the gorgeous beach at **Stumpys Bay**.

At the northern end of the park **Musselroe Bay** has a boat ramp, and up at **Musselroe Point** there is the largest of several middens, which are testament to the historic Aboriginal presence in the area.

It's necessary to drive out of the national park and return to the fork in the road from Gladstone in order to see its southern section. There's a twisty track to Eddystone Point and a short walk up to **Eddystone Lighthouse**. It was built in 1889 with granite quarried from behind the beach below.

Make a point of going down to **Ansons Bay** or **Policemans Point** and pause to admire the Bay of Fires from its northern end. The sheer scale and emptiness take the breath away every time.

Across to Bridport

Return to Gladstone and take the road towards Bridport and then turn off to the north coast at **Tomahawk** ❼. There is a caravan park, a store and miles and miles of flat empty

beach with a few rocks here and there to break it up. Fishermen keep busy and everyone else walks, plays cricket and makes the best of another stretch of unsullied coastline. As one of the brochures puts it, in a vain attempt to flesh out Tomahawk's appeal: "Popular fishing, camping and fishing area. Caravan and camping ground with a shop."

Bridport ❽ is the big smoke after so much emptiness. It is a fishing and holiday town with its full share of shacks and caravans. Attempts are being made to remarket it, and the opening of the remarkable new **Barnbougle Dunes Golf Links** (tel: 6356 0094; www.barnbougledunes.com) in 2004 has raised the profile of the area considerably *(see page 51)*.

Barnbougle is a public access course with very reasonable green fees considering that serious golfers rate it as a world-class facility. It is set amongst the sand dunes 5 km (3 miles) east of Bridport and, as with all links courses, the weather can play a big part in a round. There is always the prospect of heavy winds

or rain blowing in from Bass Strait and spoiling that crucial chip to the ninth. Accommodation is available and there is even a shuttle bus from Launceston Airport.

The other supplement to Bridport's beaches and fishing is the **Bridport Wildflower Reserve**, which has a scenic walk and is at its best in September and October.

Scottsdale

It is an easy 19-km (12-mile) run down to **Scottsdale** ❾, the largest town in the northeast. The emphasis is very much on timber, and this is reflected in its landmark attraction, the **Forest EcoCentre** (daily 9am–5pm, 9am–3pm winter; free; tel: 6352 6458). Forestry Tasmania built this drum of timber, glass and steel, which looks as if it has crashlanded in a field on the edge of town. At a bit of an angle, too. Inside it's almost disappointing to find that, under the wacky exterior, there's a box-like office building, used by Forestry Tasmania administration.

The ground level is open to the public and includes conventional

Map on page 154

BELOW: Scottsdale's striking Forest EcoCentre.

Painted poles are Lilydale's way of persuading travellers to stop.

BELOW: proceed with care at Bridstowe Estate Lavender Farm.

displays, soundscapes and numerous video presentations to explain the history and development of the area with special emphasis on the local timber industry. Sustainability is the keyword and the building itself is said to be "wood-wise and energy-smart". Jargon aside, the centre is designed to use half the energy of a conventional building of the same size. There is a shop selling innovative wood products and a café. The building also acts as the local visitor centre.

King Street has a few worthwhile heritage buildings, including "**Beulah**", which was the family home of one of the pioneer families in Scottsdale. At No. 46 is the National Trust-listed Federation-style **Annabel's**, which operates as a restaurant. **St Barnabas Church** and the old **Post Office** are also worth a look, but, unless you are drawn to the **Doll and Bear Cottage** and its cuddly contents (52 King St; daily 9am–5pm; admission charge; tel: 6352 2011), there is little in town for the visitor looking for distraction.

Better to walk up to the summit of **Mount Stronach** or drive west on the B81 to Nabowla and, up a short side road, to the **Bridestowe Estate Lavender Farm ⑩** (daily; Nov–Apr 9am–5pm; May, Sept–Oct 10am–4pm; June–Aug by appointment; free except Dec–Jan; tel: 6352 8182).

Originally set up in 1921, Bridestowe has become one of the largest commercial lavender farms in the world. Tightly planted parallel rows of flowers roll across 48 hectares (120 acres) of open fields, creating patterns and symmetries that might, were you to stretch a point, be dubbed a living art installation. Even outside the peak flowering time of December and January, the setting warrants a visit. In the summer months there are guided tours and explanations of the process that sees tons of the harvested flowers distilled down into each drum of lavender oil. At other times a video tells the story.

A shop sells all things lavender, including honey from bees on the estate, and there is also a café.

WARNING
BEES AT WORK
PLEASE DO
NOT WALK
BETWEEN ROWS

Lilydale

A winding road through the hills leads to **Lilydale** ⑪. On the final approach, at a picturesque picnic area, a walking track leads to **Lilydale Falls**. It's a nice stroll through the trees, and the falls, although comparatively small, reward the effort.

Visitors to Lilydale itself are unlikely to need to leave the main street. The unique selling point is the parade of power-supply poles which have been attacked by various local artists and are now covered in whatever the pole equivalent to a mural is called. They take local themes for inspiration and, while some are accomplished, others are obviously the work of school or playgroup projects. Or of the naïve school.

The historic **Bardenhagen's General Store** (1888) has similar daubs on its interior walls. Elsewhere on the main road there are well-preserved Victorian shops and houses, offset by Mount Arthur in the background. Antique and craft shops do their best to attract tourists.

Off the road westwards to Lalla is **Walker's Rhododendron Reserve**, set up by Frank Walker at the end of the 19th Century. There are exotic trees and extensive gardens, featuring rhododendrons more than 60 years old, and vibrant displays of daffodils and other spring bulb flowers. (Sept–mid Dec, Apr–May daily 9am–6pm; Mid Dec–Mar Sat–Sun 9am–6pm; free.)

From Lilydale it is a 30-km (19-mile) drive to Launceston. ❑

Map on page 154

Honey is produced all over Tasmania. Each area's distinctive flavour depends on the local flora.

RESTAURANTS

Restaurants

Angasi
64a Binalong Bay Rd,
Binalong Bay
Tel: 6376 8222
Open: L & D daily. **$$$**
There are few places anywhere in the world as stunningly beautiful as the Bay of Fires. Angasi takes full advantage of the view – order fresh oysters, Tasmanian crayfish or the fresh catch of the day while sipping a crisp Tasmanian Riesling on the deck.

Weldborough Hotel
Tasman Highway,
Welsborough
Tel: 6254 2223
Open: L & D daily. **$**
Wacky menus entice

tourists inside to find out what is going on. Some good pub grub available here.

Gladstone Hotel
Chaffey St, Gladstone
Tel: 6357 2143
Open: L & D daily. **$**
A very traditional hotel in one of Tasmania's most interesting mining areas, serving honest food such as roasts and good steaks.

Joseph's
Bridport Resort, 35 Main St,
Bridport
Tel: 6356 1238
Open: D Tues-Sat. **$$**
A beautiful resort and dining room overlooking the sparking waters and pure-white sands of the northeast.

Cafés and pubs

Berries Café
Main St, Derby
Tel: 6354 2520
Open: L daily. **$**
A good place for a coffee and a snack in this historic old mining town.

The Flying Teapot Garden Café
1800 Bridport Rd, Bridport
(3 km/2 miles south)
Tel: 6356 1918
Open: L Wed-Sun. **$**
Some 3 km (2 miles) from Bridport, this is possibly the only café in Tasmania where you taxi your plane to the front door. Non-aviators also welcome!

Holy Cow! Café
St Columba Falls Road,
Pyengana
Tel: 6373 6157
Open: L daily. **$**

Attached to the Pyengana cheese factory, this is a great place to stop for cakes and biscuits cooked on the premises and very good coffee. You can also sample Pyengana cheddar here.

Pub In the Paddock
St Columba Falls Road,
Pyengana
Tel: 6373 6121
Open: L & D daily. **$**
This Pyengana icon has been a draw for tourists for many years. People come for the incongruity of the location, the country cooking and the nice, cold beer.

● ● ● ● ● ● ● ● ● ● ● ●
Prices for three-course dinner per person with a half-bottle of house wine.
$ = under A$50
$$ = A$50–A$75
$$$ = over A$75
L=lunch, D=dinner

LAUNCESTON AND THE TAMAR VALLEY

The third oldest city in Australia has a gracious, well-kempt air and plenty to keep visitors occupied, while an excursion up the Tamar Valley offers gorgeous countryside and a host of bacchanalian temptations

Visit Launceston and you find a city of elegant Victorian buildings, comfortable houses and lush parkland, all shaped by the Tamar River and its two sidekicks, the North Esk and South Esk. It is a relaxed, friendly place doing its best to shake off the image of the staid, rather dull cousin to the more outgoing Hobart, 200 km (125 miles) to the south. There is some way to go yet, and with a population half the size, Launceston will never compete on level terms in every area. Nor would it want to.

However what it does well, it does very well. Food, for instance. Strong arguments could be made that it has the best restaurants in the state, especially now that star chef Meyjitte Boughenout has left Strahan's Franklin Manor and moved to Queensland.

And new developments, such as the Inveresk precinct, demonstrate the city's commitment to attracting visitors, not just from Tasmania, but from mainland Australia and beyond. The blockbuster exhibition of French painting that was curated at the Queen Victoria Museum's new Inveresk Art Gallery in 2005 attracted hundreds across the Bass Strait. That these numbers haven't been sustained is no real surprise, but it does point up the anomaly of investing millions of dollars in creating world-class museums and exhibition spaces in a city of just 98,000 inhabitants.

There is plenty more to the city, not least the spectacular Cataract Gorge, just a few minutes' walk from the centre; few other cities have such natural wonders in such close proximity. And in the Tamar Valley, it has a readily accessible swathe of peaceful countryside, dotted with vineyards and market gardens, ideal for relaxing and indulgent days out.

Maps: pages 164, 172

LEFT cruising up Cataract Gorge.
BELOW: Boag's Centre for Beer Lovers in Launceston.

Early settlers

It is at the mouth of the Tamar Valley that the history of **Launceston** ❶ begins. Back in 1798 Matthew Flinders and George Bass were the first Europeans to discover the river, naming it Port Dalrymple. The name today applies to the tidal estuary of the Tamar, which extends inland past George Town and Beauty Point. after Alexander Dalrymple, an eminent hydrographer in the British Admiralty. Six years later came the first settlement in a pre-emptive move by Governor Philip Gidley King in Hobart, who was concerned at French interest in Van Diemen's Land.

King sent Colonel William Paterson and a small force of men to the area and they set up the first camp at what is now George Town, formally staking a claim to the north of the island in November 1804. Not long afterwards an expedition came upon the current site of Launceston. Paterson moved his base there in 1806 and came up with the name Patersonia for the settlement. The name was changed the following year in deference to Governor King's birthplace. It should be noted

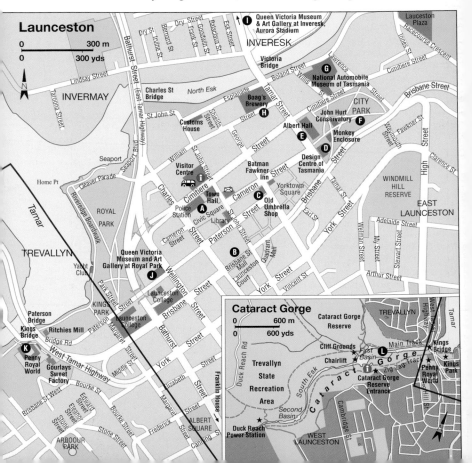

that for this Launceston, unlike its namesake in Cornwall, all three syllables are pronounced. The main military base moved back to George Town in 1819, but it was Launceston that continued to prosper.

In 1824 it was declared a township and, more significantly, took over from George Town as the main settlement in the north. Its growth was fuelled by the wheat and wool industries for which it became a key port, although it was still officially classified as a military town and headquarters of the Van Diemen's Land northern military command.

The population grew steadily, and following the official end of military control in 1846, a spate of new houses and roads were built. The discovery of gold at Beaconsfield in the 1870s cemented its status and led to a further flurry of construction. This is when the Launceston of today began to take shape and explains why, although it is the third oldest city in Australia after Sydney and Hobart, it has a smaller proportion of Georgian-style buildings than might be expected.

Civic Square

It is the lavish civic and domestic buildings from the latter half of the 19th century which give Launceston much of its character, and any exploration of the city is bound to take in a good number of them. The **Visitor Centre** (Mon–Fri 9am–5pm, Sat 9am–3pm, Sun 9am–noon; tel: 6336 3133) on the corner of Cimitiere and St John streets has maps and a self-guided heritage walk – which numbers the sights in an apparently random order.

In the next block south from the Visitor Centre is the grand **Post Office**. It was built from 1888 to 1889 and its distinctive clock tower was added in 1903. It faces the imposing **Town Hall** with its serried white columns.

The Town Hall is on a block which forms the **Civic Square Ⓐ**, a pedestrianised concourse surrounded by a disparate group of buildings. It includes **Macquarie House**, an 1830 stone warehouse of stark simplicity compared to its Italianate municipal neighbour.

Passing through the square, look

The coat of arms on Launceston's Town Hall features a pair of Tasmanian tigers.

BELOW: Cameron Street – a typically well-preserved street in central Launceston.

A detail of a seat in the Tasmanian Wood Collection.

down Cameron Street, opposite, for a taste of pure Victoriana: brick terraced houses with ornate ironwork opposite the dominant Supreme Court. Turn left onto Charles Street, past the next block and left again down **Brisbane Street Mall** Ⓑ. This is the heart of downtown shopping in Launceston and features many of the prime chain stores from the mainland as well as smaller local outlets. The atmosphere is relaxed and friendly enough to melt the staunchest of shopping phobics.

Leaving the traffic-free section and continuing eastwards, the **Quadrant Mall** curls off to the right, and boasts more classic 19th century structures. On the next block, just past the Princess Theatre and on the opposite side of the road, is a lane through to **Yorktown Square**, a modern development attempting to create a small-scale Victorian shopping atmosphere with predictable results. More rewarding is to exit onto George Street, turn right and seek out the **Old Umbrella Shop** Ⓒ (Mon–Fri 9am–5pm, Sat 9am–noon; free). Built in

1860, it was fitted out as an umbrella shop in 1918 and was managed continuously by the Shott family until the National Trust took it over in 1978. Umbrellas going back 100 years are on display, but it is the decor and fittings of the shop itself which create the atmosphere.

Turn right down Cameron Street past the **Batman Fawkner Inn** where the eponymous gentlemen planned their respective voyages across Bass Strait to Port Phillip Bay, where, ultimately, Batman founded the settlement which would become Melbourne. At the end of the street are the grand iron entrance gates to City Park.

Before going in, turn right and investigate the **Design Centre of Tasmania** Ⓓ housed in an appropriately imaginative complex on the edge of the park. Inside is the **Tasmanian Wood Design Collection** (daily 9.30am–5.30pm; admission charge; tel: 6331 5506; www.twdc.org.au), which showcases some impressive and genuinely innovative approaches to the use of wood in furniture and decorative

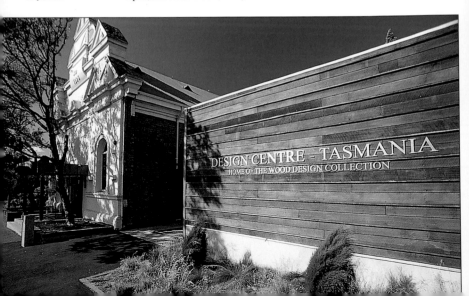

Map on page 164

objects. There are also changing exhibitions of work in other media, including paper, ceramics, textiles and jewellery. The adjoining shop sells work by some of Tasmania's best designers.

Turning back to the park gates and again refraining from going through them, have a look at **Albert Hall** ⓔ, an imposing pile built for a great colonial exhibition in 1891. Inside, if somebody can be persuaded to let you in, is an unusual water-powered concert organ.

City Park

Launceston's **City Park** ⓕ is the archetypal Victorian public garden. The grass is trimmed and the paths wind daintily from one feature to the next, be it the **Jubilee Fountain** in its ornate cast-iron splendour, the **Lithgow Rotunda** which is just crying out for a brass band to play in it, or the **John Hart Conservatory** with its carefully nurtured hothouse flowers. The duck ponds add to the ambience, and only the **Monkey Enclosure** is out of keeping. Not for the concept: the Victorians were great ones for transporting exotic fauna to display cages for the delectation of the genteel, but because it's a gleaming new construction. Pragmatism dictated it should be thus; it was discovered that the macaque monkeys, which had been housed in the park for years, were potential carriers of the Hepatitis B virus and so a new enclosure had to be designed sharpish to ensure there could be no simian-human contact.

Leave the park by the Cimitiere Street exit, on the opposite corner to the Design Centre, and across the road is the **National Automobile Museum of Tasmania** ⓖ (daily Sept–May 9am–5pm, June–Aug 10am–4pm; admission charge, tel: 6334 8888). There is nothing too sophisticated here, just rows and rows of cars from the oldest vintage models to shining new showroom examples. There are racing cars, a couple of pedal cars, and upstairs a similar mixture of old motorbikes. One section is reserved for a themed exhibition, the space often devoted to one marque, and this is changed every few months.

BELOW: nostalgia at the National Automobile Museum.

Track back along Cimitiere Street, turn right at the lights and take the first left down William Street. The whole block on the right is taken up by **Boag's Brewery** , which various tourist authority publications claim makes the world's best beer. Find out if this unlikely claim stands up to scrutiny by taking a brewery tour. It's a chance to see the brewing and packaging processes (while wearing natty fluorescent "VIP" vests), followed by some comprehensive sampling. You even get a bit of local cheese thrown in.

If time or timings are against you, there is still the **Boag's Centre for Beer Lovers**, which has displays and memorabilia from the brewery as well as a merchandise outlet (Mon–Fri 8.45am–4.30pm; free; tours Mon–Fri 9am; admission charge; tel: 6332 6300; www.boags.com.au).

Inveresk Cultural Precinct

Return to Tamar Street, turn left and cross the bridge. On the right is a vast open space with railway lines weaving across a large car park. The old railway workshops and surroundings have been converted into the **Inveresk Cultural Precinct**, whose keynote feature is the **Queen Victoria Museum and Art Gallery at Inveresk** (daily 10am–5pm; free; tel: 6323 3777; www.qvmag.tas.gov.au). This complex occupies one third of the main workshop – the rest being taken up by the Academy of the Arts, under the auspices of the University of Tasmania and TAFE Tasmania – as well as a collection of former workshops and foundries behind it.

The main **Art Gallery** houses *Aspects of Tasmanian Art*, a selection of works from the museum's collection designed to provide an overview of Tasmanian art from early colonial times onwards. Also to be found are Aboriginal artefacts, including intricate shell necklaces, as well as items from the Pacific islands and the museum's Asian collection. There is a sense of restraint, the work hung sparsely and to good effect. The **Ian Potter Gallery** houses temporary art exhibitions.

A café is sited under a huge old

BELOW: an artist at work in the Blacksmith Shop in the Queen Victoria Museum and Art Gallery at Inveresk.

crane, and it is the industrial heritage which is to the fore in the remaining spaces. The **Railways in Tasmania** gallery is full of locomotives, carriages and equipment from the days when rail was pre-eminent, and there are a few automotive and aeronautical pieces, which would also have been serviced by the workshop's engineers.

A small but affecting room devoted to migration to Tasmania leads out into a courtyard adjacent to the Traverse Way. This is a central track past a motley line of huts housing various specialist departments. Rolling stock would be mounted on a platform and then trucked along the rails to the wheel shop, paint shop, or other workshop according to need. The rolling platform is still there.

The various workshops have explanatory boards outside and a few are open for inspection. The highlight is the **Blacksmith Shop**. This large, filthy-looking barn of a building has been left intact, with tools and machinery abandoned as if the workers have just nipped out

for a break. It is highly atmospheric, especially with the "soundscape", which recreates the racket of the workshop as it would have sounded at full tilt, with grinders, drills and hammers assailing your eardrums. Elsewhere in the precinct there is a commercial art gallery, bar and parklands.

A short distance to the north is **Aurora Stadium**, also known as York Park. This is used for major sporting events, such as the 2003 Rugby World Cup tournament and, primarily, AFL, or Aussie rules as it's better known. Overseas visitors should try to see a live match of this free-flowing, full-blooded sport. The season runs from March to September. Tasmania does not have a team of its own but the Hawthorn and St Kilda teams from Melbourne each play a couple of "home" games here each year.

Penny Royal

Cross the bridge back towards the centre of the city and turn right along the bank where the **Riveredge Boardwalk** runs all the way round

Map on page 164

Railways in Tasmania flourished in the 19th century, but decline set in and the final regular passenger service ran in 1978.

BELOW LEFT: Chinese Temple detail. **BELOW RIGHT:** dinosaur head. Both items are in the Queen Victoria Museum and Art Gallery at Royal Park.

Fort Island with its defensive cannons at Penny Royal World.

BELOW: a short trip on the *Sandpiper* is part of the programme at Penny Royal World.

to Cataract Gorge. The overbearing white building with its Palladian portico is the **Customs House** of 1885. Past that, beyond the bridge carrying the East Tamar Highway, is the new **Seaport** development, complete with restaurants, bars and a marina. Pass round Home Point, where the North Esk River joins the Tamar, and follow the edge of Royal Park to Park Street, where the Tamar Yacht Club is based. Leave the waterside and turn left on Paterson Street and left again on Wellington.

The second building along is the **Queen Victoria Museum and Art Gallery at Royal Park ❿**, the sister to the museum at Inveresk. This is much more traditional in layout and presentation. There are display cases of stuffed animals, dinosaur skeletons and, in the ceramics section, historic porcelain artefacts propped up on shelves. Its **Discovery Plus** gallery is a large child-friendly space with a lot of hands-on activity available – much better than the rather half-hearted **PlayZone** at Inveresk. Of note here is a **Chinese Temple** from Weldborough *(see*

page 156) and the **Planetarium** (daily 10am–5pm; free; admission charge for Planetarium; tel: 6323 3777; www.qvmag.tas.gov.au).

Either rejoin the Riveredge boardwalk or follow Paterson Street westwards. Just before the flyover, **Ritchies Mill** sits by the water. The mill ground flour for 137 years and now houses a gallery, shop and one of Launceston's best restaurants: Stillwater *(see page 180)*.

On the other side of the road an old windmill can be seen behind an attractive property of weather-beaten stone. The windmill is old but its setting is new; it was transplanted from an original site near Cressy, 30 km (19 miles) to the south. It comes under the aegis of the complex just beyond the flyover, **Penny Royal World ⓚ**. Here, under towering rocky cliffs, where a waterfall crashes down, another old mill has been extended into a small theme park (daily 9am–4.30pm; admission charge; tel: 6331 3377; www.penny royalworld.com.au).

Visitors are directed to their "barge", a boat that travels automat-

ically along a canal through underground gunpowder mills and then a cannon foundry. Mannequins demonstrate various parts of the casting process as an audio commentary fills in the detail. Outside, a small sloop sails out on a mini lake and visitors can help fire the cannons. It's not as naff as it sounds. OK, it is, but great fun nonetheless. There are motel rooms which overlook the site and lucky guests may see the waterfall being turned off after closing time.

An original Launceston city tram links this site to another down the road, where there are windmill and cornmill museums and the small, working **Gourlays Sweet Factory**. The tram isn't always running.

Cataract Gorge

It is a very short stroll from here to King's Bridge over the South Esk River at the mouth of **Cataract Gorge ❶**. Pathways run either side of the river and fitness levels, as much as anything else, are likely to determine which one you take. The Zig Zag track on the south side is steep and testing but climbs high to give terrific views, whereas the track on the north side stays much lower and any inclines are gentle. The views here are still good because this is a natural wonder which looks splendid from any perspective. Serious photographers might want to look at taking the Zig Zag trail in the morning and the Main Walk in the afternoon, that way getting the best angles of sun on rock.

The Main Walk takes only a few minutes to get to the **Cliff Grounds** area above the First Basin, just as long as you don't dawdle and insist on stopping at each lookout to take in the view. The trouble is, turning each corner reveals another heart-stopping vista and, before you know it, an hour has passed. The Cliff Grounds were laid out as formal gardens in Victorian times, perhaps as an antidote to the untamed forces of nature which didn't always know their place. The picturesque **Lithgow Rotunda** now contains interpretive displays.

Paths head off to various lookouts and there is also a café in which to

Map on page 164

BELOW:
Cataract Gorge.

Sailing the Gorge

Once you've walked along Cataract Gorge, sampled the chairlift and had a dip in the pool, it's time for a little relaxation on board one of the small cruise ships that sails as far upstream as it can get, cliffs towering above on either side. There is a choice of vessel: the modern *Tamar Odyssey* or the *Lady Launceston*, an ersatz 1890s pleasure cruiser. Both offer commentary and refreshments and, depending on the package, the chance to sip some champagne as the sun drops down behind the hills. Contact Tamar River Cruises; Home Point, Launceston; tel: 6334 9900; www.tamarrivercruises.com.au.

It's easy to navigate the Tamar Valley Wine Route by following the distinctive signs.

BELOW: There's plenty of wine tasting pauses on offer on a journey up the Tamar Valley.

replenish energy, perhaps with one of the local peacocks for company. After that, it's time to cross to the other side of the basin. There are two methods of doing this: the **Alexandra Suspension Bridge** offers a bouncy walk over, or there is the **Basin Chairlift** which, it is proudly claimed, contains the longest single chairlift span in the world.

Once across, there is a grassy area to relax in with a good-sized open-air swimming pool. This is a popular picnic spot, especially at weekends. The pool is open from November to March and is free, but there are no attendants.

Another walking track goes further upstream to the Second Basin and on to the **Duck Reach Power Station** which opened in 1895. It was instrumental in making Launceston the first city in the world to be lit by hydroelectricity. The walk is about 90 minutes return.

The chairlift stops operating in the early evening but there is access to the reserve around the clock. Floodlighting at night makes it an attractive spot for that romantic sojourn.

One of Launceston's other major sights is 8 km (5 miles) to the south of the centre. **Franklin House** (413–19 Hobart Road, Youngtown; Oct–Mar Mon–Sat 9am–5pm, Sun noon–4pm; Apr–Sept daily 9am–4pm; admission charge; tel: 6344 7824) was opened to the public in 1961 by the Tasmanian National Trust, which had been set up specifically to raise money to buy it. It is a Georgian house built in 1838 with convict labour for a local brewer. It was sold 4 years later and became a boys' school. Now the house has been restored to its original state with contemporaneous furniture and fittings, and the gardens are worth a visit in themselves.

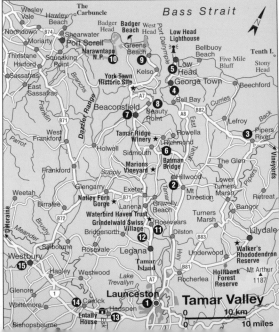

Maps: pages 164, 172

The Tamar Valley

The Tamar River is the artery that first gave life to Launceston and now, long after most of the river traffic has dried up, the flow has been reversed. A trip up the beautiful Tamar Valley is on the itinerary of the majority of visitors to the city, whether it be to take in the historic sites, the fruit farms or, increasingly, the vineyards.

There is an acknowledged **Tamar Valley Wine Route**, complete with uniform signage (blue grapes on a yellow background), which takes in over 20 wineries. This entails a loop up through Lilydale *(see page 161)* to Pipers Brook and then west, across Batman Bridge, and back to Launceston. Leaflets are available at visitor centres.

The main road up the east side of the valley (A8 East Tamar Highway) quickly leaves the city behind and bounds through rolling, sometimes wooded, countryside. There are a few turnoffs down to the water. Take the one at Mount Direction, 25 km (15 miles) north, and follow it round to **Hillwood** ❷, where the well-established **Strawberry Farm** (daily 8am–5pm) is worth a stop for a spot of indulgence, with free wine and cheese tastings to go with the berries. Look out for the bright red, if rusting, steam locomotive parked outside.

Stay on the attractive coast road until it rejoins the highway and continue north towards George Town. About 5 km (3 miles) before the town, the B82 veers off to the east – this is the road to take for some serious wine tasting. The **Pipers River** ❸ area is as renowned as the Tamar Valley for its cool-climate wines, with the emphasis on sparkling, riesling and chardonnay varieties. Although the very first wine growing in Australia was attempted here, the modern era dates from 1974 and the establishment of **Pipers Brook Vineyard**. Others soon followed. There is a self-drive tour through the vineyard ending, inevitably, at the tasting room where Ninth Island wines are also on offer (1216 Pipers Brook Road; daily 10am–5pm; tel: 6382 7527; www.pipersbrook.com).

Nearby is the **Jansz Wine Room**

BELOW:
a home maid – time has stood still at the Grove in George Town.

Detail of the Departures and Arrivals *installation by Christina Henri at the Watch House in George Town.*

BELOW:
Low Head Pilot Station.

and Interpretive Centre where this well-regarded sparkling wine is showcased in a modern tasting centre (daily 10am–5pm; tel: 6382 7066; www.jansztas.com). Elsewhere in the area **Dalrymple Vineyards** (daily 10am–5pm; tel 6382 7222; www.dalrymplevineyards.com.au) and **Delamare Vineyard** (daily 10am–5pm; tel: 6382 7190; www.dalrymplevineyard.com) also offer tastings. On the way back to the west the **Bay of Fires Winery** (daily 10am–5pm; tel: 6382 7622; www.hardywines.com.au) can be found just south of Pipers River.

Historic settlements

George Town ❹ is where settlement on the Tamar River commenced after Paterson's first landing in 1804. Its fortunes fluctuated over the years with a boom in the 1830s, when it was the major trading port on the north coast. A decline set in in the 1840s, until there was a flicker of prosperity in the 1860s when a landing point for the Bass Strait telegraph cables was established, and in the 1870s gold was discovered at Lefroy, a little way inland. By 1900 there were 5,000 inhabitants. It's close to that figure now, with the aluminium plant at Bell Bay the main economic driver.

A good visitor centre on the way into town can supply a brochure for a self-guided heritage trail. This takes in all the significant historic buildings, many of them from the 1830s and 1840s, and all in a good state of repair; this is a town with a real pride in its past. A highlight is the **Watch House**, a museum with a model village showing George Town in the early 19th century, and an installation, *Departures and Arrivals*, which is a simple, moving tribute to the women who served in the town's female factory. There is also a cell fitted out as it would have been when the building was used as a lockup (Macquarie Street; Sept–May Mon–Fri 10am–4pm, Sat–Sun noon–2pm; June–Aug Mon–Fri 10am–3pm, Sat–Sun noon–2pm; donation requested).

The Grove is a handsome *c.*1835 house, complete with maids' quarters in the attic, done up throughout in period style, as are the guides who provide access when not serving in the café. Formal gardens complete the picture (25 Cimitiere Street; Sun–Fri 10.30am–4pm; admission charge; tel: 6382 1336).

Around 5 km (3 miles) further north at the mouth of Port Dalrymple is **Low Head ❺**. The **Pilot Station** feels a little like a village, with its scattering of white-painted National Trust-listed houses clustered around a green, white picket fences keeping everything in order. One of the buildings in the John Lee Archer-designed Pilots Row now houses a **Maritime Museum** (daily 9am–5pm or "late"; admission charge; tel: 6382 1143; www.lhhp.com.au), stuffed with displays and mementoes celebrating the pivotal role played by the station from the

Map on page 172

early days of settlement onwards. Pilot boats still go out to guide ships through the tricky waters of the Tamar. Some of the cottages are available as holiday accommodation and the beaches make it an attractive proposition for families.

The **Low Head Lighthouse** (1888) is at the top of the peninsula where there are views across the Tamar on one side and to immaculate beaches stretching along the northeast coast on the other. The foghorn is tested each Sunday at noon. On the hill to the south of the lighthouse is a reconstructed mast with semaphore signal arms, the first stage in a relay to the pilot station and on, by stages, to Launceston. It was set up at the behest of merchants wanting progress reports on their ships, which could sometimes be delayed for days by adverse tidal conditions.

Other local attractions include the tiny weatherboard **Christ Church** opposite the Pilot Station entrance, and the **penguin rookery**. (Low Head Penguin Tours; daily, dusk; admission charge; tel: 0418 361 860; www.penguintours.com.au.)

Divers rave about the area, a rare spot where there is a range of habitats, including a steep drop off very close to land, providing a profusion of marine life.

Across the Tamar

The western side of the Tamar Valley is more populous, although largely unspoiled. For foot and bike passengers there are ferries from Low Head and George Town to Beauty Point (Nov–Apr Wed–Sun three times daily; tel: 6383 4479; www.shuttlefishferry.com.au), but for drivers there is a short drive south to the B73, which crosses **Batman Bridge ❻**.

The bridge is distinctive for being suspended from a tower at only one end; a pragmatic design resulting

from the ground only being firm enough on one bank.

Either take in the **Tamar Ridge Winery** at Kayena (Auburn Road; daily 10am–5pm; tel: 6394 7000; www.tamarridgewines.com.au), or pass through Sidmouth on the way to the West Tamar Highway and turn right to **Beaconsfield ❼**. It wasn't until 1879 that the town was given this name and by then, under other identities, it had already been the centre of limestone quarrying and iron ore extraction before the defining moment at the beginning of the 1870s when serious gold mining commenced. By 1900 it was the third largest town in Tasmania. The decline came when problems of water seepage proved insurmountable and the mine closed in 1914.

Today's technology has allowed mining to start up again, although the accident that led to worldwide coverage of the plight of two miners trapped underground for two weeks in 2006 has put its future in doubt. Either way, it is the residue of the old workings that creates the centrepiece of the town's main

Batman Bridge spanning the Tamar is the only vehicle crossing point north of Launceston.

BELOW: Marions Vineyard is one of several wineries situated on the banks of the Tamar.

Steam engine outside the Grubb Shaft Museum, which is located in the old pit-head buildings

BELOW: miner's cottage at the Grubb Shaft Museum in Beaconsfield.

tourist atttraction: the **Grubb Shaft Museum** (daily; Oct–Apr 9.30am–4.30pm, May–Sept 10am– 4pm; admission charge; tel: 6383 1473). The main buildings – the boiler house and engine houses – contain equipment, minerals and historical displays linked to the mine as well as broader exhibits, including steam engines and a reconstructed post office. An external walkway takes in some of the ruins of the old mine and leads to the water wheel, which powers the ore stamper. Press the button and prepare to be deafened. A platform allows views over the modern working mine, while outside the main complex there is an original miner's cottage, a general store and an old school.

Beauty Point ❽ is a sleepy little place only enlivened by the presence of the **Australian Maritime College**. Until, that is, you get to Inspection Head Wharf, where two well-presented enterprises compete for your attention. **Seahorse World** is part farm, part research centre and part tourist attraction (daily 9.30am–4pm; tours every half hour;

admission charge; tel: 6383 4111; www.seahorseworld. com.au). Guided tours of the stables, or tanks as they call them, explain the lifecycle of the creatures and the threats they face from over-fishing. The display occupies a bright, modern centre with an attractive waterfront café.

Platypus House offers a similar species-specific attraction (daily 9am–4pm; admission charge; tel: 6383 4260; www.platypushouse. com.au). Given the difficulty in spotting a platypus in the wild, this is the easy way to see them frolicking in and out of the water. Echidnas as well as various frogs, lizards and insects complete the picture, and are all covered in the hour-long guided tours.

The highway continues to **York Town**, significant as the site of an early encampment on the Tamar but little else, and on to the small waterside settlements of **Kelso** and **Greens Beach** ❾. The latter, particularly, has an appealing tree-lined foreshore and an endless shallow beach. Numerous holiday houses have been erected along this stretch by those in the know. Stay

with the road and it enters the eastern end of the **Narawntapu National Park ⑩**. The road runs out near a viewpoint across **Badger Beach**, which stretches endlessly away to the east. It's another of those glimpses of paradise that Tasmania seems to throw off effortlessly.

It's possible to reach the other end of the beach by a dirt road (C721) which leaves the highway shortly before York Town. The beach is safe for swimming and good for fishing.

South of Batman Bridge

The best way to see the West Tamar Valley south of Batman Bridge is to take the C728 coast road just before the crossing. Some 5 km (3 miles) south is **Marions Vineyard**, one of the more picturesque wineries yet strangely not on the official wine route (Foreshore Drive, Deviot; daily 10am–5pm; tel: 6394 7434; www.marionsvineyard.com). It's well worth a stop for both the wines and the setting. Not far to the south there is a good short walk to be had up the boulder-strewn **Supply River** to the ruins of the state's first water-driven flour mill; and then it's one panorama after another as the road meanders past the boats bobbing off **Gravelly Beach**.

There is a brief return to the highway before the turnoff to **Rosevears ⑪**, where there's a choice between the historic **Rosevears Hotel** and its fabulous views across the river, or the **Rosevears Estate** winery and its equally fabulous views across the river (Rosevears Estate Winery Cellar Door and Restaurant; daily 10am–5pm; tel: 6330 1800; www.rosevearsestate.com.au).

The **Waterbird Haven Trust** is a sanctuary on the Tamar River mudflats where formal introduction can be made to all the birdlife that has been flitting across the river views (Rosevears Drive; daily 9am–dusk; tel: 6394 3744).

For an altogether more bizarre experience, take the road off to the west of the highway to **Grindelwald ⑫**, where a resort hotel has been created as a Swiss alpine village, complete with chalets, a church and a main square. The word "why?" rises unbidden but, if you can accept the initial premise, it has been executed as well as it could be and is an intriguing place to spend half an hour.

Final stop on the way down to Launceston is **Tamar Island**. A boardwalk from a car park just off the West Tamar Highway runs to a futuristic information centre and then across to the 7-hectare (17-acre) island. It is a 4-km (2½-mile) wheelchair-friendly return walk across this low-lying wetlands reserve and provides a chance to spot lots of birds and other wildlife.

West of Launceston

To the west of Launceston lie a handful of colonial villages of interest.

Hadspen ⑬ has some significant Georgian structures, including the **Red Feather Inn**, a chunky

BELOW: tackling the Westbury Maze.

sandstone construction of 1844, and the **Gaol** (*c*. 1840). The main lure, however, is **Entally House** (daily 10am–4pm; admission charge; tel: 6393 6201), situated a short distance to the east. This grand mansion, built around 1819 on the banks of the South Esk River by shipping magnate Thomas Haydock Reibey, has been preserved with Regency furniture and detailing. The grounds contain formal flowerbeds, a walled garden and an ancient conservatory, all kept in shape by an army of venerable volunteers. There are also stables, a coach house and a chapel. In an unusual move, Gunns, the giant forestry company, took over management of the site in 2005 and there is talk of a restaurant and retail outlet. The volunteers are keeping a wary eye on the trees.

It is but a short drive west to the tiny settlement of **Carrick** ⓮, which is also chock-full of listed buildings. Most notable is the old **Mill House**, its four bluestone storeys covered in ivy. Up the hill alongside it are the desiccated remains of **Archers Folly** and beyond it the **Tasmanian Copper and Metal Art Gallery** (Mon–Fri 9.30am–5pm) where various metals are wrought, overwrought even, into extravagant artworks and ornaments.

Westbury

Westbury ⓯ is another 15 km (9 miles) to the west. On the approach along the Meander Valley Road you may be delayed at **Westbury Maze** (10 Meander Valley Road; daily 10am–5pm; admission charge; tel: 6393 1840), where the traditional box hedge has been used to channel explorers up a succession of dead ends. For those who escape there is a tearoom. Further up the road **Fitzpatrick's Inn**, a lovely old colonial hostelry from the 1830s, offers rooms and a restaurant.

Opposite the inn is the rambling collection of old transport that makes up **Pearn's Steam World** (65 Meander Valley Road; daily 9am–4pm; admission charge). Two huge barns are crammed with work-

BELOW: the greenhouse at Entally House.

Map on page 172

ing steam traction engines, tractors, agricultural machinery and anything else that the Pearn brothers (Jack, Verdun and Zenith) could lay their hands on over the decades. Steam, it appears, was not a prerequisite. It is a ramshackle place, clearly founded on enthusiasm and sheer obsession, and has all the advantages and drawbacks that go with that.

The centre of Westbury is as close to old England as it gets in Australia. There is a village green, overlooked by the archetype of an Anglican church (**St Andrew's**, 1836), there are oaks and elms, hawthorn hedge-rows and, once a year, a maypole is erected. Admittedly this comes out for the St Patrick's Festival in March, which might raise eyebrows in the mother country, but then a good proportion of the soldiers and convicts to settle in the area were from Ireland. That one of the town's superfluity of historic buildings is **George Best's House** (*c*.1850) is anachronistic coincidence.

At the southern end of the green, the **White House** (Tues–Sun 10am– 4pm; admission charge; tel: 6393 1171) is an old corner store and working bakery with adjoining stables and coach house. Built about 1841 by Thomas White, it is now run by the National Trust and includes, along with the regulation antique furniture and china, some vintage vehicles and a comprehensive toy collection. The enormous Pendle Hall doll's house – all 20 rooms of it – is truly astonishing in its detail.

Westbury was laid out in 1828 under the direction of Governor Arthur to be a major stopover on the route from Hobart to the northwest and many of the buildings date from this period. An Irish Army detachment was stationed here – the village green was originally the parade ground – but then growth stagnated. It seems, however, that everything that was built has been immaculately preserved, and a random stroll through the tree-lined streets reveals one gem after another. The free *Find Yourself in Historical Westbury* map has a good self-guided historical walk. ❏

The White House on the village green in Westbury.

BELOW: the Swiss-style resort at Grindelwald.

RESTAURANTS, CAFÉS AND BARS

Restaurants

Launceston

Cataract Bistro
135 Paterson St
Tel: 6334 1355
Open: L & D daily. **$$**
Despite the slightly function centre-like atmosphere, this is one the best places in town for a good-quality casual meal. A menu of French-leaning bistro specialities – slow-cooked onion soup, cured trout, pork sausages and apple tart.

Dockside Café and Wine Bar
27 Seaport Boulevard
Tel: 6331 0711
www.launcestonseaport.com
Open: L daily, D Mon-Sat. **$$$**
Very popular dining room within the Seaport precinct, its outside tables are especially coveted in warm weather.

Elaia
240 Charles St
Tel: 6331 3307
Open: L & D daily. **$$**
You can drop in here all day, but stylish Elia is much more than a café. It's good for an informal

lunch or dinner, with a good range of light and substantial dishes.

Fee and Me
190 Charles St
Tel: 6331 3195
www.feeandme.com.au
Open: D Tues-Sat. **$$$**
Launceston dresses up to go to Fee and Me – its grand dining rooms, meticulously prepared dishes, good service and excellent glassware and crockery ensure the full dining experience.

Fish 'n' Chips
30 Seaport Boulevard,
Tel: 6331 1999
Open: L & D daily. **$**
Great place to take the kids for a quick, almost self-serve, waterside fish and chip experience. BYO.

Hallam's Waterfront
13 Park St
Tel: 6334 0554
Open: L & D daily. **$$**
Seafood is the speciality here – find out what's fresh and order it simply cooked.

Jail House Grill
32 Wellington St
Tel: 6331 0466
www.jailhousegrill.com.au
Open: L Fri, D daily. **$$**
Just the place when you're ready for a serious piece of chargrilled meat.

La Cantina
63 George St

Tel: 6331 7835
Open: L & D daily. **$$**
Something of an institution, La Cantina has an extensive menu of all the old favourites you expect to see in a long-established Australian-Italian restaurant. BYO.

Luck's
70 George St
Tel: 6334 8596
Open: L & D daily. **$$**
A small place with oodles of style. There's a great wine list and an interesting menu.

Market Square
St John & William Sts,
Launceston
Tel: 6333 7555
Open: L & D daily. **$$$**
Some of the best hotel dining around, Market Square adds to the appeal of the boutique Cornwall Hotel as a place to bunk down for the night – stylishly of course.

Me Wah
39-41 Invermay Rd, Invermay
Tel: 6331 1308
Open: L & D Tues-Sun. **$$**
Arguably the best Chinese food in the state. Dumplings, abalone and duck are recommended.

Mud Bar and Restaurant
28 Seaport Boulevard
Tel: 6334 5066
Open L & D daily. **$$**
One of the most satisfying dining experiences in

town, with delicious pasta dishes, big grills served with garlic and rosemary roast potatoes, and delicious desserts. A relaxed tone coupled with the waterside location always works a treat.

Novaro's
28 Brisbane St
Tel: 6334 5589
Open: D Mon-Sat. **$$**
An intimate Italian dining room with some good Italian wines to match the food. BYO.

Smokey Joe's Creole Café
20 Lawrence St
Tel: 6331 0530
Open: L & D daily. **$**
The mood here is casual and informal. Lively flavours and fresh ingredients; try the house-smoked ribs.

Star of Siam
Paterson & Charles Sts
Tel: 6331 2786
Open: L & D daily. **$**
Lively Thai restaurant in a convenient city location. BYO.

Stillwater River Café
Ritchies Mill, Paterson St
Tel: 6331 4153
Open: L daily, D Mon-Sat. **$$$**
Don Cameron is one of the state's most innovative chefs and Stillwater one of its most awarded restaurants. His largely Asian-inspired dishes

are beautifully balanced and always exciting.

Tamar Valley

Daniel Alps at Strathlynn
95 Rosevears Drive, Rosevears
Tel: 6330 2388
Open: L daily. $$
If you're keen to try some of the best food in the north, make sure you schedule lunch here when you're touring the Tamar vineyards. Beautiful food, sourced from regional producers, in a magical location.

Hobnobs
47 William St, Westbury
Tel: 6393 2007
Open: L Sun, D Wed-Sat. $$$
On Sunday at lunchtime it's a good old-fashioned roast. For dinner Hobnobs offers a small, interesting and regularly changing menu, featuring local produce.

The Mill Inn
67 Bass Highway, Carrick
Tel: 6393 6922
Open: L & D daily. $
This old mill has a beautiful riverside location, which is especially pleasant on a warm afternoon.

Pier Hotel
5 Elizabeth St, George Town
Tel: 6382 1300
www.pierhotel.com.au
Open: L & D daily. $$
Located in an historic hotel that's had quite a makeover in recent years, the dining room

has plenty of choices – including seafood, pasta, salads, pizza, and steak.

Rosevears Estate
1a Waldhorn Drive, Rosevears
Tel: 6330 1800
www.rosevearsestate.com.au
Open: L Wed-Sun, D Fri-Sat. $$
A light and spacious restaurant perched on the hill overlooking the Tamar, with a menu designed to appeal widely.

Cafés and Bars

Launceston

Caffe Fiore
65-7 Cimitiere St
Tel: 6331 5146
Open: L daily. $
A tiny Italian café serving up a mean gnocchi.

Croplines Coffee Roasters
1 Brisbane Court
Tel: 6331 4023
Open: L Mon-Sat. $
Devoted to tea and coffee (literally, there's virtually no food), you're guaranteed a good pour here. Probably the best-made coffee in Launceston.

Cube
28 Seaport Boulevard
Tel: 6334 5066
Open: B daily. $
Breakfast venue for the Peppers Hotel, Cube opens early for hotel guests and the public. The outside waterside tables are relaxing.

Fresh on Charles
178 Charles St, Launceston
Tel: 6331 4299
Open: L Mon-Sat. $
Has more the feel of an alternative neighbourhood drop in centre than a café. But one with very good (late) breakfast options and delicious light lunches built around the freshest produce. BYO.

Metz
119 St John St
Tel: 6331 7277
Open: L & D daily. $
A good people-watching bar and cafe, Metz is one of Launceston city's most popular watering holes.

Pierres on George
88 George St
Tel: 6331 6835
Open: L & D Mon-Sat. $
Now probably serving its fourth generation of lunching ladies, Pierre's was Launceston's first

taste of café society and it's still going strong.

Tant pour Tant
226 Charles St
Tel: 6334 9884
Open: L daily. $
Patisserie and café producing Launceston's most perfect pastries.

Ursula's Wine Bar
63 Brisbane St
Tel: 6334 7033
Open: L & D Tues-Sat. $$
If hotels are not your drinking scene then Ursula's provides a pleasant alternative.

Tamar Valley

Koukla's
285 Gravelly Beach Rd, Gravelly Beach
Tel: 6394 4013
Open: L & D daily. $
All-day dining overlooking the Tamar with a definite Greek flavour. Dinner is also available. BYO.

RIGHT: staples on Seaport Boulevard, Launceston.

THE NORTH AND NORTHWEST

An A-road links all the main coastal settlements to the west of Devonport, and every one of them has something to offer the visitor. Some side trips inland provide relief from the sea, sand and seafood

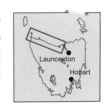

or many travellers to Tasmania, the first port of call will be **Devonport** , the set-down port for the two *Spirit of Tasmania* ships which operate out of Melbourne. It is by no means the most attractive place in the state, but neither should the first-time visitor make a swift getaway.

The ships dock on the industrialised east side of the city. You need to cross the bridge over the Mersey River for things to get interesting. Once on the west side, if you stay by the banks of the river and go north, the concrete peters out and lush grasslands make for an attractive foreshore. At the point where the Mersey feeds into Bass Strait, the road bends left and there stands the **Devonport Maritime Museum** (Tues–Sun, 10am–4.30pm summer, 10am–4pm winter; admission charge; tel: 6424 7100). It occupies the old pilot station and features a host of model ships of all eras along with ships' bells, flags and other mementoes.

Aboriginal Centre

As you follow the road around the coast, the promontory on the right is Mersey Bluff and at the end of it is a lighthouse. Before you reach that, however, there is the **Tiagarra Aboriginal Culture Centre and Museum** (daily; 9am–4.30pm;

admission charge; tel: 6424 8250). In this simple building, springing from the earth, you can get an overview of the Aboriginal presence in Tasmania and examples of arts, crafts and tools to go with the photographs and illustrations. The centre is especially renowned for its collection of 10,000-year-old rock carvings, some of which are displayed on a walking trail around the bluff. This underscores the tribes' profound links with the land in a way that housing the sculptures in a

LEFT Furner's Hotel in Ulverstone.
BELOW: penguin, Penguin.

An unusual mail cow. Wacky mail boxes can be found all over the state but the heaviest representation is in Wilmot.

museum could not possibly achieve.

Continuing on what is becoming a circuit around the city, the terminus for the **Don River Railway** is near the point where the Don River runs under the Bass Highway on the city's southwest corner. There is a collection of locomotives and carriages, restoration work to look at and regular short trips to Coles Beach near the Bluff. Note that the steam locomotives only run on Sundays and public holidays; diesels run the rest of the time (trains daily 10am–4pm, hourly; admission charge; tel: 6424 6335; www.donriverrailway.com.au).

Heading east and just to the south of the highway lies **Home Hill**, the erstwhile home of the only Tasmanian Prime Minister, Joseph Lyons, who served from 1932 to 1939 when he died. His widow, Dame Enid, subsequently became a member of the House of Representatives before becoming the first woman federal cabinet member, in 1949. The house is now run by the National Trust and is preserved as Dame Enid left it (77 Middle Rd; Jan–Apr Tues–Thur, Sat–Sun 11am–4pm; May–Dec Tues–Thur, Sat–Sun 2–4pm; admission charge; tel: 6424 3028).

Completing the circuit, head back up the bank of the river and inland just two blocks to the **Imaginarium Science Centre**, a hands-on, fully interactive, child-friendly introduction to the basic scientific principles underpinning everyday life (19–23 MacFie St; Mon–Thurs 10am–4pm, Sat–Sun noon–5pm; admission charge; tel: 6423 1466).

The final destination is the **Devonport Regional Art Gallery** in Stewart Street, which has changing exhibitions of mostly contemporary Australian art (Mon–Sat 10am–5pm, Sun 2–5pm; free; tel: 6424 8296).

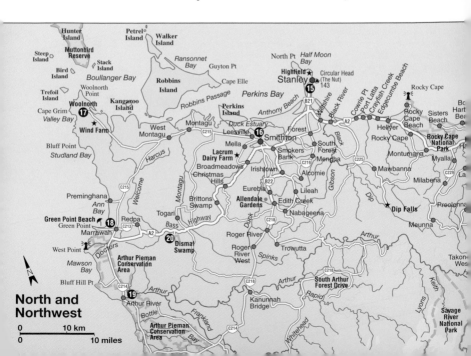

North and Northwest

Around Devonport

From Devonport, the Bass Highway leads east to **Latrobe ②**, all of 7 km (4 miles) away. As you come into Gilbert Street, immaculately preserved Victorian-era shops, banks and houses are lined up one after another. Seventy-six of them are heritage listed. Much of the pleasure is to be had just wandering up and down the street, dropping into cafés or shops, perhaps watching one of a number of artists or craftsmen at work in their studios/shops. For every jarring moment, like the tacky and poorly executed oversized platypus which should be enough to deter you from investigating the **Platypus Experience**, there's a tiny original architectural detail, or a dusty treasure to be found in one of the numerous antiques shops. For those who are interested in platypus, sightings of the real thing are a strong prospect at the Warrawee

Map below

Forest Reserve, 4.5 km (3 miles) south of town on the Mersey (daily 9am–dusk; free).

Back in Gilbert Street, the **Court-house Museum** preserves a historic courtroom and a hefty collection of old documents and photographs (Fri, Sun 2–5pm; admission charge). For a differently educative experience visit **Reliquaire**, a treasure trove of assorted mannequins, toys, automata, games and junk, which is part museum, part shop (daily 9am–5.30pm; free; tel: 6426 2599).

Altogether different in its appeal and the one attraction not in Gilbert Street, the **Australian Axeman's Hall of Fame** is to be found along the bank of the Mersey. This celebrates the achievements of champion woodchoppers over the years, with particular emphasis on the Foster family. David Foster, who has won more than 1,000 championships in his time, runs the place

Knotty but nice. Wooden figure outside the Platypus Experience.

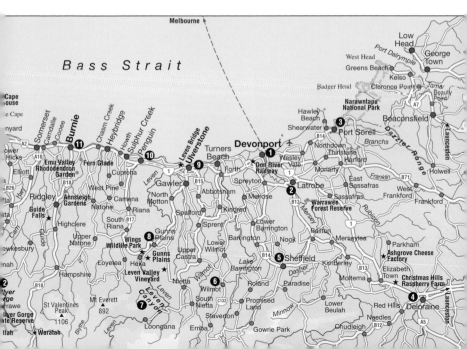

Careful with that axe...

I t is probably no surprise that, in the annals of wood chopping, six of the 13 "Legends of the Sport", inducted from all of Australia, are Tasmanians. This is a state, after all, where forestry has been central to political and economic life since its foundation. Perhaps the surprise is that wood chopping attracts sufficient following to make the Axeman's Hall of Fame in Latrobe a major tourist draw.

Legend has it that the sport originated in 1870 when two men in a bar in Ulverstone on Tasmania's north coast had a £25 bet on who could cut down a tree the quickest. Woodchop competitions subsequently became a staple of the annual agricultural shows, which evolved to become focal social gatherings for communities across the country, and to some extent still are.

As its popularity grew the rules were codified so that there are now three main categories of competition: for Standing Block the log is fixed vertically and the competitor chops at shoulder height, cutting a "scarf" or wedge shape from one side, then the other, until severing the two halves; in the Underhand category the block is horizontal in a cradle and the chopper cuts a flat platform before standing on it and cutting down between his feet, again working from one side and then the other; the most difficult and demanding category is Treefelling in which the axeman has to cut holes in a 4.6 metre (15 ft) trunk and insert boards to take him up to a point 3 metres (10 ft) off the ground where he then has to start the serious chopping. Once the first scarf has been cut he has to repeat the process the other side and then chop right through. Besides the axe work, there are one-man and two-man crosscut sawing competitions. And as for axe-throwing... let's leave that for another time.

Competitions are held in most countries where there is a timber industry and many of the participants work in the business even though technology has generally negated the need for hand-wielded axes and saws. The keenest followers are in the US and Canada, New Zealand, the UK, Ireland, Spain and a number of countries in Central Europe. Australians are reckoned to be the best at hardwood chopping while the Spaniards tend to dominate endurance events.

The Axeman's Hall of Fame is run by, in every sense of the word, a giant of the sport: David Foster. "The Foster Experience" section of the building makes it clear that it's something of a family affair. David started with his father, George, in the 1970s and the two of them won the World 600mm Double-Handed Sawing Championships for 11 years running. Brother Peter partnered David to the title for the next ten years. On his own David is the first man to have won over 1,000 championships, including 183 world titles, and was Australian Axeman of the Year an astonishing 9 years in a row. He still chops competitively and on occasion will demonstrate his skills at the Latrobe centre.

Nowadays the sport has less of a profile in Australia than in the heady days when it was a staple on TV. Yet the World Championships still sell out at the Royal Easter Show in Sydney. And there's a good chance that current star performer, Matthew Gurr, will take an award or two. Naturally, he's a Tasmanian. ❑

LEFT: David Foster, champion chopper.

and lays on chopping demonstrations for visiting groups. There's a museum, display area and café (daily 9am–5pm, closed Tues May–Aug; admission charge; tel: 6426 2099).

Northeast of Latrobe is **Port Sorell ❸**, a holiday resort popular with locals. It rather sprawls along the waterfront and is an eclectic mix of densely packed caravan parks, campsites, traditional fibro shacks, which are rapidly being replaced by concrete and brick mansions, and some old weatherboard houses. The further north on Hawley Beach you go, the more exclusive the dwellings. But in Port Sorell it's really all about the beach, whether as somewhere for the kids to play, a quiet spot for fishing, or a launching point for water craft. Wander along any of the beachfronts in early evening and the smell of barbecues is overwhelming.

To get away from development, travel across the bay by boat or drive around the bottom to reach **Narawntapu National Park**, where spotless white beaches may be all yours. Wildlife is plentiful too, with kangaroos and wombats in evidence at dusk.

Deloraine and Sheffield

Rejoin the A1 as it heads south towards Launceston. As you are approaching Elizabeth Town, signs announce the **Ashgrove Cheese Factory** on the right-hand side of the highway. Between August and May you can see the cheese being made, and even outside this period you can inspect the maturing rooms, with their strangely alluring rows of whole cheeses. There are free tastings and countless varieties on sale (Mon–Fri 7.30am–6pm, Sat–Sun 8am–6pm; free; tel: 6368 1105; www.ashgrovecheese.com.au).

If you need an antidote to all this richness, there's the **Christmas**

Hills Raspberry Farm Café on the other side of Elizabeth Town, where 500-gram punnets to take away are good value. If you linger, everything on the menu displays an imaginative, if relentless, devotion to the fruit. The simple chocolate-dipped raspberry works as well as anything, although the super-calorific ice cream gives it a run for its money. Make up your own mind on the basis of extensive empirical research. A stroll round the attractive gardens and lake might provide some guilt-alleviating exercise (daily 7am–5pm; tel: 6362 2186).

Deloraine ❹ is a small town with plenty of character and well worth a few hours of exploration. It also makes a good base for exploring the many natural attractions in the area. This is the starting point for journeying along the Great Western Tiers, which constitute the northern edge of the World Heritage-listed central plateau region. From the northwest you enter town past the **Great Western Tiers Visitor Centre** (daily 9am–5pm; tel: 6362 4377), which can supply a brochure

Map on pages 184–185

Deliberate on the delicious delights at the Deloraine Deli.

BELOW: jetty jumping in Port Sorell.

One of the best murals in Sheffield is found at the High School in Henry Street.

with a walk highlighting the historic buildings in town, and a self-drive route for the further flung features. There is also a sculpture trail with some powerful works, especially in the parkland around the river.

But before doing any of this, have a look at the **Deloraine Museum**, housed in the old Family and Commercial Inn, which is part of the Visitor Centre complex. Exhibits track the life of the inn and the local history. Within the same complex is **Yarns Artwork in Silk**; somebody had the idea of gathering together hundreds of people who would spend thousands of hours producing four huge silk panels depicting the Great Western Tiers in each season and, by doing so, create a tourist attraction. There is an explanatory audiovisual presentation every half hour (daily 9.30am–4pm; admission charge; tel: 6362 3471).

Outside, start walking down the hill, following the first series of sculptures, to the **Meander River**, where the walking tour begins. There are several well-preserved Georgian and Victorian structures,

all set off by the picturesque river and hills. Many of the buildings are now given over to the antiques or arts trade, which flourishes here and reaches its apotheosis in the annual Tasmanian Craft Fair each October.

The **Lost in the 50s Diner** with its vast collection of "petrol memorabilia" is eccentric but unmissable for anyone with the slightest interest in that decade (2 Station St; tel: 6362 2978).

Some 23 km (14 miles) northwest of Deloraine is the unprepossessing township of **Railton**. In an effort to liven up its profile, it's making a concerted attempt to become known as the topiary town, so you can follow a trail to a few dozen examples of straggly hedges being trained over wire frames. Like your uncle wearing his comedy Groucho mask, it's all bit contrived and faintly embarrassing.

Better to continue on to **Sheffield** ❺ for a lesson in how to make a stick-on theme work. In 1985 the town was suffering as the local rural industry faced long-term decline. The townsfolk decided to follow the

example of a town in Canada, which had begun promoting murals and as a consequence had drawn in curious visitors and their wallets. John Landis was commissioned to paint the first wall, which he finished in 1986. Since then he and a dozen or so other artists have turned Sheffield into an alfresco art gallery, the "town of murals".

Again, you can follow a trail. Not all the work is accomplished but much of it is (don't miss the mural at the high school in Henry Street) and has been embraced by the town, partly because the subject matter reflects local interests and history. There's now an annual Mural Fest every March or April in which nine artists submit outlines according to a prescribed theme and are then given a week for the paint-off in Mural Park. Judges choose a winner but all the entries remain in the park for the next year.

There are some points of interest beyond the walls as well. **Slaters Country Store** in Main Street has preserved much of the interior of a Victorian clothing store, including "Grandma" Slater's elevated office to which all the cash and sales dockets were sent in cylinders along the wires of the flying fox; she would return the cylinders with the change. Staff in the shop will demonstrate how it works if you ask.

More recent technology is in evidence at **Tiger's Tale** where "animatronics equal to or better than seen at Disneyland" bring thylacines to an approximation of life. It must be left to those who have actually been to Disneyland to judge whether the promotional claim is accurate (38a Main Street; daily 9am–5pm, admission charge; tel: 6491 1075; www.tigerstale.com.au).

The **Kentish Museum** has the usual historical artefacts and a special display devoted to Gustav Weindorfer, who did so much to open up Cradle Mountain (93 Main Street; Mon,Wed 1–4pm; Tues, Thurs, Fri 1–3pm admission charge; tel: 6491 1861).

To the west of Sheffield is Lake Barrington, site of international rowing competitions. On its far side, accessible by a longish drive around

Map on pages 184–185

BELOW: Damian Rossiter at work in Sheffield's Mural Fest.

the lake's southern end, is **Wilmot** . The town's claim to fame is Coles Store, the first to be founded by G. J. Coles, whose name now adorns hundreds of rather larger and less characterful stores around Australia. There are also several "character" mail boxes, apparently to meet the region's gimmick quota.

Some seriously winding and steep roads lead through Upper Castra and Nietta to **Leven Canyon**. A short walk from the car park brings you to a lookout perched precipitously over a deep canyon gouged out of the rock. It's also possible to drive down to the bottom where experienced walkers might want to follow the River Leven through the gorge if there are 10 hours or so to spare.

Northwards the land becomes as fertile as anywhere in the state and bounteous crops create a lush landscape. Vineyards and hop gardens feature and you can visit **Leven Valley Vineyard** (Wed–Mon 10am–5pm) on the C124 towards **Gunns Plains**. It is a beautiful unsullied area with just a couple of tourist sights. **Gunns Plains Cave** is best known for its glow-worms but there are intricate formations of stalactites as well, which can be seen on guided tours (daily 10, 11am, noon, 1.30, 2.30, 3.30pm; admission charge; tel: 6429 1388).

Otherwise there is the **Wings Wildlife Park** where native mammals, such as Tasmanian devils, quolls and wombats, can be seen alongside a wide range of domesticated farm animals. There is a fish display, where you can feed the exhibits, and an animal nursery. Some of the attractions are under cover, but there are fishing, rafting, swimming and bush-walking opportunities within the grounds when the weather is amenable (daily 10am–4pm; admission charge).

Ulverstone and Penguin

We return to the coast now and first stop is **Ulverstone**, where the Leven River finally joins the sea. This is an unpretentious town with the emphasis on family holidays and beaches. There are several parks, most of them along the waterfront,

BELOW: the tranquil arable land of Gunns Plains.

and prime among them is **Shropshire Park**, on the east side of the river, named after a battle cruiser sunk during World War II. Nearby **Anzac Park** also has several memorial gardens and features linked to the war. Indeed, this is something of a theme in the town when you consider that one of its main icons is the **Shrine of Remembrance**. Incorporating an earlier 1910 memorial, this hefty and entirely disproportionate structure sees a clock mounted on three towering pillars (the three services) and incorporates everything its architect could throw at it in 1953. It might have looked more at home in post-war eastern Europe.

A short walk from here is the **Ulverstone History Museum**. The displays within can be seen at limited times (Tues, Thur, Sat, Sun 1.30–4.30pm; admission charge). Perhaps as good a sense of the history of the town can be gleaned simply by wandering around the centre and reading the excellent "Stories of Ulverstone" information boards. Look down too for sculpted power access plates in the pavements. There are a handful of fine buildings, including the superbly restored **Furner's Hotel** on the corner of Reibey and King Edward streets, with its red-brick and wrought-iron detailing.

You can rejoin the highway now; however, the more appealing option is to cross the Leven Bridge and follow the coast road west for the quick hop to **Penguin** ⑩. On the way there is a lookout to Goat Island and the remnants of past foreshore mining activity at Penguin Silver Mine.

There are a number of towns along the coast with their own penguins and viewing opportunities, but having your town actually called Penguin offers a distinct advantage. Just in case anyone misses the point, there is a chunky concrete model standing on the foreshore and all the

waste bins look like, yes, penguins. If you want to see the real thing, backtrack towards Ulverstone and join a tour at Penguin Point (Sun–Fri July–April, dusk; admission charge; tel: 6437 2590).

The beaches are the main daytime attraction except for alternate Sunday mornings when the 300 stalls at the large covered **Penguin Old School Market** bring in people from all over the region with the promise of crafts, fine food and drink, fresh produce, plants and activities for children (2nd and 4th Sun 9am–3.30pm).

Burnie

The Bass Highway begins to get less attractive as it continues west, which is good preparation for **Burnie** ⑪. The town is dominated by the largest container port in Tasmania and a huge paper factory with a constantly replenished mountain of woodchips. The town's business and shopping centre has some nice old Victorian brick and stone buildings, but they are generally overwhelmed by cheap 1970s and '80s develop-

 Map on pages 184–185

Ironwork on Ulverstone's ornate Furner's Hotel.

BELOW: the Edge of the World marked by a poem.

ment. To visit the main supermarket and its associated shopping complex, right in the centre, you have to enter airless tunnels or drive round and round ramps up to the multi-storey car park. One local's take on the highlight of Burnie was: "maybe the woodchips".

Part of the problem is that most of the rest of the state is unsullied by botched development, and much of what disappoints about Burnie wouldn't draw comment in Australia's mainland cities. However, once you get used to the environment, there is plenty to do. The **Pioneer Village Museum** is linked to the council-run Visitor Centre. Inspired by a museum in York in England, a 1900 street scene has been recreated in a large hall. It is evening time and so the streetlights and shop signs are lit. You can peer into the Emu Bay Inn, a wash house, a carpenter's shop or a dentist's. You can see what's available in the store, check the proofs in the print shop. You can even pat the plastic horse. It's a step up from other museums displaying similar material in unin-

Burnie is home to the largest container port in Tasmania.

BELOW: recreated street in the Pioneer Village Museum.

spiring cabinets (Mon–Fri 9am–5pm, Sat–Sun 1.30–4.30pm; admission charge; tel: 6430 5746).

Across the Civic Centre Precinct lies **Burnie Regional Art Gallery** where the works on display are largely contemporary Australian, with an emphasis on the local (Mon–Fri 10am–4.30pm, Sat–Sun 1.30–4.30pm; free; tel: 6430 5875).

The city's West Beach is dominated by the industrial backdrop. However, at its western end, the **Little Penguin Observation Centre** introduces the "aaah" factor. There is a wall and fence with viewing slots through which the nightly waddle up the beach to the burrows can be observed. Five burrows have been built into the wall and so sometimes (mainly spring) you can see, via a cunning mirror arrangement and infra-red light, adults sitting on the eggs during the day as they have to for 35 days during incubation or, later, chicks nesting inside. Information boards provide assessments of the percentage likelihood of seeing penguins at dusk each day; summer is best (daily 24 hours; free).

The **Australian Paper Mill** offers visitors the chance to see what goes on inside its vast premises. Guided tours take you through the whole paper-making process (Mon–Fri 2pm; free; over 10s only; tel: 6430 7777). Right at the other end of the scale is the **Creative Paper** operation. Here everything is hand made and punters can muck in. There is a shop with heaps of products and a display of life-size paper people sculpted by Ruth Rees and Pam Thorne (East Mill Studios, Old Surrey Rd; summer: daily, 9am–4pm; tours 10am, noon, 2.30pm; winter: Mon–Sat 10am–4pm; tours 11am, 2.30pm; admission charge; tel: 6430 7717; www.creativepapertas.com.au).

After the city's, by Tasmanian standards, urban excesses, it's a relief to find that there are several

Map on pages 184–185

ways of getting back to nature. A short drive along the Emu River valley leads to **Fern Glade**, a prime destination for platypus-spotting. There is a riverside walk between two gorgeous picnic spots and you may be lucky, if you keep an eye on any bubbles rising or look for splashing near the banks, to see a flash of platypus. Locals advise that the best place to spot these creatures is just down from the road bridge, and our research bears this out.

Tracking further south along the Emu River, if not delayed by the myriad temptations at the **Lactos Cheese Tasting Centre** (Mon–Fri 9am–5pm, Sat–Sun 10am–4pm; free), you should find the **Emu Valley Rhododendron Garden**. This is at its best from mid-September to mid-November, although at any time of year there is plenty to see among the lakes, bridges and cultivated lawns (Aug–Feb daily 10am–4pm; admission charge).

Still further south, about 9 km (5½ miles) from Burnie, **Annsleigh Gardens** features a conservatory surrounded by English-style gardens. There are tearooms for those who didn't overdo the cheese. (Sept–May daily 9am–5pm; admission charge.) **Guide Falls** is a pleasant stop 6 km (3½ miles) down the road and there is an alpaca farm to visit too.

Wynyard

It is necessary to return to Burnie in order to keep moving westwards. Somerset is notable for little other than being the starting point for the A10 road linking the northwest with the west coast and with Cradle Mountain. It is another drive full of scenic vistas culminating, after 40 km (25 miles) or so, in the picnic spot in **Hellyer Gorge ⓬** just after the bridge. There is a short loop walk through the forest and along the banks of the river.

But, staying on the coast, the next stop is **Wynyard ⓭**. The town, which hosts Burnie Regional Airport, is compact and low key. The hyperbole in the title of the new **Wonders of Wynyard Exhibition Centre** doesn't appear to be quite appropriate to its surroundings, but

BELOW: Fern Glade, a pretty place for platypus.

Boat Harbour Beach is yet another pristine setting for a lazy summer holiday.

the staff are enthusiastic and may drag the townsfolk with them towards a new dawn of razzamatazz and self-promotion. The main drawcard is a collection of veteran Fords restored by local man, Francis Ransley. There's also a clutch of Japanese dolls and a tribute to the founder of the Alexander Technique, another local: Frederick Matthias Alexander (daily 9am–5pm; admission charge for car collection; tel: 6443 8330).

Much of Wynyard's attraction lies in its setting on the estuary of the Inglis River. **Gutteridge Gardens** is one of the best places to appreciate this. The wharf and bobbing yachts are at one end and tranquil grasslands leading down to the river are at the other.

The scenery becomes more dramatic when you cross the river and find the beach at **Fossil Bluff**. The elements are constantly eroding the soft sandstone cliffs here and revealing fossils some 20 million years old. Look carefully at low tide and you should find some. Across to the northwest the more rugged cliffs of **Table Cape** are evident.

BELOW: Fossil Bluff.

It's well worth making your way to the **Table Cape Lighthouse** for spectacular views along the coast. The lighthouse was built in 1888 and is still in action today, partly to warn sailors of possible peril but mainly as a subject for photographs. If you visit in spring the surrounding fields are filled with tulips in flower, culminating in the Wynyard Tulip Festival in early October at **Table Cape Tulip Farm** (end Sept–mid Oct daily 9am–4.30pm; admission charge; tel: 6442 2012).

There is a whole series of beautiful beaches along this stretch of coast. One of the best is **Boat Harbour Beach**, ⑭ where the sea is impossibly blue as you drive down from the hills, and the beach, when you get there, stretches away seductively to the encircling rocks. There is one resort, which is scheduled for redevelopment, and a few beach houses for rent, but for now there is a lovely relaxed atmosphere to the place, and the solitary café doesn't appear to have any difficulty in dealing with every demand that the current level of visitors can throw at it.

Sisters Beach is 8 km (5 miles) long and makes Boat Harbour Beach look positively overcrowded by comparison. It is found within **Rocky Cape National Park**, which contains a number of established walking paths and the opportunity to inspect a couple of caves used by the Aboriginal people over thousands of years and now deemed of cultural significance. Visitors are asked not to go inside the caves.

Stanley and The Nut

The road now sticks to the coast and a strange plug of land is seen emerging across the water to the right. This is "The Nut" and you are approaching one of Tasmania's most attractive villages, **Stanley** ⑮.

The Nut, formally known as Circular Head, is a volcanic formation, almost sheer on three sides, pushed up in this fashion, oh, about 13 million years ago. You can climb up the 150 metres (500 feet) to the top and walk round the rim with wonderful views in every direction, or there is the option of taking the **chairlift**. Bearing in mind that it gets very windy here and that there's only a metal bar holding you in, the chairlift is not for the nervous (daily; Oct–May 9.30am–5.30pm; Jun–Sept 10am–4pm; admission charge).

Down at sea level there are good beaches either side of The Nut: **Tallows Beach**, the more sheltered and safer for youngsters is on the southern side, and **Godfreys Beach** faces north.

Many of the buildings in town date back to the days when the Van Diemen's Land (VDL) Company established its headquarters here in 1825 in an, as it transpired, doomed attempt to set up a merino wool industry *(see panel on page 198)*. A visit to the one-room **Stanley Discovery Museum** will help with the history of the town and, if you're in luck, the volunteer looking after you may be a direct descendant of the first director of VDL (Church St; daily 10am–4pm; admission charge; tel: 6458 1145).

While we're dwelling on the past, the cemetery on the lower slopes of The Nut overlooking Godfreys Beach is picturesque and fascinating. Its graves include that of colonial architect John Lee Archer who was responsible for numerous seminal buildings, including Parliament House and Anglesea Barracks in Hobart, the bridge at Ross and, in Stanley, the plan of the town. He ended his days there as magistrate.

Alexander Terrace forms a necklace of delightful weatherboard cottages along the base of The Nut. They include **Joe Lyons' Cottage**, where the great man was born, and it's a rather more modest affair than Home Hill in Devonport. It is now a museum devoted to Lyons and Dame Enid, his wife (daily 10am–4pm, winter 11am–3pm; donation).

The end of Alexander Terrace is where Stanley's prime industry,

Map on pages 184–185

BELOW:
the Nut at Stanley.

fishing, begins to make itself felt. Marine Park has an old light station and maritime memorials, while **Hursey Seafoods** hints at the town's principal produce with a 3-metre (10-ft) crayfish over the door. The bluestone building by the park is the original VDL Company store.

A road winds round to the wharves where the fishing fleet is based. There is a lacklustre aquarium, or rather **Seaquarium**, in which a good proportion of the exhibits are available for purchase and the pot (daily 9.30am–4.30pm; admission charge).

More rewarding wildlife encounters are to be had on either a penguin and platypus tour (times vary; tel: 6458 2038) or on a Stanley Seal Cruise, which visits scores of seals basking on nearby Bull Rock (daily; Oct–Mar 10am, 1.30, 4.30pm; Apr–May 10am, 3.30pm; Jun–Sept 10am; admission charge; tel: 0419 550 134).

A little away from the town, on the hill at the far end of Godfreys Beach, sits **Highfield** (Sept–May daily 10am–4pm, June–Aug limited times – call ahead; night tours book by 5pm; admission charge; tel: 6458 1100). The house was built for Edward Curr and begun in 1832. Later additions included stables, a cowshed and other service buildings. Much of the original furniture can be seen in the house but you're as likely to be looking out at the magnificent view across the beach to Stanley and The Nut. You guide yourself around the site during the day and can join a tour at night when the emphasis is on storytelling.

To the End of the World

Returning to the main A2 from Stanley, turn west to **Smithton** ⑯, the area's administrative centre and focus of the dairy, logging and vegetable-growing industries. The Duck estuary is quite attractive and there are views across it from the lookout on top of **Tier Hill**, but there is little else to detain you.

The C217 south goes to **Allendale Gardens**, where for more than a quarter of a century Max and Loraine Cross have been creating 6 hectares (15 acres) of formal gar-

BELOW: Joe Lyons' Cottage on Alexander Terrace, Stanley.
RIGHT: a mutant crayfish waits to pounce on customers emerging from Hursey Seafoods.

Map
on pages
184–185

dens and opening up paths through the rainforest. There is a whiff of new age about some of the concepts (the Mother Garden is under development) but you can just concentrate on the landscape and the sensory overload in the fragrant rose garden. Young girls can seek out the ceramic figurines in the fairy glade (daily 9am–5pm, later in summer; admission charge; tel: 6456 4216).

Carry on even further south and you can follow the South Arthur Forest Drive, which takes in various waterfalls, walks and lookouts in Forestry Tasmania-run reserves. Pick up a leaflet at visitor centres or at Dismal Swamp.

Returning to Smithton, take the partly unmade road that leads to the northwest tip of the state. **Woolnorth** ⓱ is part of the VDL company's original allocation of land and it is still farmed by an outfit bearing that name even though ownership now resides in New Zealand. To get access you need to book onto one of three guided tours. The shortest lasts an hour and only covers a wind farm operated by Hydro Tas-

mania. Without getting bogged down in statistics, there are 37 windmills at present, with plans for more. Each can theoretically power over 700 houses. Much is made of the idea that the air, when blowing from the west, is the cleanest in the world, having lost all its pollutants in the 14,000 km (8,700 miles) trip from Argentina. Less is made of the fact that it's usually blasting full tilt straight at you.

The half-day tour adds a leisurely ride around the bullock farm and shearing shed, a visit to an odd homestead supposedly designed in the shape of an aircraft, and a view of Cape Grim which may or may not be the site of a massacre of Aboriginals, driven over the cliff by white settlers; it depends who you talk to. It's a starkly beautiful place. The full-day tour adds lunch and a visit to Woolnorth Point, the most northerly spur on mainland Tasmania (daily if enough interest; admission charge; tel: 0417 390 241.)

There is a good dirt road from Woolnorth to **Marrawah** ⓲, a tiny settlement of no significance itself,

The shearing shed on the Woolnorth Estate.

BELOW:
windfarm overlooking Cape Grim.

Map on pages 184–185

A giant insect is one of several sculptures on the trails at Dismal Swamp.

BELOW: boardwalk at Dismal Swamp.

but the area's beaches are the draw-card. In fact the first one is off the road 8 km (5 miles) before Marrawah. There is no sign so you'll need to calculate which turnoff you need in order to get down to **Preminghana**. This is Aboriginal land and the site of notable stone rock carvings. Sadly you have to make do with photographs as the originals have been buried in the sand to stop damage by tourists. However, it's worth a visit just for the view.

West of Marrawah itself, **Green Point Beach** has huge seas and attracts top-class surfers; they have to be. If you don't surf yourself, go and watch the ones who can.

There's more surf down at **Arthur River** and a great place to watch it from: the End of the World, as Gardiner Point has been renamed. The appeal is elemental, as you gaze out across whole trunks of trees that have washed down the Arthur River to be met by waves that have washed them straight back up onto the shore. Just by the bridge over the deceptively serene-looking river is the jetty where you can join day cruises each morn-ing along one of the most unspoiled rivers in Tasmania – the four-hour trip in the pristine wilderness includes a rainforest walk, and the chance to see spectacular birdlife including sea eagles (daily 10am; tel: 6452 5088; www.arthurrivercruises.com).

If you return towards Marrawah and turn right onto the A2 Bass Highway just before getting there, it's only a short distance to the remarkable **Dismal Swamp ⑳**. This is part rain-forest walk, part sculpture park and part adventure playground. The site is in a sinkhole where blackwood trees thrive in the rare confluence of conditions that suit them. Board-walks weave in and out of the trees and every now and then you come across one of the various site-specific sculptures commissioned from lead-ing artists. There is also a giant curl-ing slide which hurls you down the 40-metre (130-ft) drop from the visi-tor centre. There are buggies at the bottom to retrieve you if your legs have turned to jelly. (daily; Nov–Mar 9am–5pm; Apr–Oct 9am–4pm; admission charge; tel: 6456 7199; www.tasforestrytourism.com.au). ❑

The VDL Company

The VDL Company has long had close links with the northwest-ern corner of Tasmania, indeed has owned great swathes of it since being granted 350,000 acres (1,400 sq. km) by George IV under Royal Charter in 1825. The original idea was to develop a great wool-growing empire from a base in Stanley (Highfield was built to act as company HQ in 1835). The enter-prise was only partially successful as conditions on the ground proved to be unexpectedly inhospitable. Today the company still runs sheep on its remaining 50,000 acres (200 sq. km) and rears beef cattle to sell to McDonalds.

RESTAURANTS, PUBS, CAFÉS AND BARS

Restaurants

Boat Harbour Beach

Jolly Rogers
Esplanade,
Boat Harbour Beach
Tel: 6445 4171
Open: L & D daily,
Sept-May. **$**
Right on the beach, it's
hard to imagine a more
relaxing place for a
restaurant. Good for
active kids too.

Burnie

Mondial
14 Cattley St, Burnie
Tel: 6432 2255
Open: D Mon-Sat. **$$**
Wonderful food prepared
under the guiding hand
of consultant chef Xavier
Mouche make this
Burnie's restaurant of
choice. The lobster float-
ing island and quail pie
are memorable.

Rialto Gallery
46 Wilmot St, Burnie
Tel: 6431 7718
Open: L Mon-Fri, D daily. **$**
One of Burnie's most
popular eating houses,
Rialto Gallery offers
plenty of Italian staples.

Deloraine

Calstock
Highland Lakes Rd,
Deloraine
Tel: 6362 2642
Open: D daily. **$$**
Unfortunately only

resident guests get to
enjoy Remi Bancal's
country French cuisine,
where each daily menu is
based around what's
available from his
kitchen garden and the
very best that local sup-
pliers can provide.
Reason enough to make
Calstock your base.

**The Deck Café &
Restaurant**
188 Tarleton St, East
Devonport
Tel: 6427 7188
www.thedeckcafe.com.au
Open: L & D daily. **$$**
Right on the riverside, the
Deck's spacious and light
dining room is Devon-
port's best option for eat-
ing out. Troy Baggett's
seasonal menus include
local seafood, some of
which is sourced from
nearby Petuna.

Deloraine Hotel
Emu Bay Rd, Deloraine
Tel: 6362 2022
Open: L & D daily. **$**
A grand late-19th-century
local pub that has some
great spots on the
upstairs lacework
balcony, which
overlooks the river.

Devonport

**Renusha's Curry and
Pasta House**
132 William St, Devonport
Tel: 6424 2293
Open: D daily. **$**

When one wants curry
and one wants pasta,
this is where you go!

Latrobe

Glo Glo's
78 Gilbert St, Latrobe
Tel: 6426 2120
Open: D Mon-Sat. **$$**
Superb food, excellent
service and a great wine
list make this one of the
region's best restau-
rants. The matching of
each dish to a wine by
the glass makes it a
good venue if you want
to learn more about
Tasmanian wines.

Penguin

Wild
87 Main Rd, Penguin
Open: L & D Wed-Sun. **$**
There's plenty of Asian
inspiration in the well-

cooked dishes that
emanate from the kitchen
of this justifiably popular
establishment. Great
beachside location too.

Port Sorell

Hawley House
Hawley Esplanade, Hawley
Beach, Port Sorell
Tel: 6428 6221
www.hawleyhousetas.com
Open: D daily. **$$**
The restaurant in this
lovely guesthouse, which
also has a vineyard, is

RIGHT: one of the options in Stanley.

open to the public. It's a formal affair with well-dressed candlelit tables in a grand dining room.

Smithton

Tall Timbers
Scotchtown Rd, Smithton
Tel: 6452 2755
Open: L & D daily. **$**
Tall Timbers resort is designed to show off Tasmania's timbers, which makes for a spectacular dining room.

Stanley

Hursey Seafoods
2 Alexander Terrace, Stanley
Tel: 6458 1103
Open: L & D daily. **$$**
The Hursey Seafoods empire includes a restaurant and a takeaway as well as a fishing and fishmonger business. You can't miss it – look for the giant lobster and tanks with live fish.

The Old Cable Station
435 Greenhills Rd, West Beach, Stanley
Tel: 6458 1312
Open: D daily. **$$**
Part of the Old Cable Station B&B, this restaurant's a little out of town, but it's well worth the trip. A feature is the wood-fired oven used for pizzas and lobster.

PRICE CATEGORIES

Prices for a three-course dinner per person with a half-bottle of house wine:
$ = under A$50
$$ = A$50–A$75
$$$ = over A$75
L = lunch, D = dinner, BYO = bring your own alcohol.

Sealer's Cove
2 Main Rd, Stanley
Tel: 6458 1414
Open: D Tues-Sun. **$**
An eclectic menu that includes salads, pasta, and a huge selection of traditional and so-called gourmet pizzas.

The Shingle Inn
25 Church St, Stanley
Tel: 6458 2083
Open: D daily. **$**
A charming dining room in the centre of town with a menu that includes cooked-to-order pies, Thai and Indian flavoured curries, a steak sandwich, braised lamb shanks, along with spaghetti bolognaise.

Ulverstone

Furner's Hotel
42 Reibey St, Ulverstone
Tel: 6425 1488
Open: L & D daily. **$**
A classic pub dining room in an imposing building that dominates the main street, Furners is very popular with locals and visitors.

Pedro's The Restaurant
Wharf Road, Ulverstone
Tel: 6425 6663
Open L & D daily. **$**
A seafood restaurant that's built on stilts over the river. The fresh fish and chips are particularly recommended.

Wynyard

Buckaneers for Seafood
4 Inglis St, Wynyard
Tel: 6442 4104
Open: L & D daily. **$**
Ask for your oysters to

be shucked to order then choose whatever fish is fresh to have with chips and you'll enjoy a memorable seafood feast.

Riverview Café and Restaurant
1 Goldie St, Wynyard
Tel: 6442 2351
Open: L Wed-Sun, D daily. **$$**
Within the Waterfront hotel, this pleasant restaurant has delightful location.

Pubs, cafés and bars

Burnie

Café Europa
2/23 Cattley St, Burnie
Tel: 6431 1897
Open: L & D Tues-Sun. **$**
A place for good coffee, breakfast or a drink, but look further afield for a substantial meal.

Deloraine

41 Degrees South
323 Montana Rd, Deloraine
Tel: 6362 4130
Open: L daily. **$**
This lovely café is a great place to relax after visiting the nearby wetlands for a glimpse of a platypus or two.

Deloraine Deli
36 Emu Bay Rd, Deloraine
Tel: 6362 2127
Open: L Mon-Sat. **$**
A favourite haunt of locals who spill out onto the pavement every morning while enjoying good coffee and savoury snacks such as porcetta-filled baguettes.

Devonport

Rosehip Café
12 Edward St, Devonport
Tel: 6424 1917
Open: L daily. **$**
An "alternative" scene with lots of healthy juices and snacks to try as well as conventional coffee.

Top End
12 Rooke St, Devonport
Tel: 6424 1466
Open: L & D daily. **$**
A large café on the edge of the town centre with lots of tables plus a food store where you can source many of Tasmania's more interesting products.

Klaas's Bakehouse
11 Oldaker St, Devonport
Tel: 6424 8866
Open: L Mon-Sat. **$**
One of the best bakeries in the region. The biscuits are particularly good, the jelly-cakes legendary and the pies worth seeking out.

Mason & Mason Interiors & Fine Coffee
38 Steele St, Devonport
Tel: 6424 8888
Open: L Mon-Fri. **$**
Good coffee and enterprising snacks in this black and white building where the café shares space with an "interiors" shop.

Molly Malone's Irish Pub
34 Best St, Devonport
Tel: 6424 1898
Open: L & D daily. **$**

RIGHT: banquets by the beach in Boat Harbour.

A typical "themed" Irish pub that is a cut above the other watering holes in Devonport. Enjoy a glass of Guinness with the locals.

Elizabeth Town

Christmas Hills Raspberry Farm Café
Bass Highway,
Elizabeth Town
Tel: 6362 2186
Open: L daily. **$**
An incredibly popular venue as tourists and locals flock here for dishes based on the berries grown here, including raspberry ice creams and chocolate-dipped raspberries.

ETC
5783 Bass Highway,
Elizabeth Town
Tel: 6368 1350
Open: L daily. **$**
This bakery and café is a popular stop with those travelling to and from the northwest coast. Enjoy good pastries, pies and sandwiches and views across the valley.

Latrobe

House of Anvers
9025 Bass Highway, Latrobe
Tel: 6426 2703
Open: L daily. **$**
This chocolate-making factory is also one of the best spots in the northwest for a hearty breakfast or good lunch.

Bicci Blue
147 Gilbert St, Latrobe
Tel: 6426 1622
Open: L daily. **$**
A pleasant place for coffee, pastries and pies. Buy a loaf of their very good sourdough bread.

Penguin

Groovy Penguin Café
74 Main Rd, Penguin
Tel: 6437 2101
Open: L Wed-Sun. **$**
A small, welcoming café where a variety of vegetarian dishes is available along with good coffee.

Madsen
64b Main St, Penguin
Tel: 6437 2588
Open: L daily. **$**
The café at this charming small hotel is worth stopping at for a quick lunch or a reviving drink after penguin-watching.

Sheffield

Coffee on Main
43 Main St, Sheffield
Tel: 6491 1893
www.coffeeonmain.com.au
Open: L & D Wed-Sun. **$$**
Located in one of the historic buildings in the centre of town, this is a city-slick experience in a friendly, country atmosphere. Good fresh produce is expertly cooked and the coffee is excellent. It morphs into a restaurant, with a small but good menu, at night.

Highlander Restaurant and Scottish Scone Shoppe
60 Main St, Sheffield
Tel: 6491 1077
Open: L & D Wed-Sun. **$**
A touristy venue with added attractions, including a piper who often plays in the restaurant, and regular visits by the local alpaca... Afternoon teas and scones are also very popular.

Stanley

The Stranded Whale Coffee Shop and Tea Rooms
6 Church St, Stanley
Tel: 6458 1202
Open: L daily, D Fri Sept-May. **$**
A relaxing place for a drink or a light snack in the heart of Stanley.

CRADLE COUNTRY

Cradle Mountain is one of the must-see destinations in Australia, and so dominates this part of Tasmania that it is easy to overlook the lower-key but equally alluring attractions that surround it

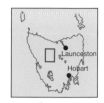

"**C**radle Country" is an amorphous concept. It has been applied to great swathes of the north coast as far along as Port Sorell in the northeast and Wynyard to the northwest, while the "official" Cradle Country route begins in Devonport. It is, then, an arbitrary judgement as to how far it stretches but always at its heart, as the name suggests, is Cradle Mountain.

It's a popular place. Close to 200,000 visitors a year have to be carefully channelled through an area of breathtaking, but fragile, wilderness. Many spend just an hour or two contemplating the fractured teeth of the summit reflected in the placid glass of Dove Lake. Some embark on one or more of the short walks that start from Cradle Valley, and just a few take on the Overland Track *(see page 206)*.

Cradle Mountain-Lake St Clair National Park plays host to these star attractions and the supporting cast, at least for the purposes of this chapter, is headed by two more national parks, each extraordinary in its own way: Mole Creek Karst and the Walls of Jerusalem.

Towards Mole Creek

Begin exploring the Cradle Country on the B12 heading west from Deloraine and after 16 km (10 miles), on entering the small settlement of **Chudleigh**, your eye cannot help but wander to the **Honey Farm** (39 Sorell St; Sun–Fri 9am–5pm; free; tel: 6363 6160). This is largely because it appears to have several very large bees flying around a virulent yellow beehive plonked on its roof. Inside you can see into a working hive, try countless different flavours of honey and end it all with some honey ice cream.

The countryside is verdant and open, with the Great Western Tiers

LEFT Cradle Mountain above Dove Lake.
BELOW: a taste of honey at Chudleigh.

looming ever larger to the south. It is only a few minutes westwards to the **Trowunna Wildlife Park** (Mole Creek Road, Mole Creek; daily 9am–5pm; admission charge; tel: 6363 6162). This is a great place to get close to a whole range of native Tasmanian fauna, notably a healthy collection of devils, wombats and koalas. Enthusiastic guides offer regular tours giving you a chance to hold or stroke the various animals. The emphasis is on conservation and many of the inhabitants are just a step away from returning to the wild after trauma or injury.

The caves of Mole Creek

To the north of Mole Creek a road loops up to **Alum Cliffs** where a 20-minute walk takes you to a lookout over a craggy forested landscape, the Mersey River threading its way far below. **Mole Creek** itself is a pleasant enough place but the real interest lies 15 km (9 miles) further on in the **Mole Creek Karst National Park ❶**, where a network of caves lies deep inside the limestone rock. This is the edge of the Great Western Tiers and the result of thousands of years of underground erosion as surface water picked up natural acids and ate through to create chambers and tunnels, some still waiting to be explored.

Marakoopa Cave is the first one you come to, a short distance south of the main road. There are two different 45-minute guided tours, both featuring a glow-worm display. Nothing beats that moment when the lights go out and there they are, specks of light pulsating in the darkness like some distant cityscape. The Underground Rivers tour follows an easy path down to the base of the cave and takes in underground streams and plunging stalactites dripping into limpid pools. The second, and marginally more physically demanding tour, lets you

Cape Barren geese are found all over Tasmania and the Bass Strait Islands, mostly around the coast.

BELOW: crowd favourite at Trowunna Wildlife Park.

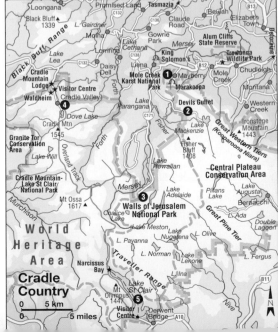

climb to the magnificent "Great Cathedral" formation and reveals the variegated strata of the "Gardens" (C170; 10am 4pm; admission charge; tel: 6363 5182 for tour times).

Further along the B12 and just to the north is **King Solomon's Cave**. This is smaller but still packs in fine formations and subtle variations of hue in the etched oranges and browns of the rock face. Access is easy and the walk is not physically demanding (C138; 10.30am–4pm; admission charge; tel: 6363 5182 for tour times).

A karst landscape doesn't just mean cave systems but also gorges and ravines; the earth has been scourged by irresistible forces of erosion and come out of it looking battered but beautiful. For a panoramic overview of this, drive along the C138 and a little way down the C171 until you reach a dirt road which winds through forest and around hills to the path to **Devils Gullet ❷**. Fifteen minutes' steady walking takes you to a metal lookout platform perched precipitously above a startling landscape. Cliffs veer off into the distance where some of the peaks in the Cradle Mountain National Park can be seen on a clear day. More than 200 metres (650 ft) below, where the Fisher River has eaten its way into the land, the forest has been scrunched up into jagged folds.

The Walls of Jerusalem

Return to the C171 and drive south, touching Lake Rowallan, to where the start of a track into the **Walls of Jerusalem National Park ❸** is signalled. There is no vehicular access to the park, nor is there a short taster walk. This is a place for serious hikers and a place to be taken seriously. As recently as 2003 there was a white Christmas here (the height of summer), so be prepared for anything and acknowledge that on a trek of upwards of six hours – and you need that time to discover the riches within – conditions can change rapidly and unexpectedly.

But having duly prepared, make the most of one of the most beautiful places in Australia. Glaciers have

Map on page 204

BELOW: the Devils Gullet.

The Overland Track

First blazed in the 1830s by surveyors, gold prospectors and fur-trappers, the Overland Track is Australia's most famous walk – a six-day traverse of Tasmania's central plateau through an ancient glacial landscape. About 9,000 hikers undertake the 80-km (50-mile) journey from Cradle Mountain to Lake St Clair each year, carrying all equipment and supplies.

The hike is not easy, but rewards are spectacular and accessible to anybody reasonably fit and well prepared. For most local bushwalkers (and an increasing number from overseas) completing the track is a rite of passage, an unforgettable expedition among stunted buttongrass moorlands, craggy snow-capped peaks, myrtle and sassafras forests, and crystalline cold-water tarns. Such is its popularity, an online booking system and a A$100 high-season (1 Nov–30 April) fee was introduced in 2005, restricting numbers to 60 hikers per day with all required to start at Cradle Valley in the National Park's north, and finish at Cynthia Bay at Lake St Clair.

Huts line the trail – seven on the main track; distances between each vary from 6.5 km (4 miles) to 11 km (7 miles) – although carrying a tent is essential in this World Heritage Area, with exposed escarpments subject to bitter weather. Hikers need equipment for all four seasons – from sunglasses, sunblock and shirt collars, to thermals, waterproofs and a woollen beanie. Warm socks, gaiters and a good sleeping bag are a must. A hiking fuel stove, medical kit and 1:100,000 map are essential. Thongs (flip-flops) are suggested, for foot relief around the huts after a long day in heavy boots.

What to carry is a delicate balance between distance, time and weight. Most walkers spend five nights on the trail, reducing the walk to 67 km (42 miles) by catching a ferry from Narcissus Hut. It's essential to pack light, to pick each item of clothing carefully and take only what's necessary. Carry enough food for an extra day in case of delays. A tip for hiking dinners is to add fresh ingredients to basic carbohydrate (pasta, rice or couscous) dishes, such as a squeeze of lemon juice on a pasta sauce on day six. Salt, pepper, curry powders and chilli are ideal – food cannot be flavoured enough after a long walk in a cold climate. Onions, green vegetables, fruit, cheese, sardines, packet soups, salami, muesli, powdered milk, nuts, sultanas, chocolate – consider all for your shopping list.

One of the walk's highlights (apart from a side-trip up Mount Ossa, at 1,617 metres/ 5,305 ft the island's highest peak) is the camaraderie around the huts each night. Everybody on the walk is equal – regardless of age, nationality or occupation – all sharing in the rigours and delights of the hike, and an experience so detached from the daily trivialities of the world outside.

For bookings, see www.overlandtrack.com.au, tel: 6233 6047 or visit the Cradle Mountain and Lake St Clair National Park visitor centres. See also www.parks.tas.gov.au for details on accommodation, transport, park entry fees and frequently asked questions. Contact Tasmanian Travel Centres for information on tour operators that offer private guided trips. ❑

LEFT: trek that track.

ripped across the surface in the past, pitting it to leave the moulds for "Solomon's Jewels", the scores of lakes that are dotted right across the park. Early explorers were clearly taken aback by what they found and, in the way of things at the time, reached for their bibles. Hence you pass through Herod's Gate on the way to the Pool of Bethesda near Damascus Gate, with King David's Peak stretching up in the distance.

It's easy to see why the pioneers were overawed. This is nature at its most alluring, where a fan of solid rock soars up from the land and beckons you onwards. Go in summer and some of the roughness of the terrain may be softened as the land is flooded with wildflowers.

Pick up the detailed map from the Parks and Wildlife Service, take a tent, allow several days and let the park work its magic. There are few facilities and there's every chance of having the place to yourself.

Tasmazia

Return north on the C171 and turn left onto the C138. Climb over the hill to the junction with the C136 and after 2 km (1¼ miles) turn right towards Sheffield and drive 12 km (7½ miles).

Tasmazia (500 Staverton Rd; daily 10am–5pm; admission charge; tel: 6491 1934; www.tasmazia.com.au) is the creation of Brian and Laura Inder, or the Laird and Lady Crackpot as they style themselves. They have taken a perfectly blameless stretch of Promised Land *(see panel on page 208)* and split it into three. Tasmazia is a collection of eight different mazes ranging from a copy of the one at Hampton Court outside London, to the Great Maze, the world's largest hedge maze. Then there's the Cage Maze, made of wood and culminating in the Thomas Crapper Memorial. Historians and trivia fans will know what

that means, and for everyone else, the clue's in the name.

The Yellow Brick Road Maze is simply a complicated footpath, aimed at children, and is actually part of the second section of the property, the Village of Lower Crackpot. This model settlement, built to 1:5 scale, has cottages, shops, a church and a "sleazy" quarter. It also has a house built upside down, another on its side, one with a chunk taken out of it and, with the help of some pointed captions and signs, it all combines to express the laird's skewed sense of humour.

The final piece of the pie is a lavender farm. Catch it in full bloom at the beginning of January. There's a café to write postcards in, then you can post them in the box outside and they will be franked as having come from Lower Crackpot.

Cradle Mountain

Backtrack to the C136 and turn right, following the winding road down to cross the Forth River and back up again, continuing on across the Middlesex Plains until the turnoff to

 Map on page 204

Fun for the kids and simple satire for the grown-ups at Tasmazia.

BELOW: the village of Lower Crackpot lies beyond the maze.

Cradle Mountain Lodge is famed for its luxury accommodation on the edge of the National Park.

BELOW: the shore of Lake St Clair at Cynthia Bay.

Cradle Valley ❹. It is 12 km (7½ miles) to the settlement and its small collection of cottages and retreats. As part of the programme to lessen the impact of so many visitors to the **Cradle Mountain-Lake St Clair National Park**, there is a car park and visitor centre, complete with café, where a shuttle bus can be boarded for the final few kilometres. The buses run regularly, stop at all the key points of interest and the drivers offer an informative commentary on the way down. Cars *can* be taken further, but it's a narrow winding road and there's little chance of finding parking at the far end unless it's a very quiet time of year.

Just past the famous **Cradle Mountain Lodge**, there is the modern, well-equipped main visitor centre (daily 8am–5pm; tel: 6492 1110). Here you can pick up all you need, whether it be park passes, permits for the Overland Track, maps or just postcards. There are also displays and screenings to provide an introduction to what you're about to see. Spend a few minutes on the delightful Enchanted Walk past

brooks and through rainforest to the Lodge, or follow the circuit to Pencil Pine and Knyvet Falls.

Behind the Visitor Centre a boardwalk runs along by the Dove River all the way to Dove Lake. Alternatively, you can hop back on the bus. Either way, it is worth stopping at **Waldheim**, the chalet built by the man regarded as the founder of this National Park, Gustav Weindorfer. The expatriate Austrian famously declared from the summit of Cradle Mountain in 1910: "This must be a national park for all the people for all time."

It may not have been until some years after his death that this finally came about, but he and his Australian wife Kate prepared the ground, helped in no small way by her spending the money on the parcel of land where they built their chalet out of King Billy pine in 1912. This first Cradle Mountain lodge attracted a handful of visitors in the early days, but curiosity was piqued and the numbers increased progressively. Waldheim, or at least the replica built after the original

Name Calling

Promised Land is one of several eye-catching place names found in the area. The story behind them begins with the Highland clearances in early 19th-century Scotland, when landlords removed hundreds of crofters from holdings they had held for generations. Some of them were placed directly onto ships to Australia. On arrival in Van Diemen's Land, many took advantage of free or cheap land and, in deference to their strong religious faith, expressed their perceived deliverance in the names they gave to their new home. So, as well as Promised Land, within a short distance there is Paradise and Garden of Eden.

Map on page 204

burnt down in 1974, is now a museum devoted to the couple and their works (daily 24 hours; free).

The lakes

The final ride or walk leads down to **Dove Lake**. The view of the mountain across the water still has the power to stop you in your tracks no matter how many times you take that path down to the lakeside. Spend the hour or two it takes to walk around the lake, to enjoy infinite variations on the same theme.

There are several other, less busy walks. The route past Lake Lilla to Crater Lake is not too demanding but offers plentiful views and attractive buttongrass terrain. More rigorous is the climb up to Marions Lookout but the view is more than worth it. The ultimate day walk – and it does take at least six hours return – is to the summit of Cradle Mountain. For these and several other options, pick up the *Cradle Mountain Day Walk Map and Notes* at the Visitor Centre. Considering that the area has more than 2,000 mm (80 inches) of rain each year,

conditions are not always going to be favourable so be sure to cover all contingencies.

At the southeastern edge of the National Park and at the other end of the Overland Track, **Lake St Clair ❺** is another easily accessible highlight. The landscape is noticeably different here, with thick forest encircling the large brooding lake. What open moorland there is is broken up by thickets of scrubby trees.

The Lake St Clair Visitor Centre (daily; 8am–5pm) is on the edge of **Cynthia Bay** at the lake's southern end. It too offers interpretive displays and is the starting point for some walks, the shortest of which is about 45 minutes return to Waters Meet along the western side of the lake. There is a regular ferry service to Narcissus Bay at the northern end and you can then spend a pleasant few hours walking back through rainforest along the western shore thereby earning the hefty meal that awaits you at the visitor centre café. Road access is via the Lyell Highway at Derwent Bridge (see *The Derwent Valley and the Wilderness*). ❏

RESTAURANTS AND BARS

Restaurants

The Grey Gum
Cradle Mountain Chateau.
Cradle Mountain Rd
Tel: 6492 1404
Open: D daily. **$$**
In winter open fires warm diners who look forward to simple fare with bush influences, and some good local wines.

Highland Restaurant
Cradle Mountain Lodge,
Cradle Mountain-Lake St
Clair National Park

Tel: 6492 1303
Open: D daily. **$$**
With a wide-ranging menu, this is the best place to dine in the Cradle Mountain area.

Laurel Berry Restaurant
100 Pioneer Drive,
Mole Creek
Tel: 6363 1399
Open: L & D daily. **$$**
The terrace is the perfect place for a coffee or light snack. Soup and a beefburger make a satisfying lunch. BYO.

Weindorfers
1447 Wellington St,
Gowrie Park
Tel: 6491 1385
Open: L & D Tues-Sun. **$$**
This institution in the shadow of the imposing Mt Roland serves nice fare in suitably rustic surroundings.

Cafés and Bars

Brushtails Bar
Cradle Mountain Chateau.
Cradle Mountain Rd
Tel: 6492 1404
Open: Daily. **$**
After a day of hiking in the wilderness this bar

is one of the first places you will head for a relaxing aperitif or cocktail.

Cradle Wilderness Café
Cradle Mountain Rd
Tel: 6492 1400
Open: L daily, D daily
Dec-Feb. **$**
Satisfying food can be found at this casual café quite close to the Lodge.

● ● ● ● ● ● ● ● ● ● ●
Prices for a three-course dinner per person with a half-bottle of house wine.
$ = *under A$50*
$$ = *A$50–A$75*
L=lunch, D=dinner, BYO = bring your own alcohol.

CRADLE MOUNTAIN

Cradle Mountain is high on the list of must-see destinations in Tasmania and it only takes one look across Dove Lake to understand why

There are some places where even the most recalcitrant slob will be driven to strap on a pair of boots, get out there and walk. Cradle Mountain is one such place. It may not be the full, multi-day Overland Track down to the bottom of Lake St Clair 80 km (50 miles) to the south; indeed it may just be the 10-minute Rainforest Walk round the back of the Visitor Centre; the thing is, it is inspirational.

Even on a rainy, windswept day – and there are plenty of those – it's where all the features of Tasmania's highland landscape come together in one satisfying whole. There are the lakes, buttongrass plains, King Billy pines and, the eye drawn back to it constantly, the chipped teeth of the mountain itself. Inevitably, the National Park attracts a huge number of visitors, but as usual, they are well managed. A shuttle bus helps minimise car use. Board walks reduce wear on the fragile environment. And there are enough Parks and Wildlife Service rangers to answer all the enquiries thrown at them. Like "How *do* I get these boots on?"

Cradle Mountain – Lake St Clair National Park
World Heritage Area

TOP: the view across Dove Lake to the serrated ridges of Cradle Mountain is one of Tasmania's top sights.

ABOVE: the designation of the Cradle Mountain–Lake St Clair National Park as a World Heritage Area came in 1982. The area is currently one of only three in the world to satisfy seven out of the ten criteria for listing.

LEFT: walkers need to make sure they're properly equipped, whether undertaking the full Overland Track or just the circuit around Dove Lake. The Visitor Centre can advise on likely weather conditions.

LEFT: the Parks and Wildlife Service recommend following the Dove Lake Circuit in a clockwise direction in order to enjoy the best views (if you can keep awake to enjoy them, that is). This is particularly good advice in the peak summer season when congestion is lessened if everybody is going the same way round.

SHORT WALKS IN THE PARK

Although the Overland Track is the celebrated walk – and busy enough that numbers now have to be restricted – the majority of visitors to the area only undertake a short stroll or two. The shortest designated walk is estimated at only 10 minutes and can be done in less. Others, for example to Marions Lookout or the top of Cradle Mountain itself, can take up to 8 hours return and involve some stiff climbing.

A copy of the booklet, Cradle Mountain Day Walk Map & Notes, sets out all the alternatives and is available at the Visitor Centre, itself the starting point for a number of walks. One of them, and an attractive option, is the Cradle Valley Boardwalk, which was opened at the end of 2003 and leads from the Centre all the way to Dove Lake in roughly 2 hours 45 minutes. There are a couple of places where it touches the road, giving hikers the opportunity to hop onto the shuttle bus if they tire or if the weather closes in.

There are two paths beginning at "Waldheim", Weindorfer's lodge, and several more starting at Dove Lake, including the Dove Lake Circuit, which everyone should tackle at least once.

LEFT: alpine, sub-alpine and heathland flowers can be found throughout the park, with the greatest variety in spring and summer.

BELOW: Cradle Mountain Lodge, on the edge of the National Park, is a good spot to relax at the end of the Overland Track. Or at the end of a large lunch in the restaurant.

ABOVE: it's only an easy short stretch from the Visitor Centre to the beginning of the 20-minute Enchanted Walk which winds along the banks of a cascading river.

LEFT: the worn shingles of the old boatshed on the shore of Dove Lake have featured in many a souvenir photo. On a more practical note, they have also provided shelter for walkers caught out by the weather. The lushness of the groundcover gives a clue to the high levels of rainfall in these parts.

THE WEST

The wet and windswept side of the island has always attracted hardy souls – from the pioneers who settled Macquarie Harbour and created the notorious prison on Sarah Island, to the miners who dug deep into the earth in Queenstown, Zeehan and Rosebery

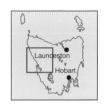

I t's not quite the *wild* west but it is remote, subject to more than its share of rough weather, and somehow at one remove to the rest of Tasmania. For a start, there are only two good roads linking the area to the rest of the state; the Murchison Highway through to the north was only completed in 1962 and the older Lyell Highway, opened in 1932, has never been the easiest thoroughfare in the depths of winter.

To the Franklin River

It is on the Lyell Highway that we start our expedition. From Derwent Bridge it is just a few kilometres west to the **Franklin-Gordon Wild Rivers National Park**, part of the huge World Heritage Area that covers much of the south and west of Tasmania. This was the scene of much turmoil between the hydro-electric industry and environmentalists in the 1980s *(see pages 44–47)* and our first stop is right at the epicentre of the dispute.

The **Franklin River** was saved from damming after a long battle and now acts as a magnet for rafters and nature lovers. There are a couple of short walks through the temperate rainforest along the **Franklin River Nature Trail** where the road crosses the river

25 km (16 miles) from Derwent Bridge. A 9 km (6 mile) drive further on you can enjoy a 30–40 minute return walk to **Donaghy's Lookout** where the bigger picture can be seen. Below is the confluence of the Collingwood and Franklin rivers and surrounding you are rocky peaks, the tallest of which, Frenchmans Cap is 1,445 metres (4,740 ft) high and marked by its white summit – not snow but quartzite (or quartzite under snow, depending on the season).

Map on page 214

LEFT Queenstown surrounded by denuded mountains.
BELOW: be prepared for bad weather.

WARNING
SUDDEN TEMPERATURE
CHANGES MAY OCCUR
ADEQUATE CLOTHING
SHOULD BE CARRIED
AT ALL TIMES

Kayaking down the Franklin River is rarely this relaxed.

There is a trail to the top of **Frenchmans Cap** but it takes four or five days and is only for the most experienced of bushwalkers. The starting point is 6 km (3½ miles) east of the Franklin River Nature Trail.

Rafters and kayakers congregate at the next stop where the highway crosses the Collingwood River 49 km (30 miles) west of Derwent Bridge. The Collingwood flows into the Franklin, which is a wild free-flowing river and rafting on it is a hazardous business as evidenced by the fatalities outlined on the *Franklin River Rafting Notes* posted by the Parks and Wildlife Service (www.parks.tas.gov.au). To follow the river to its full extent can take up to 14 days and involves not just braving white water but also strenuous humping (or portage as its known) of the raft across rocks and other obstacles where the river is not navigable. Experience is essential, which is why most people go with professional operators.

After 56 km (35 miles) of driving through the national park, you emerge for a run downhill to a crossing over Lake Burbury and then, after following the shore for a while,

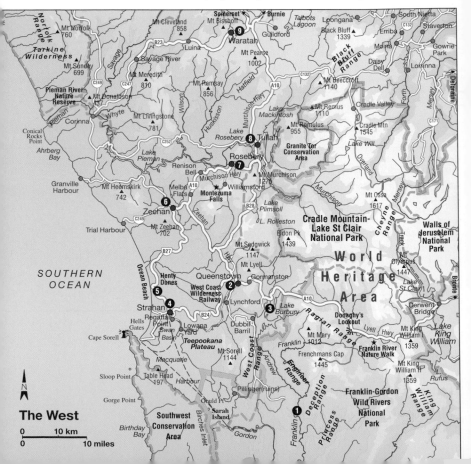

The West

0   10 km
0   10 miles

the climb up through the pass towards Queenstown. The scenery begins to change dramatically as you near the top. Soon you're in a haunting, desolate moonscape devoid of vegetation.

Gold was first found in the area in 1881 and soon creeks all around Mount Lyell were yielding small quantities of the precious resource. The discovery of the "Iron Blow" ore seam two years later saw the next development as prospectors recognised the need for a more systematic approach to extracting the metal. The Mount Lyell Gold Mining Company was established in 1888 and five years later the Mount Lyell Mining and Railway Company, as it had become, began to mine copper, which had emerged as the more viable metal. Silver was also detected and the area boomed with over 5,000 people living in and around Queenstown by the end of the 19th century.

This is when the workings began to take their toll on the surroundings. Trees were being scythed down to fuel the smelters, and sulphur, a by-product of the smelting process, was in turn poisoning the remaining flora and rendering the ground infertile. Rain washed away any remaining topsoil and the result is clear to see to this day.

Bare slopes of brown, ochre, orange and cream create a strange desert landscape, which, particularly when touched by early-morning or late-afternoon sunlight, can glow with an otherworldly beauty. It will, apparently, take hundreds of years to return to its natural state.

Queenstown

The road corkscrews down through this desolation until suddenly arriving in **Queenstown ❷**. This is the archetype of a mining town. Even without the barebacked hills crowding in on it, there's something about the generally unkempt utilitarian structures and the plethora of unadorned workaday pubs that typifies a no-nonsense, male-dominated community. And that's not altogether unattractive. If it's an antidote to heritage in aspic you're looking for, then this is the place.

Map on page 214

BELOW: the road spirals down from the mountains into Queenstown.

The Miners Siding *is another sculptural installation by Stephen Walker (see page 128).*

BELOW: mine equipment outside the Galley Museum.
RIGHT: inside the museum.

Which is not to say that there aren't some interesting and attractive places to be discovered here. As you come into the main part of the town the **Galley Museum** occupies an old hotel on your left in Driffield Street (1 Driffield St; Oct–Mar Mon–Fri 9.30am–6pm, Sat–Sun 12.30–6pm; Apr– Sept 10am–5pm, Sat–Sun 1–5pm; admission charge; tel: 6471 1483). This is an old-fashioned enterprise, with cabinets crammed full of every imaginable remnant of life and work in the area as well as an extensive display of photographs from the early days.

Over the road is the **Miners Siding**, a series of sculptures linked by a stepped water feature leading down to a mining family group. Continue on past this and the large cream-painted building ahead of you is the terminus for the **West Coast Wilderness Railway**. The 37 km (23 miles) of track from Queenstown to Strahan on the coast had not been used since 1963 until, with the aid of a massive federal government grant, it was refurbished and relaunched as a tourist attraction in 2002. It was originally known as the Abt railway, after Dr Roman Abt, who developed the third-rail rack and pinion system used on the steep final section into Queenstown.

Today the journey takes four hours and incorporates stops for a short boardwalk incursion to a patch of rainforest and either honey tasting or gold panning, depending on the direction in which you are travelling. Steam is only used for the upper 8 km (5 mile) section of the track, with diesel power employed for the run into Strahan. There is some blinding scenery on the upper reaches as you wind around deep gorges above the river (bookings tel: 1800 628 288; call for times; www.federalresorts.com.au/west-coast-wilderness-railway.php).

Opposite the station on the corner of Orr Street is the **Empire Hotel**. It has a welcoming bar and dining room and a National Trust-listed staircase made from local blackwood, which was shipped to England, machined, and then returned for construction in the hotel in 1904. While you're at the Empire, you

may want to enquire at the office of Douggie's Underground Mine Tours; they organise guided visits to either the Copper Mines of Tasmania underground mine (one of only two working underground mines in the country to allow visits) or there's a surface tour of the original century-old Mount Lyell Copper Mine (2 Orr St; tel: 6471 1472; call for times and prices).

It is worth strolling around the rest of the town to take in the old pubs and shops, the weatherboard houses and maybe the view from the top of **Spion Kopf**, a bluff overlooking the town. (Park by the old mine engine – the narrow track runs out shortly afterwards.)

Strahan

Take the road which runs south out of town along the banks of the Queen River. When it emerges from the attractive wooded valley, it begins to climb the side of Mount Jukes before coming out to a stunning lookout over **Lake Burbury** ❸, with Frenchmans Cap and several other peaks arrayed behind it.

This is another artificial lake created by the hydro company dams in 1992. The good dirt road leads down to the shoreline where you can settle in for a spot of fishing or simply savour the views, which are magnificent in every direction. You can spend hours without seeing another living thing apart, perhaps, from an eagle or two wheeling overhead. Take a picnic.

Retrace your steps and follow the Lyell Highway out of Queenstown, across more buttongrass plains and down to **Strahan** ❹, which began life as a timber town and grew in stature when the railway lines from Zeehan and Queenstown allowed it to thrive on the back of the copper industry. Strahan (pronounced *strawn*) is still an active if small fishing port and there's usually a boat or two unloading crayfish in the morning. Tourism is its main industry now, however. Thousands visit every year to cruise on Macquarie Harbour and dip a toe in the Gordon River – which flows into the harbour – tantalisingly on the edge of the wilderness and the World Heritage Area.

The Empire Hotel, a Queenstown institution, has a National Trust-listed staircase inside (see also picture on page 246).

BELOW: Lake Burbury.

From September to May, Wilderness Air (tel: 6471 7280) operates scenic flights by seaplane from Strahan Harbour. The 80-minute flight follows the rivers Franklin and Gordon and includes a landing at Sir John's Falls. Alternatively, sail up the Gordon River or around the west coast on a 60ft ketch with Strahan-based West Coast Yacht Charters – tel: 6471 7422, www.tasadventures.com/wcyc

BELOW: Strahan harbour with one of the Gordon River excursion boats.

The Visitor Information Centre (Esplanade; tel: 6471 7622; open daily 10am–7pm) has an exhibition, *West Coast Reflections*, covering the history of the area, culminating in Strahan's role as the hub of the Franklin Dam protest movement.

Backing onto the visitor centre is a small performance space where there are nightly renderings of *The Ship That Never Was*, a terrific piece of rough theatre put together by the Round Earth Company. It tells the fascinating story of one of the last escape attempts from the penal settlement on Sarah Island and, in the process, gives some insight into the barbaric conditions under which the convicts laboured (daily 5.30pm, extra shows end Dec–Jan 8.30pm; tel: 6471 7622; admission charge).

The play acts as good preparation for the cruise out onto **Macquarie Harbour** (World Heritage Cruises, daily 9am; tel: 6471 7174; or Gordon River Cruises, daily 8.30am; tel: 1800 628 288). Macquarie Harbour is vast. It is 50 km (31 miles) long, covers 285 sq. km (110 sq. miles) and could contain Sydney

Harbour several times over. But the entrance, the first destination on the cruises, is narrow and treacherous and known as Hell's Gates. As soon as the ship has navigated this tricky passage, the seas start throwing you about and, depending on conditions, you get some idea of the force of the Roaring Forties which are such a feature of this coast. Don't worry; it's only the briefest of tasters before you're back into the tranquil harbour, pausing for a quick look at the circular cages of the salmon farms before sailing down to the far end and the set down on **Sarah Island**.

In 1822 Sarah Island was established as a prison to take the worst offenders in Van Diemen's Land and, as a handy by-product they could be set to work to exploit the stands of Huon pine. Convicts were made to row to the mainland, chop down the massive trees all day and then row back again; others were put to work in the island shipyard turning the pine into vessels. The regime was relentless, unsurpassed in its harshness, and a good number of the inmates didn't survive it.

Today just ruins remain, but if the winds and the rains are present, as they usually are, it's possible with the help of a good imagination to go some way to understanding the grimness of life in Macquarie Harbour. Ultimately the settlement only survived for 11 years before the convicts were moved down to the new prison at Port Arthur.

The cruise continues with a dawdle up the lower reaches of the **Gordon River** where thick forest presses right down to the water's edge and the dark mirror of the water creates vertical symmetry. A small jetty allows access to a boardwalk that nibbles its way into a tiny section of the rainforest.

On returning to Strahan, have a look around Morrisons sawmill next to the Visitor Centre to see how Huon pine is worked and then just stroll around the village. Consider a sightseeing flight on a seaplane (see *Tips, opposite*), or contemplate the almost too-perfect agglomeration of buildings around Strahan Village. Then come to realise it *is* too perfect; they are all part of a resort hotel as is the pub, the fish and chip shop, and much else. Federal Resorts runs this as well as Gordon River Cruises and the West Coast Wilderness Railway. Strahan is as much a company town as any of the mining settlements where the local economy is over-reliant on one employer.

For somewhere where you can set your own agenda, carry on round Risby Cove to People's Park, pass under the old-fashioned sign and follow the trail for 40 minutes or so to **Hogarth Falls**.

Zeehan and Beyond

If you drive due west from Strahan you arrive at **Ocean Beach**, a 40-km (25-mile) stretch of blissful sand. You can get a different take on it if you follow the B27 north for 14 km (7½ miles) and clamber up onto the

massive 30-metre (100-ft) high **Henty Dunes** ❺, which stretch off for kilometres behind Ocean Beach.

Keep going north for another 70 km (43 miles) to **Zeehan** ❻. In 2005 *Australian Traveller* magazine nominated Zeehan as the ugliest town in Australia – a particularly harsh judgement considering that it's not even the ugliest town in Tasmania (and the planners of Burnie, let's face it, have fought hard for their title). There is some sprawl but there are a couple of attractions which more than make up for it and the town has even been classified by the National Trust!

At the beginning of the 20th century, 20 years after silver had been discovered and on the back of the subsequent boom, Zeehan was the third-largest town in Tasmania, capable of filling the 1,000-seater **Gaiety Theatre** and attracting Enrico Caruso and Nellie Melba to perform. The building is undergoing long-term renovation but you can usually gain access for a quick look around, enough to understand what a grand place it must have been in

Long-running theatrical production The Ship That Never Was *plays nightly at the Strahan Visitor Centre.*

BELOW: a wave on the sand at Henty Dunes.

Map on page 214

Guides will take you round the mine at Rosebery.

BELOW: close-up of a wheel assembly at the West Coast Pioneers' Museum in Zeehan.

its heyday. If the front door is closed you may be able to get in via the **West Coast Pioneers' Museum** (Main St; tel: 6471 6225; daily 9am–5pm; admission charge).

This stimulating museum is housed in the picturesque School of Mines and Metallurgy (1894) as well as some neighbouring buildings, like the preserved old courthouse and police station. Obsolete locomotives and mining machinery try to ward off rust out the back. Inside there is a comprehensive mineral display, mining memorabilia and material illuminating the history of the pioneer settlers in the west.

For guided tours of Zeehan, with an introduction to the intriguing Spray Tunnel (a dripping narrow passage cut through the rock of a local hill), contact Silver City Tours (129 Main St; tel: 0438 716 389).

Just 24 km (15 miles) up the road is another working mining town: **Rosebery ⑦**. Historically gold, lead and copper have all been mined around Rosebery, but it is the Pasminco Zinc Mine in the foothills of Mount Black that effectively runs

the town today. There is not a lot for the visitor beyond some more mining relics, which include an aerial ore bucket ropeway running above the road on the approach to town.

Five km (3 miles) south of town lies the starting point for a walk to **Montezuma Falls**, the state's highest. It takes around three hours return.

Tullah ⑧, another 13 km (8 miles) up the road, is another examining town with understated appeal. Tullah Lakeside Chalet occupies the most attractive plot in the neighbourhood, perched on a promontory on the shore of Lake Rosebery. There are walks down by the waterside and seats under the trees offering prime views of the waterbirds at work. Tullah's tourist attraction is **Wee Georgie Wood**, a restored steam engine that used to be the town's only link with the outside world. It operates sporadically (Sept–Apr, Sun or Sat, hours vary; tel: 0417 147 015).

The Tarkine Wilderness

The final stop is still further up the Murchison Highway and west along the B23 where **Waratah ⑨** sits lonely and windswept on the edge of the **Tarkine Wilderness** – a large roadless expanse of beautiful forest and moor extending to the Arthur River and the west coast. Waratah's raison d'être is Mount Bischoff where tin deposits were discovered in the 1870s sufficient to produce 90,000 tons of the metal over the next 50 years. A revival in mining since the early 1980s was not big enough to wake the town from its slumbers. There are some attractive old weatherboard structures in a pretty setting and **Philosopher Smith's Hut** next to the **Waratah Museum** in Smith Street is worth a look. (Smith was the man who discovered the tin.) The friendly Roadhouse proprietors can supply a self-drive tour map. ❑

RESTAURANTS, CAFÉS AND BARS

Restaurants

Queenstown

Empire Hotel
Driffield St, Queenstown
Tel: 6471 1699
Open: L & D daily. $
The Empire Hotel has a long tradition on the west coast providing shelter for weary travellers for over 100 years. The food is standard pub fare.

Rosebery

Mount Black Lodge
Hospital Rd, Rosebery
Tel: 6473 1039
Open: D daily. $
The Blue Moon restaurant at this west coast retreat is the best place for a meal in Rosebery.

Strahan

Risby Cove
The Esplanade, Strahan
Tel: 6471 7572
www.risby.com.au
Open: B, L & D daily. $$
A pleasant dining room right on the stunning harbour looking out at the port of Strahan where you can drop in for breakfast, for coffee or for a full evening meal.

Franklin Manor
The Esplanade, Strahan
Tel: 6471 7311
www.franklinmanor.com.au
Open: D daily. $$$
This venue sources its produce locally where possible, and the ocean trout is always good.

Tullah

Tullah Lakeside Chalet
Farrell St, Tullah
Tel: 6473 4121
Open: B, L & D daily. $$
Nestling on the shores of Lake Rosebery this rustic chalet offers clean, comfortable accommodation and pleasant meals.

Waratah

Bischoff Hotel
Main St, Waratah
Tel: 6439 1188
Open: L & D daily. $
Good, home-style meals are available in this grand hotel in the beautiful west coast mining village of Waratah.

Zeehan

Hotel Cecil
Main St, Zeehan
Tel: 6471 6221
Open: D daily. $
Dining options in Zeehan are limited, so a steak at the Hotel Cecil is one of your best bets.

Cafés and bars
Strahan

Banjos Bakehouse
The Esplanade, Strahan
Tel: 6471 7794
Open: B, L & D daily. $
Banjos bakery and café is a Tasmanian success story. You'll find them all over the state, serving pastries, breads, sandwiches and coffee. This one, in the middle of town, does a roaring trade at breakfast. Pizza is available at night.

Hamers Hotel
The Esplanade, Strahan
Tel: 6471 7191
Open: L & D daily. $
This bar at this historic waterfront hotel has been a local watering hole for many years. These days it's also a busy, informal bistro.

Morrisons Seafood and Tassie Treats (Strahan).
2 The Esplanade, Strahan
Tel: 6471 6321
Open: L & D daily. $
On the edge of the wharf, just beyond the centre of town, Morrisons serves fish and chips and wood-fired pizza, as well as fresh fish you can cook yourself.

Regatta Point Tavern
The Esplanade, Strahan
Tel: 6471 7103
Open: L & D daily. $
Near the West Coast Wilderness Railway terminus, this is the pub not run by Federal Resorts. Sturdy pub grub.

PRICE CATEGORIES

Prices for a three-course dinner per person with a half-bottle of house wine:
$ = under A$50
$$ = A$50–A$75
$$$ = over A$75
L = lunch, D = dinner, BYO = bring your own alcohol.

RIGHT: fresh crays on the wharf at Strahan.

BASS STRAIT ISLANDS

**The ultimate getaway for anyone
seeking peace and quiet: hop on a light
plane to either Flinders or King islands and
surrender to the leisurely tempo and raw beauty**

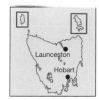

"If there's someone on the beach, just go to another one." It was a Flinders Island local who came up with that one but it could equally well apply to King Island, the other of the two larger and more populated islands to be found in the Bass Strait, the body of water separating Tasmania from mainland Australia. The two lie at the northeastern and northwestern tips of the state respectively and are surrounded by numerous smaller islands, many of them occupied by nothing other than seals and birds.

A visitor who appreciates the rest of Tasmania as a place for a quiet sojourn from urban life might like to consider that these islands can appeal to a mainland Tasmanian in the same way. They are so very quiet and so very peaceful that, at times, you can feel cut off from the rest of humanity.

However, visitors are noticed, word gets around and you may arrive in a settlement for the first time to be told: "Heard you were coming". Somebody you talk to in the normal run of things will divulge that they saw you elsewhere earlier in the day. You are being watched.

Another local, on King Island this time, responded to the observation that it must be quite difficult for someone living there to have an affair, with: "It happens all the time. Everyone knows about it but nobody cares." Before we inadvertently open up the islands to a whole new stratum of tourism, however, it's time to consider their more conventional attractions.

Flinders Island

The Furneaux Group of islands off the northeastern tip of the state is made up of the remnants of a land bridge that once joined Tasmania to the mainland. The last remaining

Maps:
pages
224, 228

LEFT: Cape Wickham lighthouse on King Island. **BELOW:** catching crabs on Flinders Island.

granite peaks are dotted across the water – tiny Swan Island, larger Clarke and Cape Barren and the main body of land, **Flinders Island**.

The peaks run down the western side of Flinders Island leaving the eastern side to tail off into flat marshland, drained after World War II to create rich farmland. The main settlement, Whitemark, is on the west coast and it is here that the visitor is likely to arrive, either on the weekly ship from Bridport or, more likely, one of the regular flights from Launceston, Burnie/Devonport or Melbourne *(see margin tip, page 225)*.

Whitemark ❶, although the administrative centre, is really just three or four streets of buildings, including the post office, council chambers, a handful of shops, a pub and a couple of churches. The school is here too, but it only offers schooling up to year 10, so older children wishing to continue their education need to transfer to boarding schools elsewhere, or families have to uproot and settle off the island. Many don't return and, not surprisingly, this tends to skew the population balance towards the elderly or to younger families. A sign on the road from the airport boasts of a population approaching the 800 mark, though locals put the figure in the six hundreds.

However many there are, they will all be familiar with Bowman's Store, which has been servicing the island's needs over several generations of the Bowman family. Upon request the current "old Mr Bowman" will lead you through to the History Room, a kind of halfway house between the public area of the shop and the living quarters of the family, where a slightly ramshackle collection of faded newspaper clippings, photographs and artefacts provides glimpses of the island's history. It's probably more rewarding just to talk to the staff of the

The Interstate Hotel in Whitemark was built in 1911.

BELOW: the beach at Whitemark looking south towards Mount Strzelecki.

Flinders and Cape Barren Islands

0   10 km

0   10 miles

shop. Before you know it, passing locals will join in and you will be inundated with advice on where to go and what to see. Another option is to walk up the road and look in at the small information centre (well, room) on the corner of the Interstate Hotel where the proprietor will offer assistance before steering you relentlessly to the collection of topaz jewellery available for purchase.

Alternatively, just pick up a free map at the airport, hire a car and drive north to **Emita ❷** where the **Furneaux Museum** provides a much more organised overview of the island and its history (daily 1–5pm summer, Sat–Sun 1–5pm winter; admission charge; tel: 6359 2010 to confirm opening). Inside a large Nissen Hut, one of a motley collection of buildings used to house exhibits, are objects salvaged from the wreck of the barque *Sydney* which ran aground in 1797 on its way from India to Sydney. When its marooned sailors clambered ashore, they represented the first Europeans to land on one of the Furneaux Islands. The anchor is the prize

exhibit. It has undergone a state-of-the-art preservation programme in conjunction with the Queen Victoria Museum in Launceston, where other relics from the wreck can be found.

Other emphasis is on the sealing and whaling which first attracted settlers to the island, and there is a reconstructed mutton-bird processing shed to cast light on another of the gruesome industries that have coloured the island's past.

Necklaces of finely threaded tiny iridescent shells represent the work of the Aboriginal population whose presence on the island has exemplified one of the darkest passages of colonial history. When the infamous "black line" was used to round up the remaining Aboriginal population of Tasmania in 1829, those captured were transported to Flinders Island between 1829 and 1834.

Colonial administrator George Augustus Robinson established a settlement just down the road from Emita at **Wybalenna ❸** with the aim of saving the final surviving Aboriginal people – all 135 of them – from extinction. Photographs in

Map on page 224

TIPS

There are weekly sailings from Bridport to Lady Barron or Whitemark on Flinders Island, taking eight hours. Departure times vary – check with the tourist office.
Flights depart from Launceston (daily), less frequently from Devonport, Burnie. There are also flights from Melbourne (Moorabin).

BELOW LEFT AND RIGHT: the Furneaux Museum at Emita has a shell collection featuring Aboriginal necklaces.

the museum give some idea of what the place looked like but there is little to be seen today other than the chapel, built by convict labour in 1838, and a cemetery just beyond it with a scattering of gravestones. None of the Aboriginal grave sites were marked, and there were many of them because by the time the survivors were uprooted and taken back to Oyster Cove on the mainland in 1847, only 47 remained.

The dirt road leading to Settlement Point provides access to some gorgeous beaches. At a parking place en route to sheltered Allport Beach you'll find the starting point for one of the branded "60 Great Short Walks" *(see margin tip, page 111)* to Castle Rock, a stark boulder rising out of the sand 2 km (1¼ miles) away on Marshall Beach. It's an easy stroll of just over an hour there and back.

A little further east is a mutton-bird or shearwater rookery where the birds are only to be seen at dusk but at any time it's a lovely spot with views out across the bay. From here northwards the island is sparsely populated and the appeal is in the subtly changing landscape and the serendipitous glimpses of vistas out to sea or up to mountains. West End Road runs off the main road and is a rougher track which winds up to the lookout at the top of Mount Tanner where, on a good day, some of the finest outlooks across Flinders and the neighbouring islands await you.

Another turnoff further north runs down to **Killiecrankie**. Fossicking for examples of clear topaz, or "Killiecrankie diamonds" as they're dubbed locally, can enliven a saunter along the spotless beach. Killiecrankie Enterprises runs the general store (daily 9am–5pm) and staff offer advice on good spots to search for topaz and also hire out sieves and shovels. Otherwise, take your pick from swimming, snorkelling, fishing or walking.

A similarly attractive beach can be found up the road at Palana. Then the road finally runs out at North East River on the northeast tip of the island. A section of the Flinders Island Ecology Trail provides opportunities to savour the bird life and pounding seas.

Map
on page
224

The only other vehicular access to the east coast of the island is much further south. Melrose Road (C801) makes its way east from just north of Melita and, perhaps with a detour up to Furneaux Lookout, you eventually come to **Patriarch Inlet** with its broad sandy expanse and wading-bird habitat.

Breaking up the flat expanse to the south are the Patriarchs, a minor range of hills. Nestled at their base is the **Patriarch Wildlife Sanctuary**. Arrive at the A-frame study centre and the house peacock will feign indifference while over-familiar wallabies bound up in the hope of illicit edible treats. It's a small enterprise and often there will be nobody there to direct your attention to specific species. It's a pleasant place for a wander nonetheless.

The C803 continues to the south of the island, offering a diversion to estuarine Logan Lagoon, a twitcher's place of pilgrimage as it's on the migration path of numerous waterfowl. However, by the end of summer it dries up leaving just a deserted muddy basin.

Lady Barron ❹ is the principal commercial port and yet tiny. Look down on it from nearby Vinegar Hill (up Barr Street and continue on the rough track past the signal tower) and take in the picturesque Franklin Sound stretching away to Cape Barren Island, which has been returned to Aboriginal ownership in recent years. A great way to explore the sound is aboard the luxurious catamaran *Resolution,* which will take you out for a few hours or a few days, depending on demand (tel: 0408 516 113).

Strzelecki National Park

The coast road west takes you past the Unavale Vineyard and its tasting room (10 Badger Corner Rd; tel: 6359 3632) and on to the main road towards Whitemark. Take the turnoff to the left after 5 km (3 miles) and after another 6 km (3¾ miles) you come to some of the most dramatic and beautiful scenery on the island. It's within **Strzelecki National Park ❺** and takes in the highest peak as well as, arguably, the island's most attractive beaches.

Inmates at the Patriarch Wildlife Sanctuary await visitors.

BELOW: rush hour at Patriarch Inlet.

There is a well-signposted track to the summit of Mount Strzelecki. It's a good couple of hours of strenuous but not difficult hiking to get to the top but the stupendous views – sometimes as far as the Tasmanian mainland – are worth it.

Recover at **Trousers Point** ❻ where the perfect white beach is lapped by rich azure waters and backed by savage granite peaks. Another of the 60 great walks strikes through woodland, along cliffs and by the foreshore to **Fotheringate Beach**. Here you'll find jagged outcrops of calcarenite, an easily eroded limestone of crushed shells, which contrasts profoundly with the smooth granite boulders encrusted with orange lichen found on Trousers Point Beach. It's also possible to drive between the two beaches.

A drive northwards takes you back to Whitemark to complete the circuit of the island. Allow time for a quick excursion inland to **Walkers Lookout** ❼ where you can savour 360-degree views which highlight the difference between the rocky west coast and the tranquil flatlands to the east. This is a good place to start and get your bearings when you arrive.

King Island

Perched beyond a smaller cluster of islands some 90 km (55 miles) off the northwest coast of Tasmania, King Island takes the full impact of the Roaring Forties and, although it's fanciful to believe that the winds have blown all the mountains off into the sea, it feels like a reasonable explanation as to why this island is so flat after Flinders.

Currie ❽ is the main settlement and, again, located midway down the west coast. It's a pleasant little town which acts as the commercial and social focus of the island. A short walk down to the picturesque

BELOW: some of the weathered calcaremite on Fotheringate Beach.

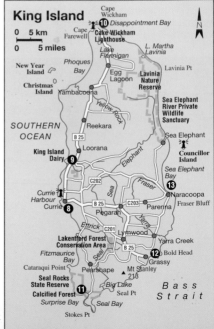

Maps: pages 224, 228

harbour, past an eccentric pottery, may well be rewarded with the sight of one of the fishing boats unloading huge crabs or succulent crayfish. You can buy them fresh off the boat.

Up on the cliff to the south sits the lighthouse. Its 312 wrought-iron pieces and cast-iron base were prefabricated in England and bolted together in situ in 1879. You can walk or drive up for terrific views over the harbour and, if you schedule your visit for the right time in the afternoon, look in at the **Historical Museum** which occupies the old lighthouse keeper's house (Lighthouse St; tel: 6462 1698; daily 2–4pm; admission charge).

Below the lighthouse, a virulently painted boathouse acts as an informal community centre and meeting place, and visitors are welcome.

If you drive south along Netherby Road, past the golf course, you come to one of the odder photo opportunities on King Island. Row upon row of black and brown bull kelp fronds hang from drying racks waiting to be processed into a dry powder for export to Scotland. **Kelp Industries**

takes tonnes of this giant seaweed from an army of collectors who harvest it from the seashore on the west of the island. It hangs out to dry for two weeks before being converted to an end product which is rich in alginates and used for thickening everything from toothpaste to paint. A visitor centre explains everything.

Carry on to the end of the road and see great swathes of kelp washed up on the rocks at **British Admiral Beach**. It's a favourite spot for surfboard riders, but you don't have to enter the water to appreciate its appeal.

About 10 km (6 miles) north of Currie, shining steel tanks trumpet the presence of the **King Island Dairy ⑨**. On mainland Australia and beyond King Island is linked irrevocably with cheese. This is where it is produced. You can visit the fromagerie to taste and buy the famous cheddar, brie and curd (North Rd, Loorana; Sun–Fri 12.30–4.30pm; closed Wed May–Sept; tel: 6462 1348; www.kidairy.com.au).

King Islanders appear to be perversely proud of being surrounded

Kelp is hung out to dry in readiness for processing.

BELOW: the last remains of the wreck of the *Shannon* can be seen on Yellow Rock Beach.

Map on page 228

Stumps from the Calcified Forest protrude from the dunes.

BELOW: although the King Island Dairy has the public profile, the beef industry is also important.

by some of the most dangerous waters for shipping in the world.

The Historical Museum in Currie (*see previous page*) gives over considerable space to the topic, and there is a Maritime Trail which allows you to track the scenes of disaster around the coast with the aid of an 18-page booklet, *Shipwrecks and Safe Havens*. The only wreckage you can actually see – unless you are diving – lies on **Yellow Rock Beach**, about 20 km (12½ miles) north of the dairy. A short walk along the final stretches of the Yellow Rock River brings you to the sweeping beauty of the sands, and a 10-minute walk to the left gets you to the rusting boiler, pistons and drive shafts of the *Shannon*, an old Murray River paddle steamer which succumbed to the waves in 1906.

Cape Wickham ❿ at the northern tip of the island also saw its fair share of shipwrecks until a massive lighthouse was built in 1861. Its construction had been delayed by squabbling between the states over who would bear the cost, and a number of vessels and lives were lost in the interim. Even *with* the lighthouse the seas were still perilous, as the plaque commemorating the wreck of the *Lock Leven* in 1871 makes clear.

Turn south now, possibly taking time out for a short detour to the northwest along a dirt road to Penny's Lagoon, where compacted sand allows a small lake to sit above sea level. The nearby Mount Lavinia Beach has many kilometres of deserted sand, ideal for fishing.

Down at the opposite end of the island, at the end of more dirt roads, a **Calcified Forest** ⓫ can be found. A few minutes' walk from the car park is a dune system with the skeletal remains of ancient roots and branches poking up from the sand. It's a fragile environment best seen from a raised platform which houses interpretive boards explaining the geological processes involved.

Grassy

Grassy ⓬ is not too far up the east coast from here, but you have to backtrack virtually to Currie and then take the main B25 for 24 km (15 miles) to get there. It's something of a sorry place, never having recovered from the closure in 1990 of the local open-cast mine where scheelite, a key ingredient in tungsten, was extracted. Crumbling houses and stores tell the story and it's unlikely that the Kelp Craft shop, where the rubbery seaweed has been fashioned into glistening brown stuffed dolphins and wallabies, will do enough to turn Grassy's fortunes around. The penguin rookery at the breakwater is the main tourist attraction.

Further up the east coast is **Naracoopa** ⓭, mostly a collection of holiday homes stretched along the beach at Sea Elephant Bay. A long jetty is enticing but unsafe and there are more memorials to shipwrecks. A plaque celebrates the welcoming of King Island into the arms of the British Empire in 1802. ❑

RESTAURANTS, CAFÉS AND BARS

Flinders Island

Restaurants

Interstate Hotel
Patrick St, Whitemark
Tel: 6359 2114
Open: L & D daily. **$$**
Very good-value A$10 meals at lunchtime or a more sophisticated "paddock delights" menu in the evening featuring local beef and wallaby. Lovely dining room too.

Furneaux Tavern
Franklin Parade, Lady Barron
Tel: 6359 3521
Open: L & D Wed–Sun. **$$**
With a chef from the acclaimed Stefano's at the Mildura Grand Hotel in northern Victoria, the restaurant here rates well above most found in pubs. Good counter meals available every day.

Cafés and bars

Sweet Surprises
Lagoon Rd, Whitemark
Tel: 6359 2138
Open: B & L Mon–Fri. **$**
Standard café fare for those who like their food fried.

Flinders Island Bakery
Lagoon Rd, Whitemark
Tel: 6359 2105
Open: B & L Mon–Sat. **$**
Wallaby pies that the locals snap up straight from the oven, interesting sandwiches and hefty cakes. Enough to fuel that climb up Mt Strzelecki.

King Island

Restaurants

Boomerang By The Sea
Golf Club Rd, Currie
Tel: 6462 1288
Open: D daily. **$$**
As close to special-occasion dining as it gets in Currie with impressive sea views as a bonus. Strong emphasis on local fish and meat.

Parers King Island Hotel
Main St, Currie
Tel: 6462 1633
Open: L & D daily. **$**
Solid, good-value pub food in this busy dining room.

Kings Cuisine at the Bold Head Brasserie
Grassy Club, Currie Rd, Grassy
Tel: 6461 1003
Open: D Wed–Mon, L Thurs–Sun. **$$**
Chef Stephen Russell has turned an otherwise dull room in the Grassy Club into the most interesting eatery on the island. Start with the seared octopus and experiment. Some of the accompaniments suffer from having to double for the club's counter meals and service needs to catch up with the standard of the cooking but still worth seeking out.

Baudins
The Esplanade, Naracoopa
Tel: 6461 1110
Open: D Tues–Sat. **$$**
Fresh crayfish is a speciality on the small menu at this dining room mainly geared to the occupants of the proprietor's holiday units. Allow for idiosyncratic service and make sure you book in advance.

Cafés

Nautilus Coffee Lounge
28 Edward St, Currie
Tel: 6462 1868
Open: B & L daily. **$**
Terrific breakfasts and lunches accompanied by the best coffee in town. Its popularity with the locals is testament to the high standards and friendly service

King Island Bakery
Main St, Currie
Tel: 6462 1337
Open: B & L daily. **$**
Interesting range of pies featuring local ingredients such as wallaby and imaginative vegetarian options.

PRICE CATEGORIES

Prices for a three-course dinner per person with a half-bottle of house wine:
$ = under A$50
$$ = A$50–A$75
$$$ = over A$75
L = lunch, D = dinner, BYO = bring your own alcohol.

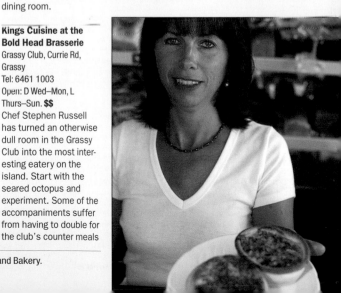

RIGHT: pies from the King Island Bakery.

GETTING THERE AND GETTING AROUND

GETTING THERE

By Air

There are no scheduled flights by international airlines to Australia's island state, so the bulk of Tasmania's visitors arrive by air from one of Australia's mainland capital cities.

Hobart/Launceston
Australia's three main domestic carriers fly direct to Hobart and Launceston from capital cities on the mainland. Flight times are about an hour from Melbourne and two hours from Sydney.

Qantas offers daily direct flights from Sydney and Melbourne to Hobart, and from Melbourne to Launceston.

Australia's two discount airlines, **Jetstar** and **Virgin Blue** offer direct flights to Hobart from Sydney, Melbourne, Adelaide and Brisbane. Jetstar also flies direct to Launceston from Sydney, Melbourne and Brisbane while Virgin Blue has direct links to Launceston from Sydney and Melbourne.

Each of these airlines regularly offers discounted airfares to passengers willing to fly at quieter times such as midweek; refunds and changes to flight times are often ruled out, or a fee is charged for making alterations.

Northwest Tasmania and the islands
Visitors starting, or ending, their journey in the northwest of Tasmania can make the short hop across Bass Strait with two of Australia's regional airlines, **QantasLink** and **Regional Express**. QantasLink flies from Melbourne to Devonport and Burnie, and Regional Express from Melbourne to Burnie.

It is possible to fly direct to several of Tasmania's islands on scheduled flights from Melbourne. Regional Express and **King Island Airlines** fly to King Island and **Airlines of Tasmania** to Flinders Island.

Airlines

Qantas/QantasLink tel: 13 13 13 (Australia), 0845 774 7767 (UK), 1800 227 4500 (N. America); www.qantas.com.au
Jetstar tel: 13 15 38 (Australia), +61 3 8341 4901 (international); www.jetstar.com.au
Virgin Blue tel: 13 67 89 (Australia), +61 7 3295 2296 (international); www.virginblue.com.au
Regional Express tel: 13 17 13 (Australia), +61 2 6393 5550 (international); www.regionalexpress.com.au
Airlines of Tasmania tel: 1800 144 460 (Australia), +61 3 6359 2312 (international); www.airtasmania.com.au
King Island Airlines tel: (+61) (0)3 9580 3777; www.kingislandair.com.au
TasAir tel: 1800 062 900 (Tasmania only); (+61) (0)3 6248 5088 (Australia and international); www.tasair.com.au

By Sea

High-speed ferries with room for 1,400 passengers and 600 vehicles offer the chance to take a more leisurely journey between Tasmania and the mainland. The other advantage is they also allow visitors to bring their own transport.

Spirit of Tasmania I and *II* make an overnight crossing of Bass Strait from Melbourne to Devonport seven days a week. In peak periods there is also a daytime crossing in both directions.

The trip takes about 10 hours and fares vary depending on the time of year, the accommodation chosen and the size of any accompanying vehicles.

The *Spirit of Tasmania III* ferry that made the 22-hour trip down the east coast of Australia from Sydney has been discontinued as of August 2006.

A limited number of discounted fares are available

on the *Spirit of Tasmania* boats. They come with the usual set of restrictions.

Some of the major cruising lines, including Cunard Line and Princess Cruises, include Hobart in their ports of call.

Spirit of Tasmania tel: 13 20 10 or 1800 634 906 (in Australia), +61 3 6421 7209 (international); www.spiritoftasmania.com.au

Cunard Line tel: 1300 725 417 (in Australia), 0845 071 0300 (UK), 1800 728 6273 (USA); www.cunard.com.au

Princess Cruises tel: 020 7800 2222 (UK), 1800 774 6237 (USA); www.princess.com

Carnival Australia tel: 13 24 69; www.carnivalaustralia.com.au

GETTING AROUND

Air

To get around Tasmania in a hurry **TasAir** has a 1-hour flight from Hobart to Burnie (Wynyard airport) Monday to Friday and **Airlines of Tasmania** a 45-minute flight from Strahan to Hobart several times a week.

But generally there is no need to fly the short distances between towns in Tasmania unless you are planning to visit one of its offshore islands. To do that, TasAir has flights from Burnie and Devonport to King Island and Airlines of Tasmania from Launceston to Flinders Island.

Operators such as **Par Avion, TasAir** and **Wilderness Air** also cater to people wanting to get a bird's-eye view of the state's wilderness areas.

Par Avion tel: 6248 5390; www.paravion.com.au

TasAir tel: 6248 5088; www.tasair.com.au

Wilderness Air tel: 6471 7280

From the Airport/ Ferry Terminal

The **Airporter Bus** meets all flights into Hobart International Airport and drops off at accommodation in the city centre and inner suburbs. Charges are A$11 for adults one way or A$19 return; children and concessions A$5. A taxi to the city centre will cost about A$30.

Launceston's airport is about 16 km (10 miles) from the city centre. The **Airport Shuttle** meets all flights and costs A$10 per adult and A$5 per child one way. Taking a taxi into town will cost about A$27.

The airport servicing Burnie is at Wynyard and the **Airbus Shuttle** meets most flights, charging A$30 for adults to central Burnie. Devonport's shuttle bus charges A$10 one way for adults and A$5 for children.

A ferry service runs from the Spirit of Tasmania terminal to central Devonport, Monday to Saturday 7.30am–6pm. Tickets are A$2.50 for adults and A$2 concession.

Airporter Bus Hobart tel: 0419 382 240 or 0419 383 462

Airport Shuttle Launceston tel: 0500 512 009 or 6343 6677

Airbus Shuttle Burnie tel: 0439 322 466

Shuttle Bus Devonport tel: 0400 035 995

Driving in Tasmania

Visiting overseas drivers are not required to obtain a Tasmanian driving licence or an International Driving Permit, provided they have an up-to-date licence from their home country. If the licence is not in English, it is a good idea to carry a translation.

Traffic drives on the left in Australia. Most of Tasmania's road regulations are based on international rules, and it is simply a matter of following the signs, sticking to specified speed limits and so on. But there are a few points that drivers should be aware of.

● Drivers must give way to the right, unless otherwise indicated, to pedestrians (keep an eye out for zebra crossings), and to all emergency vehicles.

● The speed limit in built-up city and suburban areas is 50 kph (30 mph) and in country areas 100 kph (60 mph) unless otherwise indicated.

● It is the responsibility of the driver to ensure that seat belts (including restraints for children and babies under 12 months) are used by passengers at all time.

● There is a 0.05 percent blood alcohol limit for drivers, which is widely enforced by the use of random breath tests carried out by the police.

● Street parking is always in the direction of travel.

Breakdown Services

The **RACT** (Royal Automobile Club of Tasmania) provides roadside service to members, and has reciprocal arrangements with motoring organisations overseas and

interstate, so remember to take membership cards. Most car-hire outlets arrange their own roadside service, but the RACT is a good point of contact for all sorts of motoring advice. There are seven branches across the state.

The **Transport Division** of the Department of Infrastructure, Energy and Resources can provide information about road rules and conditions.
RACT tel: 13 11 11 for roadside assistance, or 13 27 22 for travel, touring and general enquiries; www.ract.com.au *(see also page 133).*
Transport Division tel: 1300 135 513 for general enquiries.

Car Hire

Self-driving holidays are one of the most popular ways to discover Tasmania. Traffic is sparse, the roads picturesque and public transport can only take you so far. If you have not already organised car hire as part of a package, you should shop around for the best deal: the smaller independent operators tend to be cheaper.

Car-hire companies have offices at airports and town centres and it's possible to hire camper vans and motorbikes, too.

An important point to consider is insurance. Many companies

have an excess charge of A\$700–1,500, which means that you pay that amount in the case of an accident. You may wish to pay a little bit extra per day to reduce the figure. When you are getting a quote from the company, ask for the full amount including insurance and charges for items such as baby restraints. Many car-hire companies do not insure normal vehicles for off-road travel, which means that the driver is liable.

For disabled drivers, all the major hire companies have a small number of cars with hand controls. To be sure of availability, you should contact them well in advance.

Vehicle Hire Companies

Avis tel: 13 63 33
Britz Campervan Rentals tel: 1800 331 454
Budget tel: 13 27 27
Europcar 13 13 90
Hertz tel: 6335 1111 (Launceston), 6431 4242 (Burnie), 6424 1013 (Devonport)
Lo-Cost Auto Rent tel: 6231 0550 (Hobart), 6334 3437 (Launceston), 6424 9922 (Devonport)
Rent for Less tel: 1300 883 705
Rentabug tel: 6231 0300 (Hobart), 6427 9034 (Devonport)
Maui Campervans tel: 1300 363 800
Tasmanian Motorcycle Hire tel: 6391 9139
Thrifty tel: 1300 367 227

Public Transport

Buses

Metro Tasmania runs an extensive network of bus services in Hobart, Launceston and Burnie. In Hobart there are an easy way to reach sights that are more than a casual stroll from the town centre such as Hobart's beaches, the Taroona Shot Tower, the Cadbury Factory and Cascade Brewery.

Buses run from 6.30am to 10.30pm Monday to Thursday

and until midnight on Friday and Saturday. There is a limited service on Sundays and holidays.

The main bus termini are at Franklin Square (bordered by Elizabeth, Macquarie, Davey and Murray streets) and Hobart Bus Mall (Elizabeth, Collins and Macquarie streets). Drop into the Metro Shop inside the Hobart General Post Office (corner of Elizabeth and Macquarie streets) to buy money-saving tickets and to pick up timetables.

In Launceston buses run from St John Street between Paterson Street and York Street, ferrying passengers to sights such as the Inveresk Railyards Cultural Precinct and the suburb of Hadspen, close to Entally House.

Services run Monday to Thursday 7am to 6 or 7pm, and Friday until 10.30pm, but are more limited on weekends, with only a few running past 7pm on Saturday.

Buses operate in the Burnie area on weekdays only from 7.30am to 6pm. Trips can be taken to Wynyard, Penguin and Ulverstone from the bus stops on Cattley Street between Mount and Wilson streets.

Devonport is serviced by the **MerseyLink Bus Service**. It operates Monday to Saturday from the Bus Interchange in Rooke Street, with services extending to west, south and east Devonport as well as Spreyton and Latrobe. It is a day service only, with limited hours on Saturday.
Metro Tasmania Tel: 13 22 01 (in Australia); www.metrotas.com.au
MerseyLink Bus Service Tel: 1300 367 590 (in Australia); www.merseylink.com.au

Coaches

Without a car, the main way to travel longer distances is on the regional coach services.

TassieLink has routes all over Tasmania in summer, travelling to popular destinations such as Cradle Mountain, Lake St Clair, Cockle Creek and Port Arthur. It does a daily express run from Hobart to the Spirit of

Tasmania Terminal in Devonport via Launceston.

The Hobart Bus Terminal is at 64 Brisbane Street, and Launceston's is at Cornwall Square on the corner of Cimitiere and St John streets.

Redline Coaches covers the northeast and east coast, including pockets that are not part of the TassieLink network such as Smithton, Scottsdale and Burnie.

Its Hobart terminal is at 199 Collins Street; Launceston's is on the corner of Cimitiere and St John streets; in Devonport at 9 Edward Street; and in Burnie at 177 Wilson Street.

On the east coast the **Bicheno Coach Service** runs from Bicheno to Coles Bay and Freycinet National Park. To do the full run costs A$11 one way and A$18 return. Bookings are essential on some services.
TassieLink tel: 1300 300 520 (in Australia) or +61 3 6230 8900 (international); www.tassielink.com.au
Redline Coaches tel: 1300 360 000 (in Australia) or +61 3 6336 1446 (international); www.redlinecoaches.com.au
Bicheno Coach Service tel: 6257 0293

Ferries

In the maritime city of Hobart it is almost obligatory to spend some time on the water. Of particular note is the Roche O'May-run ferry *MV Cartela*, a

steamer built in 1912, which does regular cruises of Hobart's historic sights, with commentary and a sample of Tasmania's gourmet goodies.

A cruise of the Gordon River and Macquarie Harbour offers the chance to explore areas of 2,000-year-old Huon pines and rainforest in the state's west.

Ferries also allow visitors to have a closer look at the islands off Tasmania's east coast.

Maria Island National Park has no shops, electricity or cars but it is possible to explore its convict ruins and stunning cliff-tops on bicycles or foot. A ferry makes the short trip from the Eastcoaster Resort at Louiseville Point seven days a week at 9.30am, 1.30pm and 3.15pm. A service from Triabunna runs seven days a week in summer at 9.30am and 1.30pm, returning at 12.30pm and 4pm. June to December there is one service a day at 9.30am, returning at 4pm. Bookings are essential.

BUS AND COACH TICKETS

Buses
Metro Tasmania
Tickets are valid for use in Hobart, Launceston and Burnie. A single ticket, which can be bought and validated on the bus, costs between A$1.70 and A$3.90 for adults depending on the distance travelled. Children pay A$1.20 for all sections.

Metro Tasmania's **Day Rover and Day Tripper** tickets allow unlimited travel on buses at off-peak times. Valid Monday to Friday 9am to 4.30pm and after 6pm. It can be used any time on Saturday, Sunday and public holidays. The Day Rover costs A$4.40 for full-fare paying adults and the Day Tripper for children is A$2.60. There are also **10-day versions** of these passes: A$35.20 for adults and A$20.80 for children. The 10-day tickets must be pre-purchased from a Metro ticket

sales agent and validated on the bus when first used.

Family Day Ticket: For A$12.30 a day, two adults and three children or one adult and four children can travel anywhere on the network. Once again this is only valid at off-peak times.

Metro 10: This gives you 10 bus trips for 20 percent less than the cost of paying for each trip separately. Unlike the other money-saving passes these tickets can be used at any time and by more than one person. Depending on the number of sections travelled, adults pay A$13.60 to A$31.20. Children pay a flat A$9.60.

MerseyLink
Single tickets cost between A$1.60 and A$2.70 for a full-fare paying adult and A$1.20 for children aged 4–15 years.

If you are prepared to wait until 9am on weekdays, you can use a **Daytripper** ticket, which costs A$4.20 for adults and A$2.60 for children. They are valid all day on Saturday.

Inter-city coaches
TassieLink
A one-way trip on the express coach from Hobart to Devonport costs A$47.90 for adults. There are four versions of the Tassie Link **Explorer Pass**, ranging from a 7-day pass which is valid for travel within a ten-day period for A$172, to a 21-day pass (for travel within a 30-day period), costing A$280.

Redline Coaches
Redline operates another pass, the **Tassie Pass**. Once again there are four options from a 7-day pass for A$135 to a 21-day version for A$219.

The departure point for the **Bruny Island** ferry service is Kettering, about a 35-minute drive from Hobart. The car ferry runs approximately hourly to Roberts Point on the island from 6.50am to 6.30pm Monday to Saturday and from 7.45am to 6.30pm on Sunday. There is an extra service at 7.30pm on Friday and departure times can vary in peak periods. Bookings are not necessary.

Roche O'May tel: 6223 1914
Maria Island Ferry from Louisville Point tel: 6257 1589; from Triabunna tel: 0427 100 104
Bruny Island Ferry Service tel: 6272 3277
World Heritage Cruises (Gordon River) tel: 1800 611 796 (in Australia) or +61 3 6471 7174 (international); www.worldheritagecruises.com.au
Gordon River Cruises tel: 1800 420 155 (in Australia) or +61 3 6225 7016 (international); www.gordonrivercruises.com.au

Trains

Regular passenger rail services ceased in Tasmania in the 1980s, but there are a few tourist/heritage railways.

The **West Coast Wilderness Railway** is a 34-km (21-mile) journey tracing an historic train line that was once used to carry copper mined in Queenstown to Strahan. The trip through the King River Gorge runs from Strahan or Queenstown and a coach is used to make the return leg. Fares are A$175 for adults or A$120 for children travelling premier class and includes the return coach trip. Tourist class costs A$97 for adults and A$54 for children – and the bus trip is extra.

In the northwest near Devonport the **Don River Railway** makes a 30-minute return trip along the banks of the river to Coles Beach. Set aside a Sunday, a public holiday or a summer day to experience the line when a steam locomotive pulls the train. Return fares are A$10 for adults, A$6 for children and A$25 for families.

West Coast Wilderness Railway tel: 1800 628 288 (in Australia) or +61 3 6471 4300 (international); www.puretasmania.com.au
Don River Railway tel: 6424 6335; www.donriverrailway.com.au

Taxis

Taxis can be hired in the street if their "Vacant" sign is lit. There are plenty of them in the major centres, but it is recommended that passengers phone for a taxi in smaller locations. There may be a small additional charge for a phone booking. All cabs use meters and tipping is not necessary. A short trip will cost A$6–7.

All taxi drivers are required to display an official photo ID licence on their car's dashboard or sun visor. Complaints should be made to the individual taxi company involved (displayed on the side of the vehicle).

If you are travelling with a child under 12 months old and you don't have a suitable restraint, ask for one when booking a cab. It is compulsory for all passengers to wear seat belts.

Tasmanian Cabs tel: 13 10 08. This will connect you to a cab company in most of the major towns in Tasmania including **City Cabs** in Hobart and **Central Cabs** in Launceston.
Taxi Combined Services tel: 13 22 27

Cycling

Tasmania's hilly terrain can make it a challenging place to cycle – but with relatively small distances between towns, the scenery, and a relatively small amount of traffic it is worth the effort.

Tasmania's longest dedicated cycleway is the 15-km (9-mile) **Intercity Cycleway** in Hobart. Major cross-country routes include the 480-km (300-mile) **Tasmanian Trail** from Devonport to Dover, and the 100-km (62-mile) **Western Explorer** route. For further information *see pages 50–51*.

Cycling South Tasmania tel: 6273 4463; www.cyclingsouth.org A very useful site for cyclists.
Bicycle Tasmania www.biketas.org.au Bike club website with all the information you'll need.
Derwent Bike Hire Regatta Grounds, Queen's Domain, Hobart Tel: 6260 4426. Hire bikes for the Hobart cycleways and beyond.
Island Cycle Tours 3 Pitt Street, North Hobart Tel: 6234 4951. Organised two-wheel tours from one to 10 days.
Rent-A-Cycle Tasmania 4 Penquite Road, Newstead, Launceston Tel: 6334 9779. Mountain and touring bikes in all sizes for hire.

A CCOMMODATION

SOME THINGS TO CONSIDER BEFORE YOU BOOK THE ROOM

OVERVIEW

There is a whole range of options when it comes to finding somewhere to stay in Tasmania. A handful of award-winning super luxury five-star establishments are to be found in the two main cities and a couple of the key tourist sites; boutique hotels are beginning to establish a toehold; plenty of pubs provide rooms of varying standards or have motel units, usually in a separate building or annexe.

Bed and breakfast operations cater for a significant proportion of visitors and tend to reflect the British model where there will be a few bedrooms for guests within a largish house and breakfast, often cooked, is provided in a communal dining room. In this respect, Tasmania is unlike mainland Australia, where the term "bed and breakfast" is often applied when a few provisions are left in a hotel or motel room along with a kettle and a toaster and the guest need never interact with another living being.

Incidentally, it is almost unheard of for tea- and coffee-making equipment and supplies not to be provided in accommodation of all levels. Usually it's in the bedroom. If it's not, try the communal room(s).

Apart from the very busiest periods around Christmas and Easter, it's usually possible to find some sort of accommodation at the last minute. Pottering is a very real option in Tasmania; see how the day goes, how far you've got and find somewhere to stay when the mood takes you. The main exception to this is Hobart, where it only takes one sizeable conference or event for beds to be at a premium unless you're prepared to settle for one of the suburbs.

The one sector of the market where it is always advisable to plan ahead is backpacker accommodation. More than one hotelier has been heard to mutter about how the introduction of regular *Spirit of Tasmania* sailings and cheap airfares from the mainland capital cities has simply led to a boom in travellers looking for deals and trying to bargain room rates down. Hostels and backpacker operations have certainly seen an increase in custom and the chances of just turning up and striking lucky from December to March are slim.

Campsites are generally well maintained and spacious. Many have idyllic rural settings and wildlife that has learned the benefit of ambling up looking cute and cuddly. The only issue seems to be the limited number of sites with facilities for caravan and motor home dwellers seeking somewhere to empty their waste tanks.

Visitor Information Centres – official ones identifiable by a yellow "i" on a blue background – can offer advice on all levels of accommodation and many of them, including the ones in Hobart and Launceston, will make bookings on your behalf. Many hotels and other establishments will offer lower rates outside the high season (roughly December–March).

The exponential increase in use of the internet in the travel industry means that most accommodation providers are at least looking at getting their own websites. Listings here include those who had sites at the time of going to press but it's worthusing a search engine to see if others have joined up. It can be a cheap and easy way of checking on room availability or on the latest tariffs.

There are also a number of clearing houses for unsold rooms and you may well get a bargain on the following websites:
www.wotif.com
www.flightcentre.com.au
www.okjack.com.au

ACCOMMODATION LISTINGS

HOBART

Hotels are listed alphabetically within price categories

The City

Hadleys Hotel
34 Murray Street
Tel: 6223 4355
Handy Central Business District hotel with sumptuous Victorian public areas and comfortable rooms. **$$$$**

The Henry Jones Art Hotel
25 Hunter Street
Tel: 6210 7700
www.thehenryjones.com
Stunning conversion of

the old jam factory on Hunter Island right on the waterfront. The art hotel concept is to have 250 or so paintings by contemporary artists hung throughout the building and if you like one, you can buy it. Otherwise it's everything you could want from a top hotel. **$$$$**

Old Woolstore Apartment Hotel
1 Macquarie Street
Tel: 6235 5355
www.oldwoolstore.com.au
New handily placed conversion, ideal for families looking for a touch of luxury. Studios, one-, two- and three-bedroom

apartments. **$$$$**

Quest Savoy
38 Elizabeth Street
Tel: 6220 2300
Solid comfort from the apartment chain can't be faulted. **$$$$**

Somerset on the Pier
Elizabeth Street Peir
Tel: 6220 6600
Exclusive luxury apartments right over the water. **$$$$**

Somerset on Salamanca
8 Salamanca Place
Tel: 6220 6600
Converted grain silos offering similar levels of comfort to its sister operation on the pier. **$$$$**

Wrest Point Hotel
410 Sandy Bay Road, Sandy Bay
www.wrestpoint.com.au
The landmark tower with the casino, this is the place to throw your money away and enjoy a bit of luxury. **$$$$**

Grand Chancellor
1 Davey Street
Tel: 6235 4535
www.ghihotels.com
It would be nice to think that a building so unsympathetic to its surroundings wouldn't

be built today. But it was, it's comfortable and looking out from it makes a stay attractive. **$$$**

Lenna of Hobart
20 Runnymede Street, Battery Point
Tel: 6232 3900
www.lenna.com.au
Classic conversion of grand old colonial house into a sizeable hotel with an award-winning restaurant. Don't be disappointed if your room is in the modern block: you're paying for the location. **$$$**

The Lodge on Elizabeth
249 Elizabeth Street, North Hobart
Tel: 6231 3830
Close to the hub of North Hobart and a pleasant place to stay. **$$$**

Salamanca Terraces
93 Salamanca Place
Tel: 6232 3900
www.salamancaterraces.com.au
Spacious modern studios and apartments right where the action is, run as an adjunct to the Lenna. **$$$**

Zero Davey
15 Hunter Street
Tel: 6270 1444
www.escapesresorts.com.au/locations_t_zero.htm
A stylish boutique hotel that has helped this become one of the streets to stay on. **$$$**

Graham Court Apartments
15 Pirie Street, New Town
Tel: 6278 1333
Helpful and friendly management make this a favourite for families and groups happy to be

north of the Central Business District. **$$**

Leisure Inn Hobart Macquarie
167 Macquarie Street
Tel: 6234 4422
Economical central hotel undergoing complete refurbishment. **$$**

Mid City Hotel
96 Bathurst Street
Tel: 6234 6333
A few minutes' walk from the centre and filled with coach parties, it's nobody's first choice, but actually represents better value than many better-placed options. **$$**

Theatre Royal Hotel
31 Campbell Street
Tel: 6234 6925
Idiosyncratic management style but good rooms in great location offer very good value. **$$**

Central City Backpackers
138 Collins Street
Tel: 6224 2404
It's cheerful, it's cheap, and you get what you pay for. **$**

Hollydene Lodge
55 Campbell Street
Tel: 6234 6434
Cheap accommodation and not far from the waterfront. It's popular with students. **$**

EAST OF HOBART AND THE TASMAN PENINSULA

Richmond

Millhouse on the Bridge
2 Wellington Street
Tel: 6260 2428
www.millhouse.com.au
A sumptuous bed and breakfast right next to Richmond Bridge with gardens running down to the river. **$$$**

Prospect House
1384 Richmond Road
Tel: 6260 2207
www.prospect-house.com.au
Just out of town this glorious old sandstone mansion has fine rooms and an acclaimed restaurant. **$$$**

Richmond Colonial Accommodation
4 Percy Street
Tel: 6260 2570
A range of lovely old cottages around town, all well-equipped and offering good value. **$$$**

Richmond Arms Hotel
42 Bridge Street
Tel: 6260 2109
An old stables behind the pub has been converted into attractive units. **$$**

Sorell

Bluebell Inn
26 Somerville Street
Tel: 6265 2804
www.sullivanscove.com/bluebell
One of the few attractions in Sorell, this is a fine old colonial pub with five guest rooms. **$$**

Eaglehawk Neck

Lufra Hotel
Pirates Bay Drive,
Eaglehawk Neck
Tel: 6250 3262
A large old Deco hotel conveniently placed just up from the Tessellated Pavement and along from the Dog Line. **$$**

Port Arthur

Cascades Colonial Accommodation
531 Main Road, Koonya
Tel: 6250 3873
Convict built cottages upgraded with some style. It has its own on-site museum too. **$$$**

Chancellor Inn Port Arthur (Fox and Hounds Inn)
Arthur Highway
Tel: 6250 2217
Bizarre mock-Tudor edifice harking back to a history that didn't occur in Tasmania. Adequate rooms or units. **$$$**

Comfort Inn Port Arthur
29 Safety Cove Road
Tel: 6250 2101
www.port-arthur-inn.com.au
Set above the historic site, you can't find a more convenient spot although you can find better rooms. **$$$**

Port Arthur Lodge
Arthur Highway
Tel: 6250 2888
A series of well-equipped cabins dotted through the trees above Stewart's Beach. It's a lovely place to stay. **$$$**

Port Arthur Caravan and Cabin Park
Garden Point
Tel: 6250 2340
Basic accommodation if you don't use the excellent camping facilities set in woods above a beach. **$-$$**

Kettering

Oyster Cove Inn
1 Ferry Road
Tel: 6267 4446
Pub overlooking bay and ferry to Bruny Island. Rooms are basic but clean. **$$**

SOUTH OF HOBART AND THE HUON VALLEY

Cygnet

Deep Bay Schoolhouse
5 Abels Bay Road, Deep Bay
Tel: 6297 8231
This is a great place to be pampered in an idyllic setting. No children. **$$**

Cygnet Holiday Park
Mary Street
Tel: 6295 1869
Capacious campground with basic facilities. **$**

Huonville

Grand Hotel
2 Main Street
Tel: 6264 1004
Basic pub rooms are good value (and there's nothing else in town!). **$**

Ranelagh

Matilda's of Ranelagh
2 Louisa Street
Tel: 6264 3493
National Trust-listed mansion with beautiful gardens and exquisite rooms. **$$$**

Franklin

Franklin Lodge
Main Road
Tel: 66266 3506
Distinguished old Federation house with four well-furnished rooms.

Geeveston

Cambridge House
Huon Highway
Tel: 6297 1561
Lovely old house with an attractive garden running down to the river and frequent platypus visits. Run by experienced chef who will supply dinner if requested in advance. **$$**

Bears Went over the Mountain
2 Church Street
Tel: 6297 0110
Teddy bear-themed B&B.
A marketing coup. **$$**

Bob's Bunkhouse
School Road/Huon Highway
Tel: 6297 1069
Well-maintained back-packers' hostel. **$**

Dover

Driftwood Cottages
Bayview Road
Tel: 6298 1441
Set above the water, with views. Units or larger houses.**$$$**

Anne's Old Rectory
Huon Highway
Tel: 6298 1222
www.annesoldrectory.com.au
Welcoming weather-board home, the archetypal B&B. **$$**

Dover Hotel Motel
Main Road
Tel: 6298 1210
Standard accommoda-tion units at this friendly pub. **$$**

Southport

The Jetty House
Main Road
Tel: 6298 3139
Guesthouse tailor-made for relaxing in this quiet backwater. **$$**

Bruny Island

Morella Island Retreats
46 Adventure Bay Road
Tel: 6293 1131
This is the luxury option, where well-equipped sumptuous cottages of varying capacity offer the perfect getaway. **$$$**

Adventure Bay Holiday Village
Main Road (C630), Adventure Bay
Tel: 6293 1270
Reasonable cabins on a large site at the end of the bay. **$$**

Captain James Cook Caravan Park
786 Adventure Bay Road
Tel: 6293 1128
Another beachside option with a handful of good cabins. **$$**

Explorer Cottages
Daniel's Bay, Lunawanna
Tel: 6293 1271
Peace and quiet and comfort in a secluded setting. **$$**

DERWENT VALLEY AND THE SOUTHWEST

New Norfolk

Woodbridge on the Derwent
6 Bridge Street
Tel: 6261 5566
Sheer luxury in this strikingly renovated place just by the bridge. **$$$$**

Glen Derwent
44 Lyell Highway
Tel: 6261 3244
Fetching National Trust-listed mansion set in elegant formal gardens north of the river. **$$$**

Tynwald Willow Bend Estate
Hobart Road
Tel: 6261 2667
Almost absurdly grand mansion dripping in ornate iron lacework. Beautiful rooms and a top-class dining room. **$$$**

All Saints and Sinners Colonial B&B
93 High St
Tel: 6261 2955
A converted inn opposite Arthur Square providing fine rooms and breakfast. **$$**

Bush Inn
49–51 Montagu Street
Tel: 6261 2256
Popular hostelry with reasonable rooms at keen prices. **$$**

Junction Motel
50 Pioneer Avenue
Tel: 6261 4029
A clean, well-run motel. **$$**

Old Colony Inn
21 Montagu Street
Tel: 6261 2731
Attractive old pub now given over to bed and breakfast. The mock tudor half-timbering extends inside. **$$**

Hamilton

McCauley's Cottage
Main Road
Tel: 6286 3258
One of the more sumptuous of several cottages for rent in this sleepy village. **$$$**

Hamilton Inn
Tarleton Street
Tel: 6286 3204
Lovely old pub undergoing long-term renovation with some reasonable rooms. **$$**

Tarraleah

Tarraleah Lodge
Oldina Drive
Tel: 6224 5524
The original Art Deco centrepiece of the old hydro settlement converted into a luxury retreat. **$$$$**

Derwent Bridge

Derwent Bridge Chalets
Lyell Highway
Tel: 6289 1000
Comprehensively equipped cabins with loads of space. **$$$**

Bronte Park Highland Village
378 Marlborough Highway
Tel: 6289 1126
Stay in the former hydro workers' camp in huts named after the nations the men came from. **$$**

Derwent Bridge Wilderness Hotel
Lyell Highway
Tel: 6289 1144
Unadorned rooms but an attractive high-beamed bar and dining room. Service on the perfunctory side. **$$**

Maydena

Giants' Table
Junee Road
Tel: 6288 2293
A collection of well-appointed cabins, some capable of taking sizeable groups. On-site café. **$$$**

Strathgordon

Lake Pedder Chalet
Gordon River Road
Tel: 6280 1166
Originally the camp for workers on the dam project, the Lake Pedder Chalet still accommodates some of them but offers clean, serviceable rooms to tourists. Substantial meals are available at the restaurant. **$$**

THE MIDLANDS AND THE LAKES

Oatlands

Waverley Cottages
104 High Street
Tel: 6254 1264
Four different self-contained houses dotted around town. **$$$**
Kentish Hotel
60 High Street
Tel: 6254 1119
Clean basic rooms in this friendly pub. **$$**
Oatlands Lodge Colonial Accommodation
92 High Street
Tel: 6254 1444
Most effusive welcome in the state at this well-run cosy B&B. **$$**
Midlands Hotel
91 High Street
Tel: 6254 1103
Cheap rooms with shared facilities. **$**

Ross

Colonial Cottages of Ross
12 Church Street
Tel: 6381 5354
www.rossaccommodation.com.au
A choice of four immaculately restored cottages sleeping between two and six. **$$$**
Ross Bakery Inn
Church Street
Tel: 6381 5246
Plenty of treats from the bakery if you choose this historic B&B. **$$$**
Ross Motel
2 High Street

Tel: 6381 5224
A rare modern building in these parts which has to be on top of its game to draw people away from the heritage choices. **$$$**
Man-O-Ross Hotel
35 Church Street
Tel: 6381 5445
You can't go wrong at this atmospheric old pub.**$$**

Campbell Town

Fox Hunters Return
132 High Street
Tel: 6 381 1602
Former pub now successfully relaunched as a B&B with generous rooms and facilities. **$$$**
The Grange
Midland Highway
Tel: 6381 1686
Set back behind the green it looks as if it should have more than its three creditable rooms. **$$$**

Campbell Town Motel and Bistro
118 High Street
Tel: 6381 1158
Unpretentious rooms with prices to match. **$**

Evandale

The Stables
5 Russell Street
Tel: 6391 8048
Three self-contained units in the heart of the village. **$$$**
Clarendon Arms Hotel
11 Russell Street
Tel: 6391 8181
Simple rooms with shared facilities in lovely old pub. **$–$$**

Longford

Brickendon Historic and Farm Cottages
Woolmers Lane
Tel: 6391 1251
www.brickendon.com.au
Have the old farm to yourself after the visitors have left and enjoy these superb wooden cottages. **$$$**
Longford Boutique Accommodation
6 Marlborough Street
Tel: 6391 2126
Nothing has been omitted in the quest to pamper the guests in this converted bank. **$$$**
Woolmers Estate
Woolmers Lane
Tel: 6391 2230

www.woolmers.com.au
Live it up on the estate in these settlers' cottages. **$$$**
Longford Riverside Caravan Park
3 Archer Street
Tel: 6391 1470
Nice riverside setting and simple cabins available. **$**

Great Lake

Central Highlands Lodge
Haddens Bay, Miena
Tel: 6259 8179
Pleasant motel units behind the lodge itself. An enticing bar and dining room where fishermen can eat their catch and explain how they caught it. **$$$**

PRICE CATEGORIES

Price categories are for a double room without breakfast:
$ = under A$70
$$ = A$70–120
$$$ = A$120–200
$$$$ = over A$200

EAST COAST

Orford

Eastcoaster Resort
Louisville Point Road
Tel: 6257 1172
Sizeable resort struggling to keep its guests happy with facilities or service. **$$$**

Orford Riverside Cottages
Old Convict Road
Tel: 6257 1655
Four well-appointed cottages that almost negate the need to step outside. **$$$**

Spring Beach Holiday Villas
Rheban Road, Spring Beach
Tel: 6257 1440
Two-bedroom units facing Maria Island, just off a fine beach. **$$$**

Maria Island

Penitentiary Accommodation Units
Darlington
Tel: 6257 1420
Simple unpowered

bunkhouses and you have to take all your supplies over with you. The upside is blissing out on this beautiful island accompanied by only a few wallabies and Cape Barren Geese. Must book ahead. **$**

Swansea

Piermont Retreat
Tasman Highway
Tel: 6257 8131
www.piermont.com.au
Magnificent stone-built cottages overlooking their own beach. This is the place to recharge the batteries between trips to the pool and the tennis court. **$$$$**

Kabuki by the Sea
Tasman Highway
Tel: 6257 8588
www.kabukibythesea.com.au
Stylish modern units hanging off the cliff by the sea with every whim catered for. **$$$**

Swansea Waterloo Inn
1 Franklin Street
Tel: 6257 8577
The mid-range offering which scores with its ocean views. **$$$**

Amos House and Swansea Ocean Villas
3 Maria Street
Tel: 6257 8656
Straightforward rooms or better-equipped villas near the beach. **$$**

Coles Bay

Edge of the Bay Resort
2308 Main Road
Tel: 6257 0102
www.edgeofthebay.com.au
Right above the beach, a mixture of sleek modern one-bedroom units with floor-to-ceiling views of the Hazards, or slightly older two-bedroom cabins where the design hasn't been honed quite so well. **$$$$**

Freycinet Lodge
Freycinet National Park
Tel: 6257 0101

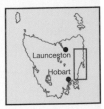

www.freycinetlodge.com.au
Terrific setting under the Hazards and looking out across the bay, this is how to do a national park in style. Cabins are scattered among the trees within easy range of the lodge with its bar and restaurant. **$$$$**

Iluka Holiday Centre
Esplanade
Tel: 6257 0115
www.ilukaholidaycentre.com.au
Expansive campsite with some good-quality cabins. **$$**

Bicheno

Bicheno by the Bay
The Esplanade

Tel: 6375 1171
www.bichenobythebay.com.au
A-frame units near the Gulch with good amenities, including pool and tennis court. **$$$**

Bicheno Gaol Cottages
81 Burgess Street
Tel: 6375 1430
Stay in the old prison and be within walking distance of all the town's attractions. **$$$**

Diamond Island
69 Tasman Highway
Tel: 6375 0100
www.diamondisland.com.au
Modern apartments a little way along the beach from town with everything you could need. **$$$**

Bicheno Backpackers Hostel
11 Morrison Street
Tel: 6375 1651
Comes recommended as the budget option. **$**

Scamander

Chancellor Inn Scamander
Tasman Highway
Tel: 6372 5255
Perfectly good hotel as long as you're looking out of it and not at it. **$$**

Surfside Motor Inn
269 Tasman Highway
Tel: 6375 5177
Standard motel units, well maintained with smooth service. **$$**

St Marys

St Marys Hotel
Main Street
Tel: 6372 2181
Standard reliable pub accommodation. **$**

Ben Lomond

Ben Lomond Creek Inn
Alpine Village
Tel: 6390 6199

www.ski.com.au/creekinn
Just six rooms available in the village unless you're part of a ski club so book well in advance when the snow's in. **$$$**

St Helens

Doherty St Helens Resort
1 Quail Street
Tel: 6376 1999
www.dohertyhotels.com.au
A full-on luxury resort with impeccable service and faultless rooms. Nice deck for drinks and meals overlooking the bay. **$$$$**

Bayside Inn
2 Cecilia Street
Tel: 6376 1466
Unremarkable motel handily placed by the wharf. **$$**

Old Headmaster's House
74 Cecilia Street

Tel: 6376 1125
www.theoldheadmastershouse.com.au
Immaculately restored Victorian house offering some class to the B&B market. **$$**

Queechy Cottages
2 Tasman Highway
Tel: 6376 1321
www.queechycottages.com.au
Stock wooden cabins (one-, two- and three-bedroom) and clean, if uninspiring, motel rooms. **$$**

Binalong Bay

Bay of Fires Character Cottages
64 Main Road
Tel: 6376 8262
Stunning collection of cottages staggered up the side of a steep hill overlooking Binalong Bay. Every facility and views to die for. **$$$**

THE NORTHEAST

Pyengana

Pub in the Paddock
St Columba Falls Road
Tel: 6373 6121
Nice simple rooms in a pretty pub. Don't forget to buy the pig a drink. **$**

Tomahawk

Tomahawk Caravan Park

Tel: 6355 2268
Good basic cabins just behind the dazzling beach. **$**

Bridport

Barnbougle Dunes Golf Links
425 Waterhouse Road
Tel: 6356 0094
Good rooms at competitive prices give golfers

no incentive to leave the course. **$$$**

Bridport Resort and Convention Centre
35 Main Street
Tel: 6356 1789
Rather tired-looking and expensive. **$$$**

Bridairre Modern B&B
32 Frances Street
Tel: 6356 1438
Perfectly serviceable rooms and impressive breakfasts. **$$**

Bridport Bay Inn
105 Main Street
Tel: 6356 1238
Decent motel rooms behind this busy pub. **$$**

Scottsdale

Anabel's of Scottsdale
46 King Street
Tel: 6352 3277

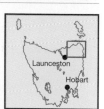

www.anabels.com.au
A National Trust-listed house (with restaurant) which you feel privileged to stay in. **$$$**

PRICE CATEGORIES

Price categories are for a double room without breakfast:
$ = under A$70
$$ = A$70–120
$$$ = A$120–200
$$$$ = over A$200

TRANSPORT
ACCOMMODATION
ACTIVITIES
A – Z

LAUNCESTON

Cornwall Boutique Hotel
St John Street
Tel: 6333 7555
It's got a lot of suites for a boutique hotel but they are all executed with such taste and intelligence that you can almost justify paying the prices being asked. **$$$$**

Hatherley House
43 High Street
Tel: 6334 7727
www.hatherleyhouse.com.au
Hard to fault this newly renovated Georgian mansion which immodestly calls itself "Australia's newest and most outstanding hip hotel". There's a combi-

nation of period feature, artwork from around the world and the sheerest of modern design. Just save up and go. **$$$$**

Peppers Seaport Hotel
28 Seaport Boulevard
Tel: 6345 3333
www.peppers.com.au/seaport
Chic modern development with a range of trendy bars and restaurants on the boardwalk below. **$$$$**

Colonial on Elizabeth
31 Elizabeth Street
Tel: 6331 6588
www.colonialinn.com.au
Built in 1847 as Launceston Church Grammar School, and now a boutique hotel, it's very welcoming and plush, if a

touch florid. Its Quill & Cane has twice been voted Tasmania's Best Restaurant. **$$$**

Penny Royal World
147 Paterson Street
Tel: 6331 6699
www.pennyroyalworld.com.au
Split between two sites, as is the fun park it's attached to, this accommodation offers very good value rooms and apartments. **$$$**

Batman Fawkner Inn
35–9 Cameron Street
Tel: 6331 7222
Central location and good cheap rooms make this an attractive choice. Includes La Primo restaurant and the Batty Bar, which can

get a bit boisterous on Friday and Saturday nights. **$–$$**

Launceston Backpackers
103 Canning Street
Tel: 6334 2327
www.launcestonbackpackers.com.au
Plenty of takers for this clean bright hostel which makes the most of its Federation house setting. **$**

THE TAMAR VALLEY

Low Head

Low Head Beachfront Holiday Village
40 Gunn Parade
Tel: 6382 1000
Extensive campsite that also contains 12 cottages. **$$**

Pilot Station
399 Low Head Road
Tel: 6382 1143
Simple cottages (Lighthouse Keeper's Cottage, Pilot's House etc) but a terrific atmospheric place to stay within the museum precinct. **$$**

George Town

Pier Hotel Motel
5 Elizabeth Street
Tel: 6382 1300
www.pierhotel.com.au
Pleasant rooms and apartments overlooking

the river and well-served by the pub's accomplished bistro. **$$$**

George Town Heritage Hotel
75–77 Macquarie Street
Tel: 6382 2655
Nothing wrong with the rooms here although the heritage element is little in evidence. **$$**

Grindelwald

Tamar Valley Resort Grindelwald
7 Waldhorn Drive
Tel: 6330 0400
High-class accommodation in nutty Swiss-themed resort. **$$$**

Rosevears

Rosevears Estate
1a Waldhorn Drive
Tel: 6330 1800

www.rosevearsestate.com.au
Lovely setting on the slopes of the Tamar Valley for a series of self-contained luxury cottages. **$$$$**

Beauty Point

Pomona Spa Cottages
77 Flinders Street
Tel: 6383 4073
Dramatic hilltop setting for these colonial-style dwellings. Every mod con supplied. **$$$**

Riviera Hotel
Lanborough Street
Tel: 6383 4153
Extremely well-renovated rooms in this old Deco pub set at the water's edge. **$$**

Westbury

Gingerbread Cottages
52 William Street

Tel: 6393 1140
Archetypal heritage cottages in attractive village setting. **$$$**

Fitzpatricks Inn
56 Bass Highway
Tel: 6393 1153
Acceptable rooms tacked on at the back of this beautiful 1833 coaching inn. **$$**

Westbury Hotel
107 Bass Highway
Tel: 6393 1151
Basic, cheap rooms but perfectly comfortable, plus country-kitchen meals. **$**

NORTH AND NORTHWEST

Deloraine

Bonney's Inn
19 West Parade
Tel: 6362 2974
www.bonneys-inn.com
High-quality B&B with a
dining room that
attracts praise. **$$$**

Calstock
Lake Highway
Tel: 6362 2642
A Georgian mansion set
in extensive gardens,
offering elegant rooms,
exquisite French cuisine
and no reason to leave.
$$$

Port Sorell

Hawley House
Hawley Beach
Tel: 6428 6221
www.hawleyhousetas.com
Another fabulously posh
mansion with rooms
available in the house
itself or the stable
block. Secluded setting
and an ambitious dining
room. **$$$**

**Port Sorell Lions
Caravan Park**
Meredith Street
Tel: 6428 7267
It can hold nearly 500
people and in the
summer clearly does.**$**

Latrobe

**Lucinda Colonial
Accommodation**
17 Forth Street
Tel: 6426 2285
Four rooms available in
this gracious National
Trust-listed 1891
Victorian mansion. **$$$**

Lucas Hotel
46 Gilbert Street
Tel: 6426 1101
Good-quality sleeps
right in the centre of
town. **$$**

Sheffield

Kentish Hills Retreat
2 West Nook Road
Tel: 6491 2484
www.kentishhills.com.au
A short hop from the
centre of town, this is a
good reliable motel. **$$**

**Sheffield Country
Motor Inn**
51–3 Main Street
Tel: 6491 1800
Solid performer in the
heart of the action. **$$**

Devonport

**Devonport Historic
Cottages**
66 Wenvoe Street
Tel: 6424 15603
Three refurbished two-
bedroom cottages. **$$$**

MacFie Manor
44 MacFie Street
Tel: 6424 1719
Six rooms up for grabs
in this extensive
Federation-style guest
house. **$$**

River View Lodge
18 Victoria Parade
Tel: 6424 7357
Traditional B&B in a
prime spot facing the
shore.**$$**

Alexander Hotel
78 Formby Road
Tel: 6424 2252
Clean functional rooms
with shared bathrooms.
$

**Mersey Bluff Caravan
Park**
Tel: 6424 8655
Plenty of space for
camping near the sea
and some cabins avail-
able too. **$**

Ulverstone

**Ocean View Heritage
B&B**
Victoria Street

Tel: 6425 5405
High-quality service and
facilities in this impres-
sive old house. **$$$**

Furners Hotel
42 Reiby Street
Tel: 6425 1488
Gloriously ornate exte-
rior isn't quite matched
by the rooms but still a
sound choice. **$$**

Lighthouse Hotel
33 Victoria Street
Tel: 6425 1197
Top end of the market in
this town, with bright
uncluttered rooms. **$$**

Penguin

The Madsen
64 Main Street
Tel: 6437 2588
Top-of-the-range B&B
where detail is every-
thing. **$$$**

Burnie

**Apartments Down
Town**
52 Alexandra Street
Tel: 6432 3219
Ten apartments drip-
ping with Art Deco style
and all the practical
trimmings you could
need. **$$$**

Glen Osborne House
9 Aileen Crescent
Tel: 6431 9866
Set in the leafy hills
above town, this is the
main heritage selection
in Burnie. **$$$**

Chancellor Inn Burnie
139 Wilson Street
Tel: 6431 4455
Not dripping in charac-
ter but a sound choice.
$$

Wynyard

Alexandria
1 Table Cape Road

Tel: 6442 4411
B&B in a nice old Feder-
ation house. Every town
should have one. **$$$**

**Leisureville Holiday
Centre**
145 Old Bass Highway
Tel: 6442 2291
www.leisureville.com.au
There are villas, cabins
and camping options in
this well-resourced com-
plex. Lots for the kids to
do. **$$**

**Waterfront Wynyard
Motor Inn**
1 Goldie Street
Tel: 6442 2351
A steady if unremark-
able motel to be chosen
for its location. **$$**

Boat Harbour
Beach

**Boat Harbour Beach
House**
12 Moore Street
Tel: 6445 0913
A house with everything
you could possibly
need, including a huge
deck with views out to
sea. Another house on
the beach is rented out
by the owners. **$$$**

PRICE CATEGORIES

Price categories are for
a double room without
breakfast:
$ = under A$70
$$ = A$70–120
$$$ = A$120–200
$$$$ = over A$200

Stanley

Abbey's Cottages
1 Marshall Street
Tel: 1800 222 397
A collection of cottages close to the centre of Stanley, all full of character and original features. Very good value for money. **$$$**
@VDL
16 Wharf Road
Tel: 6458 2032
www.atvdlstanley.com.au

The old Van Diemen's Land Company store has been transformed into an ultra-stylish two-suite guesthouse with a vast open-plan communal area. **$$$**
Hanlon House
6 Marshall Street
Tel: 6458 1149
A good B&B with sea views and room for up to 12 guests. **$$$**
Stanley Village
15–17 Wharf Road

Tel: 6458 1404
Down at the bottom of Alexander Terrace and facing out onto the water, this is a well-situated good-quality motel. **$$**
Stanley Cabin and Tourist Park
Wharf Road
Tel: 6458 1266
Just set back from the beach, this popular park is ideal for an outdoorsy summer holiday. **$**

Smithton

Tall Timbers Hotel Motel
3–15 Scotchtown Road
Tel: 6452 2755
www.talltimbershotel.com.au
A symphony to timber indeed, this very woody establishment has rooms in a range of styles and prices as well as a gym, heated pool, bistro and bar. **$$**

CRADLE COUNTRY AND THE WEST

Mole Creek

Mole Creek Guest House
100 Pioneer Drive
Tel: 6363 1399
www.molecreekgh.com.au/
A "boutique bed and breakfast" operation with five sumptuous rooms in a 19th-century hotel. **$$$**

Cradle Valley

Cradle Mountain Chateau

Cradle Mountain Road
Tel: 6492 1404
A modern luxury hotel that doesn't look bedded down in its surroundings yet, it has everything you would expect for the money and in time will probably develop some character. The unfortunate conjunction of faux regency furniture and the clean modern architecture is probably delaying that process. Pop in for a look at the

Wilderness Photographic Gallery if it's open. **$$$$**
Cradle Mountain Highlanders
Cradle Mountain Road
Tel: 6492 1116
Wooden cabins with a real homely feel provide just the right amount of comfort for the rustic setting. **$$$**
Cradle Mountain Lodge
Cradle Mountain National Park
Tel: 6492 1303
One of the iconic hotels, it has guest cabins spread through the surrounding woodland and beside a small lake. The cabins' décor is becoming dated but the real charm has always resided in the lodge – leather sofas, rich wooden panelling and an open fire. The bar is like an old-fashioned pub filled with tired hikers, and the restaurant turns out gourmet creations for those who don't need to rip into hearty pies and chips. **$$$$**
Cradle Mountain Tourist Park and Campground
Cradle Mountain Road

Tel: 6492 1395
Cabins, dorms, campsites; it's all here if you're looking for a budget option. **$$**

Queenstown

Man ov Ore
39 Cutten Street
Tel: 6471 1200
Stay in this late Victorian house for that *fin de siècle* sensation of limitless indulgence. **$$**
Empire Hotel
2 Orr Street
Tel: 6471 1699
Great old pub with well-maintained high-ceilinged rooms upstairs. **$**

Strahan

Franklin Manor
The Esplanade
Tel: 6471 7311
Grand mansion offering

very upmarket bed and breakfast. There's an haute-cuisine restaurant as well. **$$$$**

Gordon Gateway
Grining Street
Tel: 6471 7165
Chalets and motel rooms with great views across to the village. **$$$**

Risby Cove
The Esplanade
Tel: 6471 7572
www.risby.com.au
Modern development with some excellent apartments, ideal for families. **$$$**

Strahan Village
The Esplanade
Tel: 6471 7019
www.strahanvillage.com.au
Dominant down by the wharf is the range of accommodation that comes under the Strahan Village umbrella. There are the cottages around the green,

rooms above Hamers Hotel, and more conventional hotel rooms up on the top of the hill terraces. With this sort of stranglehold it's understandable that prices are high. Some of the motel rooms up the hill are dingy. **$$$**

Strahan Caravan and Tourist Park
Corner Andrews and Innes streets
Tel: 6471 7239
Well laid out park with some good cabins. **$$**

Strahan Youth Hostel
43 Harvey Street
Tel: 6471 7255
Cheap and pretty basic bunk rooms or A-frame huts. **$**

Zeehan

Heemskirk Motor Hotel
Main Street
Tel: 6471 6107
Characterless but

adequate motel. **$$**

Hotel Cecil
Main Street
Tel: 6471 6221
Unpretentious simple rooms in the hotel and some impressive cottages out the back. **$**

Rosebery

Mount Black Lodge
Hospital Road
Tel: 6473 1039
The favourite place to stay for atmosphere and comfort. Reasonable restaurant too. **$$**

Tullah

Tullah Lakeside Chalet
Farrell Street
Tel: 6473 4121
Clean and bright rooms but the appeal is the main chalet with its bar, restaurant and pleasant views over the lake. **$$**

Waratah

Bischoff Hotel
Main Street
Tel: 6439 1188
Nice old pub with some decent rooms. **$**

BASS STRAIT ISLANDS

Flinders Island

Healing Dreams Retreat
855 Trousers Point Road
Tel: 1800 994 477
Beautiful modern house operating as an upmarket B&B, with the option of bringing a chef in in the evenings. Its Californian owner originally kept the place meat- and alcohol-free but Flinders

PRICE CATEGORIES

Price categories are for a double room without breakfast:
$ = under A$70
$$ = A$70–120
$$$ = A$120–200
$$$$ = over A$200

wasn't ready for that. Now, if she were to tackle that name. **$$$$**

Flinders Island Cabin Park
1 Bluff Road, Whitemark
Tel: 6359 2188
Good brick cabins with ultra-helpful owner to direct you round the island, possibly in one of his cars. **$$**

Interstate Hotel
Patrick Street, Whitemark
Tel: 6359 2114
Good rooms to be had at this quiet pub. **$$**

Furneaux Tavern
11 Franklin Parade, Lady Barron
Tel: 6359 3521
Excellent cabins up the hill behind this welcoming modern pub. **$$**

King Island

Baudins
The Esplanade, Naracoopa
Tel: 6461 1110
Modern wooden units cover all the bases without excitement. **$$$**

King Island Holiday Village
Blue Gum Drive, Grassy
Tel: 6461 1177
16 different units and cottages around town. **$$$**

Parers King Island Hotel
7 Main Street, Currie
Tel: 6462 1633
Neat, clean and spacious en-suite rooms in this modern pub. **$$**

Boomerang by the Sea
Golf Club Road, Currie

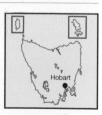

Tel: 6462 1288
The rooms are good and the views are even better at this cliff-top retreat. **$$**

King Island A-Frame Holiday Homes and King Island Gem Motel
95 Main Street, Currie
Tel: 6462 1260
Striking huts that can sleep up to six in comfort, plus conventional motel rooms. **$$**

ACTIVITIES

The Arts, Nightlife, Shopping, Sports and Festivals

The Arts

Art Galleries

Tasmania's environment attracts and inspires many artists. The best way to stay in touch with what's happening on the Tasmanian art scene is to buy a copy of *Art Almanac*, a monthly pocket-sized booklet that lists galleries and their current exhibitions. The publication costs A$3 and is available at good bookshops and galleries. Some of the better-known public and commercial galleries are listed below:

Academy Gallery
University of Tasmania, Invermay Road, Launceston
Tel: 6324 4450
Open Mon–Fri 9am–5pm. Closed public holidays.
A mix of emerging and established contemporary artists.
Art Mob
29 Hunter Street, Hobart
Tel: 6236 9200
Open daily 10am to late.
Exhibits internationally renowned Aboriginal artists.
Bett Gallery
369 Elizabeth Street, North Hobart
Tel: 6231 6511
Open 11am–6pm Mon–Sat.

Tasmanian artists of national repute as well as Aboriginal art from around the country.
Burnie Regional Art Gallery
Willmot Street, Burnie
Tel: 6431 5918
Open Mon–Fri 10am–4.30pm, weekends and public holidays 1.30–4.30pm.
Contemporary Art Services Tasmania (CAST)
27 Tasma Street, North Hobart
Tel: 6231 6231
Open Wed–Sun noon–5pm.
An incubator for upcoming contemporary artists.
Criterion Gallery
12 Criterion Street, Hobart
Tel: 6231 3151
Open Tues–Fri 10am–6pm, Sat 11am–5pm
Emerging contemporary artists in painting, sculpture and new media.
Despard Gallery
15 Castray Esplanade, Battery Point, Hobart
Tel: 6223 8266
Open Mon–Sat 10am–5pm, Sun 11am–4pm
Features the work of Tasmanian artists in a range of media, from painting and sculpture to photography and jewellery.
Devonport Regional Gallery
45–47 Stewart Street, Devonport
Tel: 6424 8296
Open Mon–Sat 10am–5pm, Sun and public holidays noon–5pm.

Inflight Gallery
237 Elizabeth Street, Hobart
Tel: 0409 016 478
Open Wed–Sat 1–5pm during exhibitions.
Artist-run space showing the innovative and the experimental.
Launceston Design Centre
City Park, Brisbane Street, Launceston
Tel: 6331 5506
Open daily 9.30am–5.30pm.
A$2.20 adults, $1.10 children, A$5.50 families.
A wide variety of design from native timber sculptures and ceramics to textiles and digital media.
Queen Victoria Museum and Art Gallery
2 Wellington Street, Launceston and 2 Invermay Road, Inveresk
Tel: 6323 3777
Open daily 10am–5pm.
Australian colonial art and the decorative arts are all part of this public gallery. Don't miss the Inveresk site, once the Launceston Railway Workshops.
Salamanca Arts Centre
77 Salamanca Place, Hobart
Tel: 6234 8414
A microcosm of artists' studios, galleries, arts organisations and theatres.
Tasmanian Museum and Art Gallery
40 Macquarie Street, Hobart
Tel: 6211 4177

Open daily 10am–5pm, closed Good Friday, Anzac Day and Christmas Day.
Tasmania's state-run gallery is home to permanent collections of jewellery and colonial art as well as models of the Tasmanian tiger.

Concerts

The responsibility for providing Tasmania with its classics falls to the **Tasmanian Symphony Orchestra**. The TSO, established in 1948, performs most of its concerts at Federation Concert Hall in Hobart or, when in Launceston, at the Princess Theatre. Its biggest gig is definitely Symphony under the Stars, when crowds flock to free summer-evening concerts in Tolosa Park in Glenorchy and City Park in Launceston.

Virtuosi Tasmania was established in 1992 to harness the casual chamber music activity of the TSO and it now performs regular concerts in venues as diverse as heritage homes, regional art galleries, shearing sheds and limestone caves.

Concerts in some of Australia's vineyards are becoming an established way of marrying the pleasures of wine and song. Tasmania's Moorilla Estate Winery is the scene of indoor and open-air concerts by contemporary and classical performers.

Tasmanian Symphony Orchestra
Federation Concert Hall
1 Davey Street, Hobart
Tel: 6235 3633 or 1800 001 190 (toll-free booking line).
Derwent Entertainment Centre
Brooker Highway, Glenorchy
Tel: 6273 0233
One of Tasmania's biggest venues, it hosts a range of crowd-pleasing entertainment from international acts such as James Brown and Billy Connolly to the latest high-profile home-grown talent.
Devonport Entertainment and Convention Centre
145–151 Rooke Street, Devonport
Tel: 6420 2900
Silverdome
55 Oakden Road, Launceston
Tel: 6344 9988
Anything goes at this 8,000 capacity venue in Launceston, from cycling to concerts.

Theatre and Dance

Tasmania's professional dance company is **Tasdance**. Originally Australia's first dance-in-education company, in 21 years it has built a strong reputation for the inventiveness and accessibility of its repertoire.

Visitors to Tasmania may also be able to catch some of Australia's best contemporary theatre and dance companies when they are on tour. Both the Sydney Dance Company and Bangarra Dance Theatre bring their performances to the island state, appearing at the Theatre Royal in Hobart and the Princess Theatre in Launceston.

The **Sydney Dance Company**, which is based at The Wharf Theatre in Sydney, did the seemingly impossible when it first started in the 1970s; it created a contemporary dance company in a city that was then vaguely suspicious of such things, and made it viable, enduring and most of all, wildly popular. The mover and shaker of the company is choreographer Graeme Murphy, who has been at the artistic helm since the beginning. The work is devastatingly skilled, funny, sensual and highly intelligent.

The **Bangarra Dance Theatre**, under the direction of Stephen Page, is a mostly Aboriginal company performing works that draw both on traditional indigenous forms and contemporary styles. Their work is highly regarded both at home and abroad.

Theatrical troupes make use of warmer summer weather to stage open-air performances. Shakespeare's works are performed in the Queens Domain in Hobart's Royal Tasmanian Botanical Gardens and on the west coast plays are performed at Strahan's open-air theatre.

Civic Theatre
Willmot Street, Burnie
Tel: 6430 5850
Earl Arts Centre
10 Earl Street, Launceston
Tel: 6323 3270 (Theatre North)
Tucked behind Launceston's Princess Theatre, this is where the city's smaller productions are staged.
Playhouse Theatre
106 Bathurst Street, Hobart
Tel: 6234 1536
Presents a mix of Shakespeare, old favourites and more modern performances.
Princess Theatre
57 Brisbane Street, Launceston
Tel: 6323 3666

An Art-Deco palace, this 1,000-seat theatre presents the best dance, comedy and classical music from Tasmania and Australia's capitals.
Tasdance
197 Wellington Street, Launceston
Tel: 6331 6644
Professional dance company.
Theatre Royal
29 Campbell Street, Hobart
Tel: 6233 2299
Australia's oldest working theatre with walls of convict-carved stone.

NIGHTLIFE

Bars

Bar Celona
24 Salamanca Square, Hobart
Tel: 6224 7557
A haunt for Hobart's movers and shakers in the art and business worlds.
Cow
112 Murray Street, Hobart
A hip bar and bistro for Hobart's 20 and 30-somethings.
Lizbon
217 Elizabeth Street, North Hobart
Tel: 6234 9133
Cool and sophisticated – think jazz and absinthe. Open to 3am Wed–Sat and midnight Mon–Tue.
Stillwater River Café, Restaurant and Wine Bar
Paterson Street, Launceston
Tel: 6331 4153
Converted 1830s flour mill with an excellent wine list. Wine by the glass until 6pm, dining only at night.
Ursula's Wine Bar
63 Brisbane Street, Launceston
Tel: 6334 7033
Tasmanian wines by the glass and tapas menu.

Traditional Pubs

Clarendon Arms Hotel
11 Russell Street, Evandale
Tel: 6391 8181

Murals on the walls depict the early history of the area.
The Duke of Wellington
192 Macquarie Street, Hobart
Tel: 6223 5206
The place to go for a few beverages at the end of the working day.
Empire Hotel
2 Orr Street, Queenstown
Tel: 6471 1567
Built in 1901. Don't miss the staircase.
Hope and Anchor Tavern
65 Macquarie Street, Hobart
Tel: 6236 9982
Hobart's oldest watering hole, still going strong.
Knopwoods Retreat
39 Salamanca Place, Hobart
Tel: 6223 5808
A waterfront institution.

Live Music and Nightclubs

Central Café Bar
73 Collins Street, Hobart
Tel: 6234 4419
A groovy chill zone just off Elizabeth Street Mall. Live bands Thurs, Fri and Sat.
Doctor Syntax Hotel
139 Sandy Bay Road, Sandy Bay, Hobart
Tel: 6223 6258
Live acoustic and alternative rock music on Sat and Sun.
Irish Murphys
21 Salamanca Place, Hobart
Tel: 6223 1119
211 Brisbane Street, Launceston
Tel: 6331 4440
Does what all Irish bars do best –

great drink, music and cráic.
Lonnie's Nightclub
107 Brisbane Street, Launceston
Tel: 6334 7889
One for your dancing shoes.
O'Keefe's Hotel
124 George Street, Launceston
Tel: 6331 4015
Stop-off for rock and blues bands.
Republic Bar and Café
299 Elizabeth Street, Hobart
Tel: 6234 6954
Draws a young, arty crowd with its range of live music from reggae to jazz on Sundays.
Royal Oak Hotel
14 Brisbane Street, Launceston
Tel: 6331 5346
Regular live rock, jazz and blues as well as cover bands.
The Saloon
191 Charles Street, Launceston
Tel: 6331 7355
Launceston's biggest live-music venue pulls international acts and DJs. Open to 5 or 7am.

In Devonport there are several live music and drinks options on King Street.

Gay-Friendly Bars

For the inside track on where to go for gay or gay-friendly venues contact the Gay and Lesbian Community Centre's recorded information line. Tel: 6234 8179. Here are some of its suggestions:
Barcode at Cafi Centro
76 St John Street, Launceston
Tel: 6331 3605
Friday nights from 8.30pm.

Flamingos
60 Argyle Street, Hobart
Alternative bar open from 9pm
Saturdays.
Lalaland at Halo
Level 1, 37 Elizabeth Street,
Hobart
Tel: 6234 6669
Dance parties on the first
Saturday of the month.
**Soak at Kaos Café and
Lounge Bar**
237 Elizabeth Street, Hobart
Tel: 6231 5699

Cinema

Most of Tasmania's cinemas
screen the latest mainstream
releases. A few show the
occasional art-house or foreign-
language film and the independent **State Cinema** is well-known
and well-loved for its eclectic pro-
gramming. Foreign-language films
usually have English subtitles.

SBS, Australia's multicultural
broadcaster, runs a film review
programme on Wednesday
evenings covering most of the
major releases. ABC has a similar
programme on Wednesday nights,
repeated on Sundays.

Burnie Metro Cinemas
Marine Terrace, Burnie
Tel: 6431 5000
CMAX Devonport
5–7 Best Street, Devonport
Tel: 6420 2111
Eastlands Village Cinemas
Bligh Street, Hobart
Tel: 6245 1033
Glenorchy Village Cinemas
Cooper Street, Glenorchy
Tel: 6273 0444
Hobart Village Cinemas
181 Collins Street, Hobart
Tel: 6234 7288
Launceston Village Cinemas
163 Brisbane Street, Launceston
Tel: 6331 5066
State Cinema
375 Elizabeth Street,
North Hobart
Tel: 6234 6318
Screens anything from surf films
to world cinema and the latest
Australian releases.

Tickets

Buying Tickets

Performance venues often sell
tickets through ticket agencies
such as Centertainment, Tick-
etek and Ticketmaster. Names
and numbers of venues are pub-
lished in all listings of what's on.
Centertainment
53 Elizabeth Street Mall, Hobart
Tel: 6234 5998
www.centertainment.com.au
Also has booking offices in
Launceston, Burnie and
Devonport.
Ticketek
Theatre Royal Hobart,
29 Campbell Street or CD Centre,
81 Brisbane Street, Launceston
Tel: 13 28 49
www.ticketek.com
Ticketmaster
Derwent Entertainment Centre,
Brooker Highway, Glenorchy;
Myer Hobart, 55 Murray Street;
Myer Launceston, 108 Brisbane
Street
Tel: 13 61 00
www.ticketmaster.com.au

Gambling

Tasmania's main venue for
gambling is **Wrest Point Casino**.
Australia's first casino, it sits on
the edge of the Derwent at Sandy
Bay and offers a choice of traditional table games and video
machine gaming. There are also
shops, cafés, bars, live shows
and a 269-room hotel which
includes some 5-star options.

The bushland setting of
Launceston's **Country Club
Casino** is the place to go in the
north of Tasmania for a turn at the
blackjack tables, a game of tennis
or a round of golf at its 18-hole
course. Accommodation, cafés
and bars are all part of the scene.
Wrest Point Casino
410 Sandy Bay Road, Sandy Bay;
tel: 6225 0112 (reception) or
6211 1750 (accommodation).
Country Club Casino
Country Club Avenue, Prospect;
tel: 6335 5777.

Tassie for Kids

Tasmania's attractions will keep
even the most demanding children happy. Few kids (or adults)
can resist the lip-smacking opportunity to see the **Cadbury Chocolate Factory** in action and taste a
few samples along the way
(Cadbury Road, Claremont; tel:
1800 627 367).

The Discovery Space at the
**Tasmanian Museum and Art
Gallery** (40 Macquarie Street,
Hobart; tel: 6211 4177) has
hands-on action and its summer
holiday programmes can include
anything from a sneak preview of
the taxidermist's latest work to
putting butterflies under the
microscope.

In Hobart the **Terrapin Puppet
Theatre** (77 Salamanca Place,
Hobart; tel: 6223 6834) introduces under-12s to the magic of
performance via Hans Christian
Andersen stories with an Aussie
twist and other contemporary
tales. The **Imaginarium Science
Centre** (Wenvoe Street, Devonport; tel: 6423 1466) has interactive exhibits that are changed
every school term.

Tasmania's wildlife can be
observed up close at the **Tasma-
nia Devil Park** (Arthur Highway,
Taranna; tel: 6250 3230),
Bonorong Park Wildlife Centre
(Briggs Road, Brighton; tel: 6268
1184) or **Platypus House**
(Inspection Head Wharf, 200
Flinders Street, Beauty Point; tel:
6383 4884).

Or you can take your chances
and try to catch them in their
natural habitat. **Narawntapu
National Park**, east of
Devonport, is one of the best
places to see wombats, kangaroos, wallabies and brush-tailed
possums, while **Fern Glade** in
Burnie and the rivers of Latrobe
and Stanley are three top spots
to see a platypus. Bicheno, on
the east coast, is one of the best
locations for fairy penguins, but
they are also found at Bruny
Island, Low Head, Burnie,
Stanley and, of course, Penguin.

SHOPPING

What to Buy

Aboriginal Art

In Australia, Aboriginal artists sell their work in art centres, specialist galleries and craft retailers and through agents. Each traditional artist owns the rights to his or her particular stories, motifs and tokens. Indigenous fabric designs by artists such as Jimmy Pike are eagerly sought. Bark paintings are the most common form of Koori (Aboriginal) art, but look out for contemporary works on board, boomerangs and didgeridoos. A Tasmanian speciality is shell necklaces, particularly those featuring the mother-of-pearl mareener shells. These can take months to complete and there are only a handful of Aboriginal women still producing them.

Antiques

Early settlers in Tasmania had an incentive to bring as much valuable furniture with them as possible – oddly, the amount of land they were granted depended on the value of the furniture they brought with them. As a result, Tasmania is a happy hunting ground for antique-lovers. **Bathurst Street** and **Battery Point** in Hobart are good places to start the search. But don't overlook the possibilities that may be found in smaller towns such as **Evandale**, **Latrobe**, **Longford**, **Ulverstone** and **Devonport**. Look also for clocks, jewellery, porcelain, silverware, glassware, books and maps.

Clothing

A distinct style of clothing has evolved in rural Australia. Driza-Bone oilskin coats, Akubra hats (wide-brimmed and usually made of felt) and the R.M. Williams range of bushwear (including boots and moleskin trousers) are good examples. Blundstone boots, made in Tasmania and renowned

for their durability, are another.

Australian merino sheep produce fine fleece ideal for spinning. All sorts of knitwear, from children's clothing to Casaveen's bright designs are available.

Wood Products

Look out for furniture, sculptures and homewares made out of Tasmanian speciality timbers such as Huon pine, myrtle, blackwood and furniture timbers such as colonial cedar and kauri. Strahan, on the west coast, is a centre for craftspeople working with wood.

Food and Drink

Local delicacies include cheese, wine, chocolate truffles and leatherwood honey. Australian wines can be bought at any pub or bottle shop, with fair quality wines starting at A$10 a bottle. Don't forget, however, that one of the pleasures of touring Tasmania is going to the source of its gourmet treasures: the farm gate, the dairy and the vineyard.

Cascade and Boag's are renowned as being two of Australia's better brewers and their beers are available throughout the state. Arguably the best of all is Hazards Ale, produced in small quantities on the east coast and only available through a limited number of outlets.

Where to Buy

Elizabeth Street Mall and the adjoining **Cat and Fiddle Arcade** and **Centrepoint Hobart Shopping Centre** form the retail hub of Hobart, with all the major department stores and retail chains. Go to **Salamanca Place** for arts and crafts, particularly on a Saturday when the market is held.

In Launceston the **Brisbane Street Mall** is home to the mainstream shopping options and **The Quadrant Mall** is the place to go for more eclectic choices. Check out the **Rooke Street Mall** and **Best Street** in Devonport, and **Mount Street** in Burnie.

CONSUMER RIGHTS

If you have a complaint or query concerning shopping, contact Consumer Affairs and Fair Trading in Tasmania (tel: 1300 654 499). Larger stores generally offer greater consumer protection. Ask to speak to a manager or customer service officer if you are unhappy with the service.

Australiana

All Goods
93 Harrington Street, Hobart
Tel: 6236 9969
A good place to buy Blundstones bushman's boots. Also in Launceston and Devonport.
Art Mob
29 Hunter Street, Hobart
Tel: 6236 9200
Specialises in shell necklaces by Tasmanian Aboriginal artists.
Australian Geographic Shop
63 Elizabeth Street, Hobart
Tel: 6234 1110
For the great outdoors.
Casaveen Knitwear
44 High Street, Oatlands
Tel: 6254 0044
Factory and retail outlet for colourful knitwear.
House of Anvers
8925 Bass Highway, Latrobe
Tel: 6426 2958
Truffles, fudge and pralines.
IXL Design
31 Hunter Street, Hobart
Tel: 6231 2288
A temple of design for furniture, homewares and ceramics.
King Island Dairy
North Road, Loorana
Tel: 6462 1348
Tastings are held in the fromagerie, daily except on Saturdays.
R.M. Williams
104 Elizabeth Street, Hobart
Tel: 6234 7877
Stockists of their bush gear.
Tasmanian Wine Centre
201 Collins Street, Hobart
Tel: 6234 9995
Waverley Woollen Mills
Waverley Road, Waverley
Tel: 6339 1106

TRANSPORT

Books

The ABC Shop
70 Murray Street, Hobart
Tel: 1300 360 111
Small but well-chosen selection.

Ancient Relics
41 Formby Road, Devonport
Tel: 6423 3316
Antiquarian and second-hand
books.

Angus & Robertson
36 Elizabeth Street, Hobart
Tel: 6234 4288
Also in Bellerive, Launceston,
Devonport and Burnie.

Astrolabe Booksellers
81 Salamanca Place, Hobart
Tel: 6223 8644
Old and rare books, specialising
in Tasmania, Australia, Aborigine,
Antarctica and maritime subjects.

Birchalls
118–120 Brisbane Street,
Launceston
Tel: 6331 3011
Tasmania's oldest bookshop,
also in Hobart (147 Bathurst
Street), Burnie and Devonport.

Book City Hobart
73 Bathurst Street, Hobart
Tel: 6234 4225

Dymocks
70 Murray Street
Tel: 6231 6656

Ellison Hawker Bookshop
96 Liverpool Street, Hobart
Tel: 6234 2322
Independent bookstore, all
categories.

Fullers Bookshop
140 Collins Street, Hobart
Tel: 6224 2488
93 St John Street, Launceston
Tel: 6334 8499
An independent bookseller with a
range of titles by local authors.

Hobart Bookshop
22 Salamanca Square, Hobart
Tel: 6223 1803

Olde Musick and Cookery Books
185 Bathurst Street, Hobart
Tel: 6231 0803
Specialises in antiquarian
cookbooks and illustrated
sheet music.

Sandy Bay Bookshop
197 Sandy Bay Road, Sandy Bay
Tel: 6223 6955
Independent bookstore.

Stories Bookshop
126 Charles Street, Launceston
Tel: 6331 5716

Tasmanian Map Centre
100 Elizabeth Street, Hobart
Tel: 6231 9043
Specialist map store.

Shopping Centres

**Centrepoint Hobart Shopping
Centre**

70 Murray Street, Hobart
Tel: 6223 2572
A mix of clothes, food and book-
shops in the centre of town.

Cat and Fiddle Arcade
51 Murray Street, Hobart
Tel: 6231 2088
Thirty-five shops set on two
levels form a passage between
Centrepoint and Elizabeth
Street Mall. Turn up on the hour
to see the clock's performance.

Eastlands Shopping Centre
Bligh Street, Rosny Park
Tel: 6244 5222
Located on the eastern shore
of the Derwent River in Hobart,
Tasmania's largest shopping centre has four department stores
and a total of 70 speciality shops
and a multi-level car park.

Northgate Shopping Centre
387–393 Main Road, Glenorchy
Tel: 6272 0122
Home to department stores and
speciality shops in Hobart's
northern suburbs.

Markets

Many towns now have a farmers'
or produce market at least once

a month where you can buy or
simply enjoy the spectacle, and
there are plenty of markets cater-
ing to people with an urge to rum-
mage through bric-a-brac and
second-hand goods. Sharp-eyed
bargain hunters will usually be
rewarded if they browse for long
enough among the huge variety
of merchandise. Most stall-
holders handle cash only, so be
prepared to bargain.

Salamanca Market
Salamanca Place, Hobart
Sat 8.30am–3pm
Weekly market set against a
backdrop of historic sandstone
warehouses: about 300 stalls
offering everything from fresh
produce and flowers to hand-
spun, hand-knitted sweaters.

Island Markets
54–56 Gormanston Road,
Moonah, Hobart
Fri, Sat and Sun 10am–4pm
This relatively new indoor market
specialises in food including live
and fresh seafood, meat and Tasmanian wine and olives.

Penguin Market
Corner Arnold and King Edward
Streets, Penguin
Sun 9am–3pm
Fresh produce, arts and crafts,
woodwork and metalwork are
sold at stalls in the Old Penguin
Primary School.

Burnie Farmers Market
Wivenhoe Show Ground, Burnie
1st and 3rd Saturday of the
month, 8.30am–12.30pm
A satisfying array of fresh produce.

ACCOMMODATION

ACTIVITIES

A – Z

Department Stores

Tasmania's main department stores are Myer and Harris Scarfe. They both offer an extensive range of goods from fashion and accessories to hardware and homeware. Target and KMart fill a similar role at the lower end of the price spectrum.

Myer
Liverpool Street and Murray Street, Hobart.
Tel: 6234 2888
108 Brisbane Street, Launceston. Tel: 6331 6233.

Harris Scarfe
91 Collins Street, Hobart.
Tel: 6235 0350
133 Brisbane Street, Launceston. Tel: 6331 5622
(Also in Burnie, Devonport, Moonah and Ulverstone.)

Target
Elizabeth Street Mall, Hobart.
Tel: 6235 2555
78 Charles Street, Launceston.
Tel: 6334 3550
(Also in Glenorchy, Burnie and Devonport.)

KMart
Corner of Best and Gunn Streets, Devonport. Tel: 6424 6401
15 Racecourse Crescent, Launceston. Tel: 6331 8444.
(Also in New Town, Rosny and Burnie.)

SPORT

Spectator Sports

The main action in Tasmania occurs on the water; otherwise the only options for watching sports are **Australian Rules football** and **international and national cricket**.

If you're keen to catch an Aussie Rules match or some cricket in Tasmania, ask your travel agent to find out about tickets prior to arrival. The ticket agency, **Ticketmaster** (tel: 13 61 00), handles international cricket matches, and tickets to Australian Football League matches can be bought online through Aurora Stadium *(see below)*.

Bellerive Oval
Derwent Street, Bellerive on Hobart's eastern shore.
Tel: 6211 4000 (Tasmanian Cricket Association)
Hosts all the major cricket matches including international ones and some Victorian Football League games.

Aurora Stadium
Invermay Road, Launceston
Formerly known as York Park, this is the venue for major Australian

Football League games and some Victorian Football League games. See www.aurorastadium.com for online bookings, or buy tickets at Launceston's Silverdome (tel: 6344 9988) or Princess Theatre (tel: 6323 3666).

Sydney to Hobart and Melbourne to Hobart Yacht Races
These famous races finish at Constitution Dock in Hobart.

Horse Racing

Tasmania's racing season hits its peak in summer, with the Hobart and Launceston Cups both held in February. There are also race meetings on Sundays throughout the year, usually alternating between Hobart and Launceston. Midweek meetings are usually held at Devonport.

Tasmanian Racing Club
Elwick Racecourse, Goodwood Road, Glenorchy
Tel: 6272 9492

Devonport Racing Club
Racecourse Road, Devonport
Tel: 6427 2070

Tasmanian Turf Club
Mowbray Racecourse, Launceston
Tel: 6326 1070

Devonport Racing Club
Racecourse Road, Devonport
Tel: 6427 2070

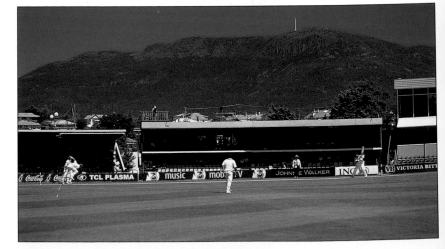

Participant Sports

Golf

Tasmania has around 80 golf courses. Most are inexpensive, well equipped and very scenic. Ask at your own golf club before leaving home about reciprocal member-ship arrangements with Tasman-ian clubs. The **Tasmania Golf Council** (tel: 6244 3600) is a good starting point for golfers from abroad looking to play a round. Included in the following list are Bothwell Golf Course or Ratho Links, the oldest golf course in the southern hemisphere, and Barn-bougle Dunes, one of the newest, which has golfers waxing lyrical.

Barnbougle Dunes
Bridport (follow the signs from the centre of town)
Tel: 6356 0094
Bothwell Golf Course
Lake Highway, Bothwell
Tel: 6259 5702
Devonport Golf Club
66 Woodrising Avenue,
Devonport
Tel: 6427 2381
Current home of the Tasmanian Open Golf Championships.
Royal Hobart Golf Club
81 Seven Mile Beach Road,
Seven Mile Beach, Hobart
Tel: 6248 6161
Tasmania Golf Club
Barilla Bay, Cambridge
Tel: 6248 5098

Tennis

Ask about equipment hire when calling to book a court. A good stop for information is **Tennis Tasmania** (tel: 6334 4237; www.tennistasmania.com.au). There are 58 tennis clubs in Tasmania and the website allows you to search for a nearby one. Courts for hire include:
Domain Tennis Centre
2 Davies Avenue, Domain,
Hobart
Tel: 6234 4805
Launceston Indoor Sports Arena
23 Racecourse Crescent,
Launceston
Tel: 6331 5333

Burnie Tennis Club
Eastwood Drive, West Burnie
Tel: 6431 3402

Swimming

Some hotels have their own pools, but they can be a bit short for a good workout. Here are a few of the local alternatives:
Burnie Aquatic Centre
Terrylands, Burnie
Tel: 6431 4768
October to end of March, Mon–Fri 6am–7pm, weekends and public holidays 10am–7pm.
Glenorchy Olympic Swimming Pool
Anfield Street, Glenorchy
Tel: 6216 6701
October to end of March, Mon–Fri 6am–6.40pm, weekends and holidays 7.30am–6.40pm.
Tattersall's Hobart Aquatic Centre
Davies Avenue, Hobart
Tel: 6222 6999
Mon–Fri 6am–10pm, weekends and public holidays 8am–6pm. 50m and 25m pools.
For a dip of a different kind try the **Hastings Thermal Pools** in the south of the state. The pools, near the Hastings Caves, are kept at a constant balmy temper-ature year round. (State Reserve, Hastings; tel: 6298 3209).

OUTDOOR ACTIVITIES

Tasmania is a great place for all kinds of outdoor activities. *See also pages 49–53 for an overview.*

Scuba Diving

There are dive operators based in Bicheno, Hobart, St Helen's and Eaglehawk Neck on the east coast, as well as George Town in the Tamar Valley, and King and Flinders islands. To make contact with a local diver, try the **Tasmanian Scuba Diving Club** (tel: 0418 138 293).

Dive companies include:
Come Dive
5929 Arthur Highway, Taranna
Tel: 6231 9749

East Coast Scuba Centre
124 Binalong Bay Road,
St Helen's
Tel: 6376 8368
Flinders Island Dive
22 Wireless Station Road,
Emita
Tel: 6359 8429
Go Dive
190 Argyle Street, Hobart
Tel: 6231 9749

Kayaking

Sea kayaking options range from day paddles in sheltered waters to exposed crossings to the off-shore islands. Some of the popu-lar spots include Bruny Island, the D'Entrecasteaux Channel, the Tasman and Freycinet peninsulas, Bathurst Harbour, Lake St Clair and the Henty and Gordon rivers.
Blackaby's Sea Kayaks
GPO Box 1138, Hobart
Tel: 0418 124 072
Twilight, half-day or extended tours in and around Hobart.
Freycinet Adventures
2 Freycinet Drive, Coles Bay
Tel: 6257 0500
Days tours and longer kayak/camping expeditions.
Roaring 40s Ocean Kayaking
Oyster Cove Marina, Kettering
Tel: 6267 5000
The sole Port Davey operator at present, leading three- and seven-day paddles with all equip-ment and food provided.

White-water Rafting

White-water rafting on the Franklin River is one of the ulti-mate multi-day rafting journeys but for those who prefer to start at a slower pace another option is the Picton River near Hobart where there are single-day trips.
Aardvark Adventures
Anfield Street, Glenorchy
Tel: 6273 7722
Rafting tours of the Huon, Picton and Mersey rivers.
Rafting Tasmania
683 Summerleas Road,
Fern Tree, Hobart
Tel: 6239 1080
Half-day, full-day or extended tours of the Derwent, Huon, Picton,

North Esk and Franklin rivers.

Water by Nature
157 Macquarie Street, Hobart
Tel: 1800 111 142
Ten-, seven- and five-day tours;
everything provided.

Sailing

Whether sailing the Derwent
River or attempting the more
adventurous route up the west
coast, getting out on the water in
a yacht is an integral part of
Tasmanian culture. Tasmanians
own more boats per head of population than in any other part of
Australia and many of their major
sporting events revolve around
boating.

To find out more about the
Tasmanian yachting scene have a
look at the **Tasmanian Yachting**
Association website (www.tas.
yachting.org.au). It has information
on clubs, events and races.
Another good point of contact is
the **Royal Yacht Club of Tasma-**
nia (Marieville Esplanade, Sandy
Bay; tel: 6223 4599). For boat
hire check the Yellow Pages
under boat charter hire.

Walking

The Tasmania Parks and Wildlife
Service has put together a
brochure on 60 walks around the
country classified as "short",
which is anything from a few minutes to a full day. There is good
signage at the start of each of
these walks.

One of the most popular multi-
day walks is the **Overland Track**
(see page 206). The five- to eight-
day trek through the heart of
Cradle Mountain– Lake St Clair
National Park introduces visitors
to its glacial lakes, alpine
shrubbery and waterfalls. If you
plan to walk in the peak period
from November to the end of April
it is necessary to book at
www.overlandtrack.com.au. The fee
for walking the track is $100 per
adult or $80 for children and
concessions.

Other multi-day walks include
the **South Coast Track** which follows a route used by Tasmanian
Aborigines and the shorter four-
day walk from Waterfall Bay near
Eaglehawk Neck to Fortescue Bay.
See also pages 49–50.

Cycling

See page 236 for details.

ADVENTURE AND WILDERNESS TOUR OPERATORS

For a useful overview of what's
available, two useful websites are:
www.discovertasmania.com.au
www.tasadventures.com

Aardvark Adventures, Glenorchy
Tel: 6273 7722
Abseiling, rafting, and caving in
Hastings Caves (with the largest
tourist cave in Australia).
Tasmanian Expeditions
Launceston
Tel: 6339 3999
www.tas-ex.com
Operates the largest range of
active and adventure holidays in
Tasmania, including bushwalk-
ing, climbing, cycling, rafting and
sea-kayaking.

CAVING
Wild Cave Tours
Caveside
Tel/fax: 6367 8142
www.wildcavetours.com
Caving for beginners in the
beautiful Mole Creek caves
surrounded by World Heritage
mountain wilderness.

HANG GLIDING
Cable Hang Gliding, Geeveston
Tel: 0419 311 198
www.cablehanggliding.com.au
Safe, 200- and 400-metre flights
from Launceston and at Huon
D'Entrecasteaux Bruny in the
south.

HORSE RIDING
Huon Valley Horsetrekking
Judbury
Tel: 6266 0343
Trail rides and overnight camp-
ing tours near Hobart.
Cradle Country Adventures
Kimberley
Tel: 6497 2154
Trail rides suitable for all levels
from beginners to advanced.

RIVER CRUISES
Gordon River Cruises, Strahan
Tel: 1800 420 155
www.gordonrivercruises.com.au
Cruises aboad the fast and quiet
catamaran, *Lady Jane Franklin II.*
World Heritage Cruises
Strahan
Tel: 6471 7940
www.worldheritagecruises.com.au
Tasmania's largest eco-tourism
cruise operator and over 100
years old. Choose between
overnight and day cruises.
(See also pages 215 and 218)

RAFTING
Water By Nature, Kingsgrove
Tel: 408 242941
www.franklinrivertasmania.com
Five-, seven- or ten-day expedi-
tions on the Franklin River.

WILDLIFE TOURS
Pepper Bush Adventures
Scottsdale
Tel: 6352 2263
www.pepperbush.com.au
Tailor-made "wilderness, wildlife
and gourmet bush tucker
encounters" for visitors seeking
an authentic Tasmanian lifestyle
experience.
Inala Nature Tours, Bruny Island
Tel: 6293 1217
www.inalabruny.com.au
Personalised wildlife tours of
Bruny Island and other
Tasmanian destinations.
Wilderness to West Wildlife
Tours, Stanley
Tel: 6458 2038
www.wildernesstasmania.com
4WD eco-tours, with wildlife
including platypus, penguins,
Tasmanian devils and wombats.

For **scenic flights**, *see* Tips *on
pages 76, 122 and 218.*

TRANSPORT

VISITING TASMANIA'S NATIONAL PARKS

You'll need to buy a pass to visit any of the National Parks, available from visitor centres, tourist information centres and Spirit of Tasmania ferries. Daily passes cost $10 per person and $20 per vehicle. Eight-week ($30 per person, $50 per vehicle) and annual passes ($60–84 depending on season) are also available. Call 6233 2621 for more information, or see the excellent Parks & Wildlife service website at www.parks.tas.gov.au. The Wilderness Society site at www.wilderness.org.au/regions/tas is a good source of information on environmental issues.

Fishing

Tasmania offers the ultimate in trout fishing, in idyllic surroundings. Offshore, the game-fishing waters stretch from Flinders Island in the north, past St Helens and all the way down the east coast to the Tasman Peninsula. Targets include marlin, swordfish, tuna and mako sharks. For more information see www.fishonline.tas.gov.au.

Bluewater Sportsfishing Charters

Georges Bay Marina, Tasman Highway, St Helen's
Tel: 6344 4134.
Game fishing and deep-sea fishing from an 11-metre flying bridge boat.

Fish Wild Tasmania

115a King Street, Sandy Bay, Hobart
Tel: 0418 348 223.
Offers one- to five-days tours, principally in trout waters.

EVENTS AND FESTIVALS

Tasmanians love a party, and the biggest knees-up of the year is the arrival of the competitors in the annual Sydney to Hobart and Melbourne to Hobart yacht races at Hobart's Constitution Dock. The celebrations begin shortly after Christmas and last over New Year.

Spring (Sept–Nov)

Blooming Tasmania, Sept–May. Floral shows, garden open days and festivals are part of this series of events which run from spring to autumn across the state.

Royal Launceston Show, Oct. Agriculture comes to town.
Royal Hobart Show, late Oct. A celebration of Tasmania's primary industries.
Tasmania Craft Fair, early Nov. See the works of Tasmania's finest craftspeople in Deloraine.
V8 Supercars Championship, mid-Nov. Symmons Plains Raceway near Launceston. Rev-heads' heaven as the souped-up Fords and Holdens mix it. Very loudly.
The Piners Festival, Nov, Strahan. Wood-chopping, punt races and a sail past of historic boats are all part of the celebration of piners on the west coast.
Point to Pinnacle Road, Run and Walk, late Nov. A 22-km (14-mile) foot race from Hobart's Wrest Point to the top of Mount Wellington.

Summer (Dec–Feb)

Sydney to Hobart Yacht Race and Melbourne to Hobart Yacht Race, 26 Dec–3 Jan. Thousands welcome the yachts at Constitution Dock.
Hobart Summer Festival, 28 Dec–8 Jan. Two weeks of performance, art and music at the waterfront.
Taste of Tasmania, 28 Dec–3 Jan, Hobart waterfront. Sample the best local food and drink.
King of the Derwent Yacht Race, 2 Jan. Competitors in the Sydney to Hobart and Melbourne to Hobart yacht races battle it out on the Derwent River.
Tasmanian Wine Show, mid-Jan.
Australia Day Celebrations, 26 Jan. Parades, concerts and fireworks.

Symphony Under the Stars, Feb. The Tasmanian Symphony Orchestra goes alfresco in Hobart and Launceston.
Australian Wooden Boat Festival, Feb in even-numbered years, Hobart. This biennial event draws wooden boat builders and lovers from across the globe.
Festivale, mid-Feb. Launceston's annual shindig celebrating excellence in the arts, entertainment, food and wine.
Royal Hobart Regatta, mid-Feb. A long weekend for southern Tasmania to join in one of the oldest maritime regattas in Australia.
Hobart Cup, mid-Feb. The culmination of the Hobart Summer Racing Carnival at Elwick Racecourse.
Launceston Cup, late Feb. Northern Tasmania's top racing event.
Evandale Fair and the National Penny Farthing Championships, late Feb. The most fun you can have on one big wheel (and a small one).

Autumn (Mar–May)

Tasmania's Readers and Writers Festival, Mar–Apr. Salamanca Place buzzes with literary activity.
Ten Days on the Island, Apr in odd-numbered years. Island-dwellers from around the world flock to this biennial event in Tasmania to celebrate their identity with art, music and drama.
Australian Three Peak Race, mid-Apr. Four-day non-stop race around Tasmania's east coast, with sailors going ashore to scale three mountain peaks.
Targa Tasmania, late Apr. International car rally covering 2,000 km (1,240 miles) in six days.
Agfest, May. Carrick's agricultural field days showcase Tasmanian food and crafts.

Winter (June–Aug)

Suncoast Jazz Festival, late June. A weekend of jazz in St Helen's.
Devonport Jazz Festival, late July. The best of Tasmania's jazz talent plus some interstate artists.
Tasmanian Living Artists' Week, late Aug. Open studios, gallery openings and workshops.

ACCOMMODATION

ACTIVITIES

A – Z

AN ALPHABETICAL SUMMARY OF PRACTICAL INFORMATION

Admission Charges

Visitors to Tasmania's national parks are charged entry fees. The daily fee, for up to 24 hours of access, is A$20 per vehicle or A$10 per person for anyone walking, cycling or travelling by coach or motorbike. A holiday pass provides entry to all national parks for up to two months and costs A$50 per vehicle or A$30 per person. In smaller or quieter unstaffed parks, there is a self-registration system but this only allows for one-day permits, so if you require a longer one, buy it from a busier park or a Parks and Wildlife Service office. Some visitor centres also stock them.

Many attractions offer family tickets which can reduce the cost of entry considerably. Entry to Port Arthur Historic site is A$24 for adults, A$11 for children and A$52 for a family ticket. The Cadbury Factory is A$12.50 for adults, A$6.50 for children and A$31.50 for families, and Penny Royal World is A$15 adults, A$6.50 for children and A$35 for families.

Admission to Tasmania's public and private galleries is generally free. The Tasmanian Museum and Art Gallery in Hobart may charge for temporary exhibitions, Launceston's Queen Victoria Museum and Art Gallery is free and the Maritime Museum of Tas-

mania is A$6 for adults, A$4 for children and A$16 for a family.

The National Trust has a heritage pass which allows entry into all its Tasmanian properties for three months. Adults pay A$25 for a pass, pensioner/concessions A$20 and accompanying children go free. There is a reciprocal arrangement with similar organisations in other countries or states, so remember to take your card with you or, once you're in Tasmania, buy a membership card in the knowledge that it can be used elsewhere.

A See Tasmania Smartvisit card can also help keep a lid on admission charges. It entitles the user to free entry to many of the

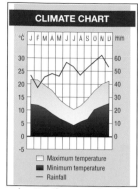

CLIMATE CHART

- ☐ Maximum temperature
- ■ Minimum temperature
- — Rainfall

major attractions as well as free tours and day passes to some of the main national parks. It comes in three-, seven- and 10-day versions starting at A$149 for adults and A$79 for children (aged 4–15) and rising to A$279 adults and A$179 children.

B udgeting for your Trip

Australia has low inflation and the basics – food, accommodation, admission charges – are still comparatively inexpensive. A plate of noodles or pasta in an average restaurant costs about A$12. A bottle of Australian wine from a bottle shop starts at about A$8, a 260ml glass of beer (about half a pint) costs from A$2.50, and a cup of coffee or tea about the same.

Bus and coach travel is quite reasonable and there are various saver tickets available to travellers which can reduce the cost further (see page 235).

Hiring (renting) a small car starts at A$35 per day. Petrol (gasoline) costs around A$1.20 per litre, more expensive than in the US but cheaper than in most European countries. A coach sightseeing tour is A$50–130 per adult, depending on the destination and length of the tour.

A bed at a backpacker hostel is usually about A$15–20 a night and a room in four- or five-star accommodation can start as low as A$200 (see page 237).

Business Hours

Banks generally open 9.30am–4pm Monday to Thursday and 9.30–5pm on Friday. Most shops are open 9am–5.30pm Monday to Thursday, 9am–5pm on Saturday and 10am–4pm on Sunday. Friday night is late-night shopping. Major supermarkets tend to be open longer hours. In Hobart the Woolworths supermarket is open 7am–10pm every day.

C limate

Tasmania has mild summer days with the average maximum temperature for January and February, the hottest months, just 21°C (70°F), and the minimum 12°C (54°F). There may still be some some days where the temperature reaches 30°C (86°F) and beyond.

In winter the average maximum temperature is 12°C (54°F) and the minimum, 5°C (41°F).

The west coast and central highlands tend to be cooler than the more temperate east coast, with temperatures generally about 5°C (17°F) lower.

Rain is also a far more likely prospect on the west coast. Its average annual rainfall of 2,400mm (93.6 inches) is about three times that of Hobart, which has the distinction of being Australia's second-driest capital city.

Crime & Safety

The lowest overall crime rate in Australia makes Tasmania an extremely safe place to travel. Just remember all the usual commonsense rules. Don't carry

large amounts of cash when sightseeing; lock cars and place any valuables out of sight even when in remote locations.

More than half the police stations in Tasmania are one-person operations so there may be nobody on duty at certain times. If a station is closed ring the 24-hour **Police Headquarters** switchboard number for assistance, tel: 6230 2111. The emergency number is 000.

Take care when driving on winding roads, particularly in the early morning or towards dusk when wildlife can present a hazard.

If you are walking in remote areas, be aware that the weather can change dramatically in a short time and take adequate clothing and equipment.

Tasmania Parks and Wildlife Service (PWS; tel: 1300 135 513; www.parks.tas.gov.au) hires Electronic Position Indicating Radio Beacons to people trekking in wilderness areas, but these should only be used in life-threatening situations. It also has excellent fact sheets with safety tips for people exploring Tasmania's remote regions by boat, four-wheel drive and on foot.

Customs

Australia has extremely strict regulations about what can and cannot be brought into the country. Before disembarking from a plane visitors are asked to fill in an Incoming Passenger Card. Australian Customs officers check the information on the cards when passengers disembark, and may initiate a baggage search. There are heavy fines for false or inaccurate claims. It is always best to declare an item if in doubt.

Strict quarantine laws apply in Australia to protect the agricultural industries and native Australian flora and fauna from introduced diseases. Animals, plants and their derivatives must be declared on arrival. This may

TRANSPORT

ACCOMMODATION

ACTIVITIES

A – Z

include items made from materials such as untreated wood, feathers or furs. The import or export of protected species, or products made from protected species, is a criminal offence. It is also illegal to export any species of native flora or fauna without a permit.

All food products, no matter how well processed and packaged, must be declared on arrival. All weapons are prohibited, unless accompanied by an international permit. This includes guns, ammunition, knives and replica items.

Medicinal products must be declared. These include: drugs that are illegal in Australia (narcotics, performance enhancers, amphetamines); legally prescribed drugs (carry your doctor's prescription with you); non-prescribed drugs (painkillers and so on); and vitamins, diet supplements and traditional preparations. **Customs Information and Support Centre** Tel: 1300 363 263 (in Australia); 61 2 6275 6666 (international); www.customs.gov.au

D isabled Travellers

Tasmania caters reasonably well for people with disabilities, but you would be wise to start making enquiries and arrangements before leaving home. A good place to begin is the **National Information Communication Awareness Network** (NICAN), a national organisation that keeps an online database of facilities and services with access for the disabled, including accommodation and tourist sights.

The **Paraplegic and Quadriplegic Association of Tasmania** (**ParaQuad Tasmania**) has a comprehensive listing of tourist accommodation with wheelchair access, as well as information on hire cars, taxis and public toilets.

The **Tasmania Parks and Wildlife Service** (**PWS**) produces

a fact sheet on the facilities provided for disabled people at national parks and reserves around the state.
NICAN PO Box 407 Curtain, ACT 2605; tel: 1800 806 769; www.nican.com.au
ParaQuad Tasmania PO Box 1528 Glenorchy, Tasmania 7010; tel: 6272 8816; www.paraquadtas.org.au
PWS PO Box 1751, Hobart, Tasmania 7001; Tel: 1300 135 513; www.parks.tas.gov.au

Duty-free Allowances

Anyone over the age of 18 is allowed to bring into Australia A$900-worth of goods not including alcohol or tobacco; 2,250ml (about four pints) of alcohol (wine, beer or spirits); 250 cigarettes, or 250 grams of cigars or tobacco products other than cigarettes.

Members of the same family who are travelling together may combine their individual duty/tax-free allowances.

E lectricity

The current is 240/250v, 50Hz. Most hotels have universal outlets for 110v shavers and small appliances. For larger appliances such as hairdryers, you will need a converter and a flat three-pin adaptor.

Embassies & Consulates

When travelling in Tasmania contact:
British Consulate General Level 17, 90 Collins Street, Melbourne, Victoria; tel: 03 9652 1600 (office hours), 02 4422 2280 (after-hours emergencies only); www.britaus.net
Canadian High Commission Commonwealth Avenue, Canberra, ACT; tel: 02 6270 4000; www.canada.org.au
Embassy of Ireland 20 Arkana Street, Yarralumla, ACT; tel: 02 6273 3022

US Consulate General Level 6, 553 St Kilda Road, Melbourne, Victoria; tel: 03 9526 5900, 03 9389 3601 (after-hours emergencies); http://usembassy-Australia.state.gov

Overseas Missions

Canada Australian High Commission, Suite 710, 50 O'Connor Street, Ottawa, Ontario; tel: 613-236 0841; www.ahc-ottawa.org (plus consulates in Toronto and Vancouver).
Ireland Australian Embassy, Fitzwilton House, Wilton Terrace, Dublin 2; tel: 01-664 5300; www.australianembassy.ie
United Kingdom Australian High Commission, Australia House, The Strand, London; tel: 020-7379 4334; www.australia.org.uk (plus consulate in Edinburgh).
United States Australian Embassy, 1601 Massachusetts Avenue, Washington DC NW 20036-2273; tel: 202-797 3000; www.austemb.org (plus consulates-general in New York, Los Angeles, San Francisco, Chicago, Honolulu, Atlanta etc).

Entry Requirements

Visitors to Australia must have a passport valid for the entire period of their stay. Anyone who is not an Australian citizen also needs a visa, which must be obtained before leaving home – except for New Zealand citizens, who are issued with a visa on arrival in Australia.

ETA visas The Electronic Transfer Authority (ETA) enables visitors to obtain a visa on the spot from their travel agent or airline office. The system is in place in over 30 countries including the UK and the US. ETA visas are generally valid over a 12-month period; single stays must not exceed three months, but return visits within the 12-month period are allowed. ETAS are issued free, or you can purchase one online for A$20 from www.eta.imml.gov.au.

Tourist visas These are available for continuous stays longer than three months, but must be obtained from an Australian visa office, such as an embassy or consulate. A fee of A$20 applies. Those travelling on tourist visas and ETAS are not permitted to work while in Australia. Travellers are asked on their applications to prove they have an adequate source of funding while in Australia (around A$1,000 a month).

Temporary residence Those seeking temporary residence must apply to an Australian visa office, and in many cases must be sponsored by an appropriate organisation or employer. Study visas are available for people who want to undertake registered courses on a full-time basis. Working holiday visas are available to young people from the UK, Ireland, Japan, the Netherlands, Canada, Malta and Korea who want to work as they travel. **Department of Immigration and Multicultural and Indigenous Affairs** tel: 13 18 81 (in Australia) or the nearest mission outside Australia; www.immi.gov.au

G ay & Lesbian Visitors

Once the most conservative of Australian states in its laws affecting the gay and lesbian community, Tasmania is now one of the most progressive. In 1994 it decriminalised gay sex putting an end to laws that had the power to put people behind bars for a maximum term of 21 years. In 2004 Tasmania became the first state in Australia to allow same-sex couples to register their relationship.

Gay and Lesbian Tourism Australia allows visitors to locate gay-owned or gay-friendly accommodation and tour operators via its website. tel: 08 8267 4634; www.galta.com.au

The **Gay Information Line** (tel: 6234 8179) is a recorded message line produced by the Gay and Lesbian Centre in Tasmania. It provides details on events, bars, nightclubs and gay-friendly cafés as well as contact details for groups across the state.

Guides & Tours

There are plenty of ways to explore Tasmania without hiring a vehicle and you may prefer to let an expert help you find some of its hidden treasures. Tours range from walking tours of Hobart's historic pubs to multi-day treks in the state's national parks and 10-day raft expeditions on the Franklin River.

The state's natural attractions have made it a breeding ground for eco-tourism options including trout-fishing, nature-watching, diving, cycling and bushwalking, and many operators are willing to tailor tour packages to individual needs. For a list of tour operators see page 256.

Specialist operators also home in on Tasmania's gourmet reputation, with tours for foodies showcasing the growing number of wineries and farms offering fine cheeses and other fresh produce.

H ealth & Medical Care

Australia has excellent medical services. For medical attention outside of working hours go to the casualty department of a major hospital or, if the matter is less urgent, look for a medical practitioner in the Yellow Pages, or ask at your hotel for advice.

No vaccinations are required for entry to Australia. As in most countries, HIV and AIDS is a continuing problem despite efforts to control its spread. Heterosexual and homosexual visitors alike should wear condoms if engaging in sexual activity. **Emergency medical assistance** tel: 000

Pharmacies

Chemist shops are a great place to go for advice on minor ailments such as bites, scratches and stomach trouble. They also stock a wide range of useful products such as sunblock, nappies (diapers) and non-prescription drugs. If you have a prescription from your doctor, and you want to take it to a pharmacist in Australia, you will need to have it endorsed by a local medical practitioner.

Local Health Hazards

The biggest danger for travellers in Australia is the sun. Even on mild, cloudy days it has the potential to burn. Wear a broad-brimmed hat and, if you are planning on being out for a while, a long-sleeved shirt made from a light fabric. Wear SPF 15+ sunblock at all times, even under a hat. Avoid sunbathing between 11am and 3pm.

Care should be taken while swimming. Rip tides resulting in dangerous conditions are fairly common, but it is not always obvious to those unfamiliar with the coastline. The best advice is to swim only at beaches that are patrolled by surf lifesavers, and to swim between the yellow and red flags. Never swim at night after a few drinks.

When hiking in remote terrain be aware that the weather can change quickly and bring protective clothing for cold, wet and windy conditions.

Snakes and Spiders

Two of Australia's most dangerous spiders are found in Tasmania, the funnelweb and the redback. Because you will not necessarily be able to identify these creatures, seek medical help for any spider bite. Dangerous snakes are also part of the Tasmanian landscape, but most will not attack unless directly provoked. Avoid trouble by wearing covered shoes when walking in the bush, and checking areas such as rock platforms and rock crevices before making yourself comfortable. Again seek medical advice for any bite.

Internet Cafés

There are a number of options in Hobart and Launceston. Here are a few:
Mouse on Mars Internet Cyberlounge 27 Salamanca Place, Hobart; tel: 6224 0513.
Nexus Games and Internet Café 46 Bathurst Street, Hobart; tel: 6234 2557.
Café Online 103 George Street, Launceston; tel: 6334 8199.
CyberKing Internet Lounge 113 George Street, Launceston; tel: 6334 2802.
iCaf Internet Café 22 The Quadrant Mall, Launceston; tel: 6334 6815.

Outside these towns internet access can often be found at the local library or at one of Tasmania's 64 Online Access Centres. Locations are often included on maps produced for tourist information. Note there may be a nominal charge for overseas visitors to use these facilities. At the State Library of Tasmania (91 Murray Street, Hobart; tel: 6233 7511) it costs A$5.50 per half hour.
Tasmanian Commmunities Online (www.tco.asn.au) has a list of the Online Access Centres.

LOST CHEQUES & CARDS

If you lose your **traveller's cheque**s or want replacement cheques, contact the following:
American Express, tel: 1800 688 022.
Thomas Cook MasterCard Traveller's Cheques, tel: 1800 127 495.
Interpayment Visa Traveller's Cheques, tel: 1800 127 477.

If you lose your **credit card**: American Express, tel: 1300 132 639.
Diners Club, tel: 1300 360 060.
MasterCard, tel: 1800 120 113 (for international visitors).
Visa, tel: 1800 450 346.
For **lost property**, tel: 6230 2277.

Left Luggage

With no passenger rail network in Tasmania and relatively small airports, you may have to hunt for left-luggage facilities or rely on the goodwill of hotel/hostel managers.

Redline Coaches has a limited left-luggage facility at its Launceston depot. It charges A$1.50 per bag and items must be collected by 5.30pm on the same day. Tel: 1300 360 000.

TassieLink Regional Coach Service provides a luggage storage facility in Hobart, Launceston and Derwent Bridge for people walking the Overland Track. The cost is A$10 per bag. Tel: 1300 300 520.

Lost Property

The loss or theft of valuables should be reported to the police immediately, as most insurance policies insist on a police report. The Police Headquarters switchboard is staffed 24 hours a day. Tel: 6230 2111. Its **Lost and Found Property** office is located at 37–43 Liverpool Street, Hobart; tel: 6230 2277.

For property lost on the major airlines or bus and coach services try the following numbers:
Qantas Baggage Services tel: 6248 5388 (Hobart), 6332 9926 (Launceston).
Jetstar Baggage Services tel: 6214 8915 (Hobart), 6398 6925 (Launceston).
Virgin Blue tel: 6248 4443.

(Hobart), 6391 8782 (Launceston).
Metro Tasmania tel: 13 22 01.
Redline Coaches tel: 1300 360 000.
TassieLink Coaches tel: 1300 300 520.

Maps

Local visitor centres (see page 265) give away useful maps of their areas, which often include information on supermarket opening times and the location of banks, ATMs, internet access and postal services.

The **Map Centre** in Hobart is the place to go for street maps, topographic maps and maps of Tasmania's national parks for walkers.
Map Centre 100 Elizabeth Street, Hobart; tel: 6231 9043.

Media

Publications

To read some local news pick up The Mercury and The Sunday Tasmanian in Hobart, The Examiner in Launceston and The Advocate in Burnie and Devonport seven days a week.

For national news look for The Australian and the Financial Review, both excellent publications at the serious end of the scale. The weekly Bulletin is a long-running magazine with good news analysis and there is also a weekly Australian edition of Time magazine.

Newsagents in the city centre and tourist districts carry some foreign newspapers and magazines.

Radio and Television

The Australian Broadcasting Commission (ABC) runs a national television channel as well as an extensive network of radio stations. ABC Television offers excellent news and current affairs, as well as local and imported drama, comedy, sports and cultural programmes. Two commercial broadcasters, Southern Cross Tasmania and WIN Television, offer news, drama, soaps, "infotainment", travel shows and, between them, coverage of all the major international sporting events. Hotels may provide access to cable television stations.

The radio stations include Triple J-FM (92.9 in Hobart and 90.9 in Launceston), providing rock and comment for the twenty-somethings. Classic FM (93.9 Hobart and 93.3 Launceston) plays continuous classical music; and Radio National AM (585AM Hobart and 94.1FM Launceston) has excellent national news and events coverage.

Commercial radio stations include Ho FM (101,7) and Sea FM (100.9) for various blends of contemporary music.

Of particular interest to overseas travellers is Australia's ethnic/multicultural broadcaster, SBS. The organisation's television channel offers many foreign-language films and documentaries, and Australia's best coverage of world news. SBS Radio (105.7) has programmes in a large variety of languages.

Money

Currency

The local currency is the Australian dollar (abbreviated as A$ or simply $), made up of 100 cents. Coins come in 5, 10, 20 and 50 cent units and 1 and 2 dollar units. Notes come in 5, 10, 20, 50 and 100 dollar bills. Single cents still apply to many prices, and in these cases the amount will be rounded down or up to the nearest 5c. Carry smaller notes for tipping, taxis and payment in small shops and cafés.

There is no limit to the amount of foreign or Australian currency that you can bring into or out of the country, but cash amounts of more than A$10,000 (or its equivalent) must be declared to customs on arrival and departure.

Banks

The big four banks in Australia are the ANZ, Commonwealth, National and Westpac. Trading hours are generally 9.30am–4pm, Monday to Thursday and 9.30am–5pm on Friday. The post office may offer limited banking services in small locations.

Credit cards and ATMs

Carrying a recognised credit or debit card such as Visa, Master-Card, American Express or Diners Club, is always a good idea when travelling. A credit card should provide access to EFTPOS (electronic funds transfer at point of sale), which is the easiest, and often, the cheapest way to exchange money – amounts are automatically debited from the selected account. Many Australian businesses are connected to EFTPOS.

Bank branches and Automatic Teller Machines (ATMs) are relatively common in the major centres in Tasmania allowing for easy withdrawal of cash. Outside these centres the options are more limited, particularly on the west coast, so it helps to plan ahead. Many small businesses are still cash only.

Exchange

Foreign-exchange bureaux are located in the centre of Hobart and Launceston so if you fly in, it is best to arrive with some Aus-tralian currency or a card that allows you to withdraw cash from an ATM.

Traveller's Cheques

All well-known traveller's cheques can be cashed at banks, hotels and similar establishments and are as good as cash with many of the larger retail outlets and the shops in major tourist areas. Smaller restaurants and shops may be reluctant to cash cheques, so you should also carry cards or cash.

Banks offer the best exchange

rates on cheques in foreign currencies; most banks charge a fee for cashing cheques.

P ostal Services

Post offices are generally open between 9am and 5pm Monday to Friday. The General Post Office (GPO) is located at 9 Elizabeth Street in Hobart and opens 8.30am–5.30pm Monday to Friday. There are also postal agencies in general stores and newsagencies.

Domestic Post

Posting a standard letter to anywhere in Australia costs 50 cents. The letter will reach a destination in the same city overnight, but may take up to a week if it is being sent to a

TRANSPORT

ACCOMMODATION

ACTIVITIES

A – Z

far-flung part of the country.

Yellow Express Post bags can be used to send parcels and letters overnight to other Australian capital cities. The cost for a letter ranges from A$4 to A$9.70 and represents very good value for money when compared with courier costs.

Postal enquiries and information tel: 13 13 18

Overseas Post

The cost of overseas mail depends on the weight and size of the item. Postcards cost A$1.10 by airmail to the UK and the US. Standard overseas mail takes about a week to most destinations.

Express Post International (**EPI**) will reduce the delivery time to four to five working days for the UK and three to six working days for the US. It is priced according to weight and size. There is also an international courier service offered by Australia Post.

EPI tel: 13 13 18
Express Courier International tel: 1800 007 678

Public Holidays

These are the state-wide public holidays in Tasmania. There can be other holidays associated with events in particular regions.

1 January New Year's Day
26 January Australia Day
March (2nd Mon) Eight Hours Day
March/April Good Friday, Easter Sunday, Easter Monday
25 April Anzac Day
June (2nd Mon) Queen's Birthday
25 December Christmas Day
26 December Boxing Day

There are four school holidays a year: the third week of December to mid-February, Easter, two weeks in June and two weeks in September. It can be particularly difficult to get discounted airfares and accommodation during the summer break.

Telephones

Faxes

There are many places from which you can fax documents, including hotels, video stores, newsagents, a variety of small businesses, and also post offices, where the rates are very reasonable.

Telephones

Local calls in Australia are untimed, and cost on average 25c from private phones and 40c from public phones. Instead of making calls from hotel rooms, which can be double or triple the price, you should aim to use public phones. Having a phonecard will make this much easier. These are widely available from newsagents and other outlets displaying the Telstra logo. Cards range in price from A$5 to A$50.

Most interstate (STD) and international (ISD) calls can be made using phonecards. These calls are timed, and can be expensive, but cheaper rates are available after 6pm and on weekends. Most overseas numbers can be dialled direct without the need for operator assistance.

If you make a phone call to parts of Tasmania outside your area, it will be charged at STD rates. You have to dial an area code to call interstate in Australia. All regular numbers in Australia (other than toll-free or special numbers) are eight digits long. Numbers in Tasmania have 6 as the first digit. The area code for Tasmania is the same as Victoria: 03. If you are calling from overseas, drop the 0.

Numbers beginning with 1800 are toll-free. Numbers beginning with 13 are charged at a local rate, even if the call made is STD. Numbers beginning with 018, 04, 015, 019 are mobile phone numbers.

Directory enquiries: 1223
Overseas assistance: 1225
Information on costs: 12552
International calls: 0011, fol-

lowed by the national code of the country you are calling.

Directories

There are two types of telephone directory in Tasmania. The *White Pages* contains business and residential numbers in alphabetical order; useful if you are trying to locate a particular number. Government numbers are also listed at the beginning of the book. Turn to the *Yellow Pages* directory if you need to find a service provider. It lists commercial operations under subject headings.

Mobile Phones

Most of the major centres are covered by a telecoms network but outside of these areas it can be difficult to get coverage, so you should not rely on a mobile phone as a safety device if you are hiking or travelling in remote areas.

Many visitors will find that they can bring their own phones with them and use them without too much trouble. Contact your provider before leaving home to find out what is involved. To hire a phone during your stay, look under "Mobile Telephones" in the *Yellow Pages*, and shop around for the best deal – this is a very competitive market. Telstra supplies free leaflets showing where their network provides coverage.

Time Zone

Tasmania is on Eastern Australian Standard Time (EST), which is 10 hours ahead of Greenwich Mean Time, 15 hours ahead of New York and 18 hours ahead of California. Daylight saving (one hour forward) operates from the first weekend in October to the last weekend in March.

Tipping

Tipping is not obligatory but a small gratuity for good service is appreciated. It is not customary to tip taxi drivers or hairdressers, except for perhaps rounding bills up to the nearest dollar. Restaurants do not automatically include service charges, but it is customary to tip waiters up to 10 percent of the bill for good service.

Toilets

Australians manage without euphemisms for "toilet". "Dunny" or "Thunder Box" is the Outback slang, but "washroom", "restroom", "Ladies" and "Gents" are all understood. Many of Tasmania's public toilets are open 24 hours, but some are restricted to daylight hours, shopping hours or only open on an irregular basis. If you get stuck try the nearest pub or service station. Toilets are generally clean and often have wheelchair access.

Tourist Information

For pre-trip planning a good starting point is **Tourism Australia**. It has a website where you can get itinerary ideas, order brochures and find a specialist Australian travel agent: www.australia.com.

There are also the state government-operated **Tasmanian Travel Centres** in Melbourne (259 Collins Street) and Sydney (60 Carrington Street); tel: 1300 655 145 (in Australia); www.tastravel.com.au

Once in Tasmania there is a network of about 20 visitor information centres dotted around the state *(see below)* where you will find maps, accommodation guides, brochures and well-informed staff to help with all your queries.

These accredited centres, marked with the blue and yellow "i", are usually open seven days a week and are always a good first stop when you reach a new town. Unaccredited centres are not allowed to use the same logo and will often employ a blue and white "i".

The **Tasmanian Travel and Information Centre** is at 20 Davey Street, Hobart; tel 6230 8233 and is open 8.30am–5.15pm Monday to Friday, 9–4pm Saturday and Sunday (December to April) and 9am–1pm on Sundays (May to November).

Websites

Here are a selection of websites that may help with pre-trip planning:
www.discovertasmania.com.au
www.tas.gov.au
www.atn.com.au
www.oztravel.com.au
www.about-australia.com
www.itsanisland.com.au

Weights & Measures

Australia uses the metric system of weights, measures and temperatures.
1 metre = approx 39 inches
1 kilometre (km) = 1,093 yards or approx 0.6 mile
16 km = approx 10 miles
1 kilogram (kg) = approx 2.2 lb
1 litre = 1.75 pints
40 litres = approx 9 imperial gallons or 10 US gallons
20°C = 68°F
30°C = 86°F

What to Wear

Be ready for any weather, no matter what the season. A warm sweater may be necessary, even in summer, and winter may call for heavy jackets, scarves and gloves. Don't forget to bring wet-weather gear, particularly if you are visiting in spring or planning to spend time on the west coast. Anywhere you go, you'll need comfortable walking shoes and you should pack proper walking boots if you are planning to do any long-distance walks.

Dress is generally casual – shorts, a short-sleeved shirt or T-shirt and trainers or sandals are fine. Even fine-dining restaurants are generally smart rather than formal, but they may draw the line at customers wearing T-shirts, tank tops, ripped jeans or thongs (flip-flops).

VISITOR CENTRES AROUND TASMANIA

Hobart 20 Davey Street; tel: 6230 8233
Launceston 14–16 St John Street; tel: 6336 3133
Devonport 92 Formby Road; tel: 6424 4466
Burnie Civic Square Precinct, off Little Alexander Street; tel: 6434 6111
Deloraine 98–100 Emu Bay Road; tel: 6362 3471
Evandale Tourism and History Centre 18 High Street; tel: 6391 8128
Exeter Main Road; tel: 6394 4454
Geeveston (Forest and Heritage Centre) Church Street; tel: 6297 1836
George Town Main Road; tel: 6382 1700
Huonville Esplanade; tel: 6264 1838
Kettering (Bruny D'Entre-casteaux Visitor Information Centre) 81 Ferry Road; tel: 6267 4494
Oatlands (Central Tasmanian Tourism Centre) 85 High Street; tel: 6254 1212
Port Arthur Port Arthur Historic Site; tel: 6251 2371
Ross (Tasmanian Wool Centre) Church Street; tel: 6381 5466
Scottsdale (Forest EcoCentre) 96 King Street; tel: 6352 6520
Sheffield 5 Pioneer Crescent; tel: 6491 1036
Stanley 45 Main Road; tel: 6458 1330
Strahan (West Coast Visitor Information and Booking Centre) The Esplanade; tel: 6471 7622
Triabunna corner of Esplanade and Charles streets; tel: 6257 4090
Wynyard Goldie Street; tel: 6442 4143

FURTHER READING

History

The Fabrication of Aboriginal History, Volume One: Van Diemen's Land 1803–47, K Windschuttle.
The Fatal Shore, R Hughes.
The Future Eaters: An Ecological History of the Australian Lands and People, T Flannery.
Manning Clark's History of Australia, M Clark.
A Short History of Tasmania, M Roe.

Biography & Memoir

The Devil in Tim: Travels In Tasmania, T Bowden.
Down Home, P Conrad.
In Tasmania, N Shakespeare.
A Man and a Mountain: The Story of Gustav Weindorfer, M Giordano.

Fiction

The Alphabet of Light and Dark, D Wood.
The Boys in the Island, C Koch.
Cape Grimm, C Bird.
A Child's Book of True Crime, C Hooper.
The English Passengers, M Neale.
For the Term of His Natural Life, M Clarke.
Gould's Book of Fish, R Flanagan.
The Hunter, J Leigh.
The Last Thylacine, T Domico.
Morality of Gentlemen, A Lohrey.
The Potato Factory, B Courtney.
The Sooterkin, T Gilling.
The Tilted Cross, R Drewe.

Food & Wine

Eat Drink Tasmania, G Phillips.
The Penguin Good Australian Wine Guide, H Hooke and R Kyte-Powell.

Wildlife

Australian Wildlife, J Kavanagh.
Green Guide: Mammals of Australia, T Lindsey.
Green Guide: Snakes and Other Reptiles of Australia, by G Swan.

FEEDBACK

We do our best to ensure the information in our books is as accurate and up-to-date as possible. The books are updated on a regular basis, using local contacts, who painstakingly add, amend and correct as required. However, some mistakes and omissions are inevitable and we are ultimately reliant on our readers to put us in the picture.

We would welcome your feedback on any details related to your experiences using the book "on the road". Maybe we recommended a hotel that you liked (or another that you didn't), or you'd like to tell us about a new attraction or any other details about the country itself. The more details you can give us (particularly with regard to addresses, e-mails and telephone numbers), the better.

We will acknowledge all contributions, and we'll offer an Insight Guide to the best letters received.

Please write to us at:
Insight Guides
PO Box 7910
London SE1 1WE
United Kingdom
Or send an e-mail to:
insight@apaguide.co.uk

The Slater Field Guide to Australian Birds, P, P & R Slater.

Art & Architecture

Art in Australia: From Colonialisation to Postmodernism, C Allen.
The Art of Australia, R Hughes.

Other Insight Guides

Titles which highlight destinations in this part of the world include:
Insight Guide: Australia, a superbly illustrated guide to all the best that Down Under has to offer.

Insight Guide: New South Wales, a detailed look at Sydney and its state, from the beaches to the remote outback.

Insight Guide: Queensland, a comprehensive guide to the sunshine state.

Insight Pocket Guide: Melbourne, a series of itineraries written by a local author guides you to the best of what has been described as the world's most liveable city.

ART & PHOTO CREDITS

Oriol Alamany/Auscape 10/11
Auscape 45
Australian War Memorial
(negative number H11609) 24
James Davis Photography/Alamy
18L, 71
Jerry Dennis/Apa 1, 2/3, 3B, 4T,
4C, 5T, 5B, 6B, 7T, 7C, 7B, 8T,
8C, 8B, 9T, 9CL, 9CR, 12/13, 16,
22, 23L, 23R, 27, 28/29, 30,
31, 32, 33, 35L, 35R, 36, 37L,
38, 39, 43, 46L, 46R, 47, 49,
51, 52, 53, 54, 55, 56, 57, 58L,
58R, 59, 60, 61, 62/63, 64/65,
66, 70, 73, 73T, 74T, 75T, 76,
77, 77T, 78, 78T, 79L, 79R, 80T,
81, 81T, 82T, 83, 84, 85, 85T,
86, 89, 90, 91, 92, 92T, 93, 94,
95, 95T, 96, 96T, 97, 98, 98T,
99, 102, 103, 105, 105T, 106,
107, 107T, 108, 109, 109T, 110,
110T, 111, 112, 112T, 114, 115,
117, 117T, 118, 118T, 119, 120,
120T, 121, 122, 123T, 124, 125,
127, 127T, 128, 129, 129T, 130,
131, 131T, 132, 133, 134, 134T,
135, 135T, 136, 136T, 137, 138,
139, 141, 141T, 142, 142T, 143,
144L, 144R, 144T, 145, 146,
146T, 147, 149, 152, 153, 154T,
155, 156, 156T, 157, 158, 159,
159T, 160, 160T, 161T, 162,
163, 165, 165T, 166, 166T, 167,
168, 169L, 169R, 169T, 170,
170T, 171, 172, 172T, 173, 174,
174T, 175, 175T, 176, 176T,
177, 178, 179, 179T, 181, 182,
183, 184T, 185T, 186, 187,
187T, 188L, 188R, 188T, 189,
190, 191, 191T, 192, 192T, 193,
194, 194T, 195, 196L, 196R,
197, 197T, 198, 198T, 199, 201,
202, 203, 204, 204T, 205, 206,
207, 207T, 208, 208T, 212,
214T, 215, 216L, 216R, 216T,
217, 217T, 218, 219, 219T, 220,
220T, 221, 222, 223, 224, 224T,
225L, 225R, 226, 227, 227T,
228, 229, 229T, 230, 230T, 231,
233, 234, 235, 236, 238, 240,
241, 242, 243, 246, 247, 249,
250, 253, 254, 255, 257, 259,
261, 263, all route map images
John Fairhall/Auscape 42
Jean-Paul Ferrero/Auscape 37R
Gavin Gough/Alamy 21
Dennis Harding/Auscape 74/75
National Library of Australia 17,
18R, 26
Newspix 25
Tony Perrottet 34
Popperfoto/Alamy 80

Galen Rowell/Corbis 213
Paul A. Souders/Corbis 44, 50
State Library of Tasmania 19, 20,
104T
Tom Till/Auscape 14
Rob Walls/Alamy 6T
S. Wilby/C. Ciantar/Auscape 48

PICTURE SPREADS

Pages 40/41: Jerry Dennis 40CR,
40BL, 40BR, 41CL, 41BL, 41BR;
Tourism Tasmania 41CR;
Rob Walls/Alamy 40/41
Pages 100/101: All pictures
Jerry Dennis
Pages 150/151: All pictures
Jerry Dennis except: Tony
Perrottet 150/151
Pages 210/211: All pictures
Jerry Dennis except: Tony
Perrottet 211BR

Cartographic Editor: Zoë Goodwin

Map Production:
James Macdonald
©2006 Apa Publications GmbH & Co.
Verlag KG, Singapore Branch

Book Production:
Linton Donaldson

GENERAL INDEX

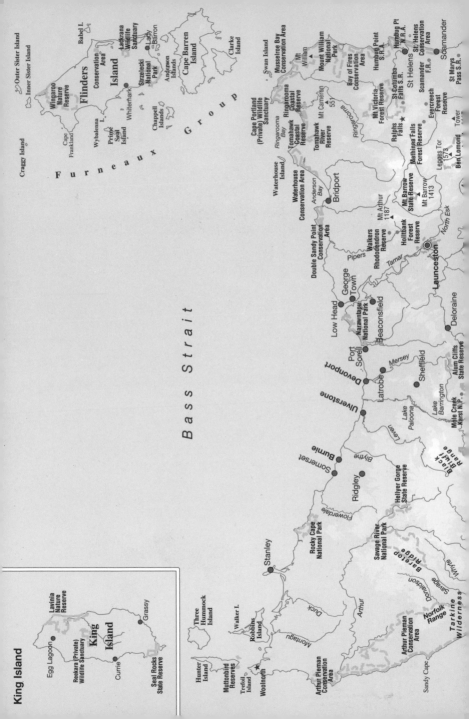